本书的出版获得国家社会科学基金"汉语篇章的韵律特征和音系表达研究"（10CYY036），国家973课题"互联网环境中文言语感知与表示理论研究"（2013CB329301）以及中国社会科学院哲学社会科学创新工程的资助，特此表示感谢

中国社会科学院文库
文学语言研究系列
The Selected Works of CASS
Literature and Linguistics

中国社会科学院创新工程学术出版资助项目

中国社会科学院文库 · **文学语言研究系列**
The Selected Works of CASS · **Literature and Linguistics**

普通话焦点的语音实现和音系分析

PHONETIC REALIZATION AND PHONOLOGICAL ANALYSIS OF FOCUS IN STANDARD CHINESE

贾 媛 著

中国社会科学出版社

图书在版编目 (CIP) 数据

普通话焦点的语音实现和音系分析 / 贾媛著 . —北京:
中国社会科学出版社,2012.10
ISBN 978 - 7 - 5161 - 1699 - 9

Ⅰ. ①普… Ⅱ. ①贾… Ⅲ. ①普通话—语音学—
研究 Ⅳ. ①H116

中国版本图书馆 CIP 数据核字 (2012) 第 263497 号

出 版 人	赵剑英
责任编辑	张 林
责任校对	张洪波
责任印制	戴 宽

出 版	中国社会科学出版社
社 址	北京鼓楼西大街甲 158 号 (邮编 100720)
网 址	http://www.csspw.cn
	中文域名:中国社科网 010 - 64070619
发 行 部	010 - 84083685
门 市 部	010 - 84029450
经 销	新华书店及其他书店

印刷装订	三河市君旺印装厂
版 次	2012 年 10 月第 1 版
印 次	2012 年 10 月第 1 次印刷

开 本	710 × 1000 1/16
印 张	16.5
插 页	2
字 数	273 千字
定 价	50.00 元

凡购买中国社会科学出版社图书,如有质量问题请与本社联系调换
电话:010 - 64009791
版权所有 侵权必究

《中国社会科学院文库》出版说明

　　《中国社会科学院文库》（全称为《中国社会科学院重点研究课题成果文库》）是中国社会科学院组织出版的系列学术丛书。组织出版《中国社会科学院文库》，是我院进一步加强课题成果管理和学术成果出版的规范化、制度化建设的重要举措。

　　建院以来，我院广大科研人员坚持以马克思主义为指导，在中国特色社会主义理论和实践的双重探索中做出了重要贡献，在推进马克思主义理论创新、为建设中国特色社会主义提供智力支持和各学科基础建设方面，推出了大量的研究成果，其中每年完成的专著类成果就有三四百种之多。从现在起，我们经过一定的鉴定、结项、评审程序，逐年从中选出一批通过各类别课题研究工作而完成的具有较高学术水平和一定代表性的著作，编入《中国社会科学院文库》集中出版。我们希望这能够从一个侧面展示我院整体科研状况和学术成就，同时为优秀学术成果的面世创造更好的条件。

　　《中国社会科学院文库》分设马克思主义研究、文学语言研究、历史考古研究、哲学宗教研究、经济研究、法学社会学研究、国际问题研究七个系列，选收范围包括专著、研究报告集、学术资料、古籍整理、译著、工具书等。

中国社会科学院科研局

2006 年 11 月

前　言

　　"焦点"（focus）是音系学、句法学、语义学、话语分析等语言学各个研究学科共同感兴趣的问题。"焦点"在不同领域中有不同的解释，在语言的形式理论描述中，它是句子中某个句法成分的一种特征，在意义上是讲话人认为比较重要，需要通过语言手段强调的成分。"焦点"可以分为常规焦点、对比焦点和话题焦点，焦点可以通过句法、词法、音系和语音等手段来体现（张伯江、方梅 1996，刘丹青、徐烈炯 1998，徐烈炯 2005)。近些年，在语音学和言语工程界，"焦点"问题也成为研究和应用的热点，随着人—机语音交互技术的发展，在语音应用上，需要机器能够听懂自然输入的言语，找到信息的焦点，并进行相应的操作，例如在进行信息检索时，能够做出正确的应答。在这一应用中，主要涉及语音识别、对话理解以及语音合成等方面对焦点问题的研究和应用。焦点是人们交际过程中，交际双方想要传递的凸显信息，对焦点信息的正确识别对言语理解至关重要，而正确设置焦点信息位置，并进行正确的声学表达，则是合成自然口语的重要保证。因此，针对焦点的各种 "接口"研究就显得非常重要了。

　　与语音接口的研究，一般关注焦点位置和非焦点位置的语音表现，探讨窄焦点和宽焦点的声学特征，林茂灿先生在 2012 出版的《汉语语调实验研究》中对这个问题进行了大量的实例分析；与句法接口的研究，探索各种句法结构与焦点的关系，以及焦点标记等；与音系接口的研究，更多偏重音系的描写，以及焦点与重音实现的关系；与篇章的接口研究，则关注信息结构与焦点的关系，以及焦点的语用功能等。贾媛的这本研究专著的特点是从语音学、音系学和句法等多个层面对普通话的焦点进行接口研究，设计了大量严格的实验对话材料，音系分析建立在大量的语音实验结果基础上。该研究通过分析不同类别和不同数量焦点声学特征，系统地考察了普通话焦点重音的声学特征，揭示了汉语焦点与重音的不对应性特征，以及多焦点句的重音和音系实现规律，并采用核心重音和核心前重音来解释重音的层级问题。

尽管该研究主要关注"汉语的焦点"问题，但它实质上也是汉语语调研究的一个非常重要的构成部分。在对各种焦点句的语音表现和音系实质研究的基础上，该研究从音系层面对汉语的语调结构进行了系统描写，提出了汉语语调描写的有限状态文法，并指出构成汉语语调的音系事件包括：核心重音、核心前重音和边界调。研究中采用的描写方式，结合了汉语声调特征的音系特征和重音的实现方式，采用原始的 H 调和 L 调，描写汉语语调的组构形式，体现了汉语语调与声调的作用关系，可以说，将赵元任先生提出的"橡皮带效应"或者"小波浪加大波浪"关系进行了解读和形式化。

吴宗济先生从 20 世纪 80 年代，就开始面向语音合成，进行了一系列的汉语语调与声调关系的研究，特别是考察了焦点（加强）位置对于语调变化模式的影响，提出了语调的语音和音系描写体系。他在世的时候，经常鼓励贾媛从音系和语音的角度，利用音系学理论，基于汉语音事实对汉语焦点和语调的开展研究。这本专著能在赵元任先生诞辰 120 周年、吴宗济先生诞辰 103 周年的时候出版，是后学们对前辈的最有意义的怀念了。

书中对焦点和重音的概念，焦点作用域，重音实现方式以及焦点和重音的对应关系等基本概念都有详细的介绍。部分内容在人机语音工程通讯会议上发表，获得了优秀论文奖，还有一些章节在国际会议上宣读，得到了很高的评价。是近年来一部难得的从语音、音系和句法等角度对汉语焦点进行系统研究的专著，相信对语言学、语音学以及言语工程领域的研究人员和研究生都将有非常重要的参考价值。

李爱军

2012 年 10 月 15 日

摘　要

本研究主要考察普通话语调结构、韵律结构以及焦点的关系，主要研究普通话不同类别以及不同数量焦点的韵律特征。内容主要涉及三个方面：(1) 焦点成分的声学特征，如疑问词引导的(主位和述位)焦点、句法标记的焦点以及两类焦点的交互作用在韵律上的表现；(2) 由不同类别和数量焦点所传达的重音的层级和音系表征；(3) 焦点和重音对应关系的理论解释。根据研究的目的，本研究采用 Pierrehumbert、Ladd、Grice、Gussenhoven 等人提出的语调音系学理论，Selkirk, Nespor 和 Ladd 等人提出的韵律层级理论，以及有关语调的优选论分析模式 (见 Gussenhoven 2005，Yip 2002)，来解释普通话的焦点的分布问题、焦点和重音的对应关系问题，以及普通话的语调音系表征模式。本研究遵循实验室音系学研究思路，将实验数据与理论分析相结合，在实验数据的基础上概括普通话的音系范畴特征。

本研究所采用的实验句子均为陈述句，实验用句根据研究目的的不同，包括单焦点句 (疑问词引导的焦点或者句法标记的焦点，如"连"标记或"是"标记的焦点)、双焦点句 (包括疑问词引导的主位焦点和述位焦点，双述位焦点以及句法标记焦点和述位焦点)、多焦点句 (多个疑问词引导的述位焦点)，以考察普通话中不同数量和不同类别的焦点句，对短语层面突显，韵律切分以及语调模式影响，为跨语言的焦点句的研究提供有力证据。

本研究以音高和时长为参数，考察由上述焦点类型所体现的不同类别的重音模式。在分析焦点成分的声学特征时，将每个音节的音高目标值 H 或 L 特征作为分析的基本单元。本研究指出：(1) 在单焦点情况下，无论焦点成分为疑问焦点或者句法标记焦点 ("是"或"连"

标记的焦点)，重音与焦点是一一对应的关系。以音高为参数，句法标记的焦点与疑问词引导的焦点的语音特征类似，其将焦点成分的音高音域显著抬高而将焦点后成分的音高显著压低。焦点成分的声调组合对重音实现的方式有重要的影响，如重音可将焦点成分的 H 和 L 调显著抬高，而以 H 调为声学特征主要体现位置，但焦点成分的声调组合不影响重音的分布。以时长为参数，不同类别的焦点都对时长有显著的拉长作用，但疑问词引导的焦点的作用比句法标记要显著；(2) 在无句法标记结构中，在双焦点情况下，由焦点所传达的重音有层级差异。在无句法标记结构中，主要发现包括以下几个方面：① 不用层级的焦点可以由不同层级的重音来体现，如由疑问词引导的焦点主位焦点和述位焦点，由于述位焦点的层级高于主位焦点，所传达的重音层级也以述位焦点为主重音；② 相同层级的疑问焦点引导的述位焦点，重音的层级也不相同；③ 双焦点对焦点之间成分的音高无压低作用；④ 在多个疑问词引导的焦点，焦点与重音不是一一对应的关系，只有最右位置的焦点可以实现为重音；⑤ 在本研究中，采用核心重音和核心前重音来解释重音的层级问题，核心重音是重音成分中主要的、非选择性成分，而核心前重音则是次要的、选择性的成分；⑥ 疑问词引导的焦点对韵律切分也有影响，可以将普通话语调切分为中间短语。(3) 在有句法标记的结构中，双焦点情况下，根据疑问词和句法标记焦点成分的组合关系主要发现有以下几点：① 疑问焦点和句法标记焦点分布于同一成分时，可以实现为核心重音，对焦点下成分的音高抬高和时长的拉长作用比单焦点更显著，对后接成分的音高压低也更显著；② 疑问焦点和句法标记的焦点可以分布于句子的不同成分上，当句法标记焦点（"连"标记焦点）位于疑问焦点之前，句法标记焦点和疑问焦点分别实现为核心前重音和核心重音，前者音高和时长变化比后者幅度小。当句法标记焦点位于疑问焦点之后，句法标记焦点则失去重读，只有疑问焦点实现为核心重音。

根据实验结果以及以往语调音系研究，本研究进一步提出了具有语言学意义的普通话语调音系表征模式。该语调模式主要描述普通话字调层面以上的语调变化模式，主要包括四类音系事件：核心重音，核心前重音，调头和边界调。其中核心重音和边界调是非选择性成分，而核心前重音和调头则是选择性成分。音系事件的语音实现是以 H 和 L 调的描述为基础的，语调的模式是以局部的音系事件为基础，按照线性的序列组合而成。核心重音和核心前重音的内在特征不同，核心重音具有唯一性特征，核心重音实现是无标记的，而核心前重音的出现却是有标记的，在普通话中只出现在双焦点情况下。在上述焦点语音实现的描述中，多焦点情况下只有一个重音出现，而在有句法标记情况下，也可以失去重音。因此，在普通话中，有焦点的位置未必由重音来表征。根据以上分析，本研究提出制约表层核心重音实现的底层原因，即节律上相对的"轻-重"关系，节律上相对"重"的成分获得核心重音，节律上相对"轻"的成分则根据焦点环境失去重音或者实现为核心前重音，如在单焦点环境下，节律结构为"重-轻"，因此，焦点位置实现为核心重音，而焦点后成分则失去重音；在双焦点以及多焦点环境下，节律结构为"轻-重"，在双焦点情况下，实现为核心前重音和核心重音，而在多焦点情况下，只有最右位置焦点实现为核心重音。

在优选论的框架下，采用普遍性的制约条件等级排列，来解释从焦点到重音的实现过程，共分为三个步骤：表层重音类型的生成包括：H*，L*，LH* 或者 H*L；重音的连接位置以及韵律切分位置。

关键词：焦点，核心重音， 核心前重音，优选论

Abstract

The subject matter of this research is the relation between intonational structure, prosodic structure, and focus in Standard Chinese (hereinafter SC). It is an investigation of prosodic effects of various kinds and different numbers of focuses in SC, on the one hand, and of the accent patterns conveyed by the focus, on the other. The research examines three aspects: (i) the acoustic manifestations of the entities bearing focus, that is, *wh*-elicited focus, *syntax*-marked focus (*lian*-marked or *shi*-marked focus), and interaction of these two kinds of focuses; (ii) the phonological representation of the accents pattern and hierarchical levels of accents induced by the focus in discussion; and (iii) a theoretical explanation of the corresponding relation between focus and accent in SC. To accomplish this aim, this research employs (a version of) the theory of *Intonation*, as developed by Pierrehumbert and colleagues, Ladd, Grice, Gussenhoven, and others, (a version of) the theory of the *Prosodic Hierarchy*, as developed in the work of Selkirk, Nespor, and Ladd and (a version of) the theory of *Optimality Theory*, as developed by Gussenhoven and Yip, among others. The chosen approach here is simultaneously theoretically and empirically based, much along the lines of laboratory phonology research, in which experimentally collected speech data is adopted to investigate questions about the abstract categories of phonological structure.

The sample sentences employed in this research are confined to declarative sentences with one or more (single, double or multiple) focuses. The inclusion of focus in the domain of research is motivated by the fact that the focus affects phrasal prominence, prosodic phrasing, and other aspects in intonation in various languages. It is expected that the present examination of focus may provide important evidences for the prosodic organization of SC.

Fundamental frequency (F_0), together with duration, is an acoustic measure that is adopted to signal the contrast in focus conditions. The underlying tonal target H (*High*) or L(*Low*) is employed in dealing with the phonetic realization of focus phenomenon. It is mainly concerned with the following aspects: (i) in the single-focus condition, regardless of the kind of focus; i.e., whether it is *wh*-operators elicited information focus, *lian*-marked focus, or *shi*-marked focus, the accent is correlated with the focus. Taking F_0 into consideration, the *syntax*-marked focus resembles the phonetic nature of the *wh*-elicited information induced focus.

Specifically, in the under-focus domain, the F_0 ranges of the focused words are expanded as the H and L tones of the focused syllables are raised. The accent that results from a *syntax*-marked focus also exerts a compressive effect on the following constituents that can extend to the every end of a sentence. The tonal combinations of the focused constituents contribute greatly to the specific manner in which an accent is manifested, that is, the accent is realized by modifying the original tonal targets H or L.

As for the durational adjustment, the focus can trigger a significant effect on lengthening; (ii) in the syntax unmarked sentence, in double focus condition, what is crucially involved in the acoustic reflection of focus is the hierarchical level of accents. Concerning the F_0 and durational pattern, the observations are threefold: (a) different levels of focus can lead to a different magnitude of pitch register raising and durational lengthening in a sentence; i.e., as between *wh*-elicited theme focus and rheme focus, the primary role is due to the rheme focus; (b) double rheme focus exhibits similar acoustic manifestations, namely, each of the focused units are characterized by F_0 lifting and durational lengthening; (c) consistent non-lowering of F_0 on the second constituent reveals the fact that the accents have a primary status; (d) the accent of multiple rheme focus displays distinct properties in comparison with the single and double focus condition in that the distribution of the accent exhibits no corresponding relation with the focus. Only the last focused constituent of a sentence serves as the anchor in realizing accent tone the surface form; (e) the hierarchical level differences of accents are adequately accounted for by the *nuclear accent* and *pre-nuclear accent* distinction in SC. The *nuclear accent* bears the obligatory and primary characteristics while the pre-nuclear tone is optional and secondary; (f) focus is also assigned the crucial role of determining the phrasing at the intermediate phrase boundary in SC; (iii) with regard to a syntax-marked sentence, the acoustic evidence for the double focus is based on the relation between the syntax-marked focus and the *wh*-elicited rheme focus: (a) they can combine together to induced a *nuclear accent* correlated with the larger F_0 excursion and durational lengthening, and a more obvious F_0 drop of the post focus constituents; (b) they may co-exist on different components. When the syntax-marked focus is located in the proceeding position of the rheme focus, these two focuses can be marked by *pre-nuclear accent* and *nuclear accent*. These two accents also observe a phonetically degree-based difference, in that the latter is marked by more obvious phonetic features than the former. Crucially, when the *syntax*-marked focus is preceded by the rheme focus, it is de-accented by the compressive effect of the preceding rheme focus.

Based on empirical investigations, as well as the existing literature on the phonological study of intonation, this study further proposes a phonological representation of the linguistically significant non-lexical configurations in SC. The grammar states that the intonation contour consists of four types of categorical phonological events; i.e., *nuclear accent, pre-nuclear accent, onset,* and *boundary tone.* Among these four entities, the *nuclear accent* and the boundary tone bear an obligatory nature, whereas, the appearance of the *pre-nuclear accent* and the onset are optional. The intonation patterns are constructed by phonological events in a linear sequence, and are represented by the primitive tonal targets *H* and *L*. The phonetic realization of any given *H* or *L* tone depends on a variety of factors (e.g.,status and number of focuses, position in an utterance) that are of essential importance to the identity of those tonal targets. Overall trends of contours (e.g., local range expansion or gradual compression of overall range) mostly reflect the operation of localized linguistic factors. The essential properties of *nuclear accent* and *pre-nuclear accent* are distinct from each other; the former is unmarked and bears a unique feature, while the latter is restricted by the focus condition in that it only appears in a double-focus utterance. Thereafter, there is a status difference between these two accents; they exhibit a primary and secondary status distinction. Evidence of 'focus without accent' and 'accent without focus' in SC further demonstrates that sentence-level accent is not only a matter of where the accent is located, but also involves a '*strong* or *weak*' relation in the prosodic structure that in turn determines the distribution of the accent in the surface form. Under a single focus condition, the metrical relation is '*s-w*' that determines the accenting and de-accenting phenomenon in the surface form. Under a double or multiple focus environment, the metrical structure is captured as '*w-s*' that determines the distribution of the *nuclear accent* in the rightmost position elicited by the focus in SC sentences.

Within the framework of Optimality Theory, a ranking of constraints in the generation of accent in the surface form is conducted in three steps: (i) the analysis of accent pattern generation, i.e., H^*, L^*, LH^* or H^*L; (ii) the association of the accents; (iii) the location of the prosodic boundary.

Key words: focus, nuclear accent, pre-nuclear accent, Optimality Theory

Abbreviations

Ad: Adverb

AM Theory: Autosegmental-Metrical Theory

BF: Broad focus

BrE: British English

Con: Constraint

C-ToBI: Chinese Tone and Break Index

DTE: Designted Terminal Element

DF: Double focus
Eval: Evaluator
F_0: Fundamental frequency
FTA: Focus-to-Accent

Gen: Generator

IPO: Instituut voor Perceptie Onderzoek in Holland (Institute for Perception Research)
IViE: Intonational Variation in English
NA: Nuclear accent
NF: Narrow focus
Obj: Object
OT: Optimality Theory
PRA: Pre-nuclear accent
RB: Rheme background
RF: Rheme focus
Sub: Subject
SC: Standard Chinese
SVO: Subject, Verb, Object
TB: Theme background
TF: Theme focus
ToBI: Tone Break Index
USFP: Unique Strong Focus Principle
V: Verb
***Wh*-elicited focus**: *Wh*-question elicited focus

Symbols

%: Boundary tone

L%: Low boundary tone

H%: Hing boundary tone

H: High target of tone

L: Low target of tone

H*: Accented high target

L*: Accented low target

*: Violation of the constraints in Optimality Theory

*!: Fatal violation in ranking constraints

☞: Optimal candidate in ranking constraints

[+LianF]: *Lian* marked focus

[+LianF & +RF]: *Lian* marked focus and rheme focus

P: Prominence

[+ShiF]: *Shi* marked focus

[+ShiF & +RF]: *Shi* marked focus and rheme focus

S-W: Strong-Weak

W-S: Weak-Strong

T: Tonal events

Table of Contents

Chapter One

Introduction

1.1   Introduction

It is generally accepted that sentence accentuation reflects in some way the intended *focus* of an utterance (by the term *focus* is meant the center of interest during the communication (Crystal 1997). However, there remains a decades-old debate on the corresponding relations between *focus* and *accent* (by the term *accent* is meant sentence accent, which is also referred to by some authors as *stress* (Cystal 1997). The major goal of this study is to examine the prosodic effects of different kinds and various numbers of focuses in Standard Chinese (hereinafter SC) with an emphasis on the relation between intonation structure, prosodic structure, and focus in SC. It is expected that the examination of focus may provide important evidences for cross-language investigation of focus phenomena, particularly the relation between *focus* and *accent*.

The present chapter provides a general view of what has been done in the relevant linguistic fields so as to facilitate an understanding of the discussion in the following chapters.

1.2   Literature review

1.2.1   Intonational phonology

Intonational phonology is a study of the patterning of linguistically significant non-lexical pitch configurations, or the phonological structure of pitch variations at the phrase or sentence level. It aims mainly to provide universal principles or rules that characterize the internal structures of intonation. The term intonational phonology did not appear until the late 1970s, and even up to the present not all the intonation researchers fully agree on its meaning. The difficulty in the study of intonation consists in various sources (both linguistic and non-linguistic sources) that add to the complexity of categorizing intonatinal patterning. Therefore, it is not easy to work out phonological principles that govern the linguistically significant pitch variations at the level of a phrase or sentence.

Ladd (1996) was the first to present a systematic discussion of intonational phonology. The AM (Autosegmental-Metrical) theory, the approach to intonational phonology he advocates, finds its main support in the growing number of studies of various languages. The following is a brief review of some of its basic assumptions, together with some of the debatable issues that are relevant to this study. The AM approach to intonation is based on the studies of Pierrehumbert (1980), and Pierrehumbert and Beckman (1988). This approach claims that *intonation* is characterized mainly by linguistically significant pitch evens and that such events can be represented by a string of categorically distinct entities. This view has at least two implications: (i) intuitively identical contours are accounted for by the same phonological representation, and conversely, intuitively different contours are represented in a differently structured string of tonal categories (Ladd 1996, Gussenhoven 1983, in particular); (ii) the phonological representation of a string of categorically distinct entities is of much help to a comparative study that aims to identify the universals in intonation patterning among different languages.

Previous studies have shown that in languages such as English, German, Italian, Bengali, and Spanish, there are two distinct types of events in a tonal string: pitch accent and boundary tone (Hayes and Lahiri

1991, Féry 1993, Grice 1995, and Prieto et al. 1995). The former is associated with prominent elements of the segmental string, and the latter is associated with the boundaries of prosodic phrases. Either type of tonal event is analyzed in terms of two distinct tonal entities—H (*High*) and L (*Low*).

1.2.2   Prosodic phonology

Prosodic phonology is a study of phonological structure and its relation to syntax. Its essential claim is that the flow of speech is hierarchically organized into prosodic domains. The basic support for the prosodic hierarchy has been the domain of operation of phonological rules. Although no single widely accepted framework has emerged in the study of this area, there are still a number of theoretical assumptions shared by many prosodic phonologists. These, together with some of the points made in different versions of the theory, are briefly reviewed below.

1.2.2.1   Syntax-phonology mapping

Prosodic structure is partially determined by syntactic structure. These two structures may or may not coincide. This is the reason why syntax does not always provide correct predications about structure sensitive phonological processes, and why a prosodic level of representation is required (refer to Nespor and Vogel 1986, Selkirk 1986, Hayes 1989 for an extensive demonstration of this point). Further, the ways in which prosodic structure deviates from syntax are systematic. This governed relation between the two structures is defined in the mapping of the relation between syntactic structure and prosodic structure: (i) syntactic structure plays a limited role in determining prosodic structure (refer to, for example, the syntactic category type, the direction recursively, the head/complement relation—Chen 1990, Inkelas and Zec 1995 for review and discussion); (ii) a set of corresponding conditions (or phrase formation rules) hold between the two structures, and a syntactic structure-prosodic structure pair has to satisfy these conditions. There are two major approaches to syntax-phonology mapping in the literature: *the end-based approach* (Selkirk 1986), and *the relation-based approach* (Nespor and Vogel 1986, Hayes 1989). The main difference between the two approaches resides in the nature of the syntactic information to which the mapping conditions are sensitive: syntactic edges of a selected syntactic phrasal rank in the former (i.e., the right or left edge of such a syntactic phrase) and the relation between heads and adjacent constituents in the latter (i.e., the presence or absence of a head/complement relation). Chen (1990) and Cho (1990) contrast these two approaches, but arrive at conflicting conclusions: Chen (1990) finds that the facts of the language under analysis fit more easily into the end-based approach, whereas Cho (1990) concludes that the relation-based approach does a better job in predicting the facts of the language observed. Chen (1990) and Inkelas and Zec (1990) also suggest that there are some languages that seem to be amenable to both approaches. In other words, speech may be categorized as consisting of phrases with particular prosodic characteristics involving demarcation (end-based mapping) and/or grouping (relation-based mapping). It must be pointed out that most research on prosodic phonology is carried out in one or the other these two approaches (refer to, among others, Rice 1987 for Slave, Condoravdi 1990, Hayes and Lahiri 1991 for Bengali, Dresher 1994).

1.2.2.2　Prosodic domains

There are differences in the inventory of prosodic domains in the prosodic phonology literature. Syntax-phonology mapping provides a prosodic representation is a hierarchy of prosodic constituents. Thus, for example, it is predicted that sandhi processes have their domains defined in terms of prosodic hierarchy. Also, the dominant rule-based approach to prosodic domains takes the rules of phrasal phonology as the determining role on the prosodic structure. Additionally, a language may have as many prosodic levels as those required by the phrasal rules (Kanerva 1990 and Condoravdi 1990). As a result, there are differences in the inventory of prosodic domains.

Related to the identification and definiton of prosodic domains, it bears on the universal hypothesis that phrasal rules are only one of the various roles of prosodic structure. Prosodic phrasing has already been shown to have a role to play in the association of the tunes of a melody, in rhythmic phenomena, and in boundary strength phenomena (refer to, among others, Hayes and Lahiri 1991 for intonation, Nespor and Vogel 1986 for rhythm, and Ladd 1992 for boundary strength). This means that various types of evidences, besides sandhi, may be considered in the identification and definition of prosodic domains.

1.2.2.3   Properties of prosodic structure

It is widely assumed that prosodic phrasing is not solely determined by the restrictive amount of syntactic information it encodes via syntax-phonology mapping. There is also an important role to be played by independent principles of prosodic structure. The Strict Layer Hypothesis (SLH) predicts a wellformedness of condition on prosodic presentations that establishes the properties of prosodic structure to which prosodic phrases have to conform. According to the SLH, ill-formed prosodic structures include multiple domains, inverted ranking of domains, skipping of levels, heterogeneous sisters, and nesting (Selkirk 1984, Selkirk 1986, Nespor and Vogel 1989). Despite its widespread acceptance, several exceptions to the SLH have been reported in the literature, and some modifications have been proposed in order to accommodate the contradicting data while adhering to the claim that prosodic structure is essentially different from syntactic structure (Itô and Mester 1992, Dresher 1994, Ladd 1992; 1996, Peperkamp 1997).

1.2.3 Focus

There is almost as much variation in the notion of focus as there are different ways of approaching focus phenomena. This fact, which has been repeatedly pointed out in the literature (refer to, among others, Szabolcsi 1981, King 1995, Kiss 1996, and Winkler 1997), is investigated in the fields of semantics, syntax, phonology, phonetics, or pragmatics, which makes it difficult to compare. Accordingly, the following discussion concerns the cross-language study of focus from different perspectives.

1.2.3.1 Focus from three different angles

Focus phenomena may be discussed from different points of views. These different points of view include, but are not limited to, the phonological perspective, the semantic/pragmatic perspective, and the syntactic perspective. Thus, authors may differ in their choice of one of the aspects as a basis for approaching focus phenomena.

The idea that the characterization of focus phenomena is an important field of phonological study has long been shared by many generative linguists. For example, as stated by Chomsky (1971), focus is seen as a reflex of phonology since it is determined by "the intonation center of surface structure." This early work thus presents what can be considered as *a phonological view of focus*. In subsequent work by other researchers, which has been dominated by either a semantic/pragmatic or a syntactic approach to focus, phonological properties are no longer seen as the determinants of focus (refer to, among others, Bolinger 1972).

The *semantic/pragmatic* view of focus includes two main trends: the *highlighting-based approach* and the *structure-based approach* (the terms are taken from Ladd 1996). In the highlighting-based approach, and according to authors such as Bolinger (1972) and Schmerling (1976), there is no agreement on the distinction between focus and accent distribution, and the validity of the bidirectional relation between focus and accent is maintained. In contrast, the structure-based approach (Gussenhoven 1983 and Ladd 1983), claims that once the focus is defined according to the speaker's intent and the context, accent distribution follows more or less automatically in accordance with language-specific rules or structural principles.

The *syntactic approach* toward focus and the structure-based version of the semantic/pragmatic view share the same concept of the structure of focus. The two views differ, however, in the role that the *syntactic approach* explicitly gives to syntactic features and the syntactic trees. The syntactic view was first proposed by Jackendoff (1972). In his view, focus is a syntactic feature relevant to both phonology and interpretation. Although Jackendoff defines focus from the syntactic perspective, he claims that *stress* is the criterion for focus assignment, and the syntactic focus marker "contains a feature marking the pitch contour" by syntactically association with the focus constituent (Jackendoff 1972).

The discussion above has shown that, whichever approach is chosen to focus phenomena, a phonological property of focus is always present. This phonological property is primarily in the form of *stress* (e.g. Culicover and Rochemont 1983) or *pitch accent* (e.g. Selkirk 1995). It is important to note that all the views of focus referred above have been elaborated mainly on the English and Gemantic languages. Therefore, the examination of the accent to the expression of the variations of focus in SC is precisely one of the central goals of the present study.

1.2.3.2   Focus in phonetic approach

As an important phonetic and phonological aspect, sentence focus is closely related with the release of new information. That is, when the sentence focus falls on a constituent, the focused constituent will distinguish itself through phonetic means, and thus results in some particular meaning. Over the past several years, great emphasis has been placed on the proper classification and characterization of the information related to focus. In the literature, two major types of focus are usually distinguished: *broad* (or *wide*) and *narrow*. Although there may be variants in the senses in which they are used, broad or wide focus is also often referred to as (*new-*) *information* focus or *presentational* focus that spreads over the entire phonological unit, and narrow focus is often referred to as *identification* or *contrastive* focus on a specific constituent (refer to, among others, Rochemont and Culicover 1990, King 1995, and Kiss 1996). The prosodic literature has approached the focus phenomena in two major ways: (i) the phonetic approach and (ii) the phonological approach. In the former, instrumental and experimental work looking for the acoustic correlates of 'focus' (broad or narrow) has provided a description of the phenomenon in terms of fundamental frequency (F_0), and sometimes also duration and intensity.

Wells (1986) and Cooper (1986), among others, are representatives of the phonetic approach. O' Shaughnessy (1979) and O' Shaughnessy and Allen (1983) report that "emphatic stress" is correlated with increased F_0 shapes reduction in the (especially) ensuing F_0 variation. These findings are generally confirmed in Cooper et al (1985). Copper et al (1985) examines the acoustics of "contrastive stress" (defined as the primary stress prompted by a trigger *'yes-no'* question designed to avoid non-contrastive and broad focus interpretations) and finds (i) a local durational effect in the form of elongation of the focused word and (ii) a more global effect on the sentence F_0 pattern in the forms of a post-focus drop on the following words and generally lower F_0 values. The presence of increased F_0 on the focused item is a matter of some dispute, as well as the less prominent acoustical cues related to focus in the clause-final position (Copper et al. 1985, Eady and Cooper 1985). Wells (1986) extends the phonetic characterization of focus to a third parameter: loudness (the perceptual correlate of force). He aims at providing an empirical basis for a definition of focus by considering features of the three dimensions of pitch, tempo, and loudness (the notion includes *information focus*, *contrastive focus*, and *emphasis*). The conclusion that Wells (1986) reached is that pitch features are the best correlates of perceived focus, namely pitch range and pitch movement, immediately followed by peak loudness (however, durational measures of/in the focused item are not included among his tempo features). Wells further remarks that there is a phonetically degree-based difference between contrastive focus and main/primary focus, in that the former is marked by more phonetic features than the latter. With the findings that cleft phrases are as phonetically marked as non-cleft equivalents (and not less marked), Wells (1986), together with many other researchers, concludes that phenomena such as pitch and stress are crucially involved in the interpretation of focus in English.

The phonetic approach to the focus phenomea in many other languages yields similar results. Dutch and Danish are illustrative examples, as shown in Nooteboom and Kruyt (1987) and in Thorsen (1975) respectively. These authors emphasize the effect of F_0 in focus signaling that, according to Nooteboom and Kruyt, overrides syntactic devices (e.g. word order) as a cue to the "given/new" distinction in Dutch. As in English and Dutch, F_0 is the prime cue for "focus" and "emphasis for contrast" in Standard Danish, but F_0 details are different among these languages. It is the F_0 reduction of surrounding rise-falls or the lifting out of the focused item in relation to the contour, and not the presence of a more elaborate F_0 movement on the focused item, that is in relation to the contour, and not the presence of a more elaborate F_0 movement on the focused item, that is the relevant cue. Further, durational differences are not important in focus signaling in Standard Danish as in English.

Toledo (1989) attempts to provide an acoustic description of focus (as triggered by *wh*-questions) in Spanish and, inspired by Wells (1986), also investigates features of pitch, intensity and duration in English. He concludes that although pitch features such as peak F_0 and pitch range may cue focus, they behave less consistently than in English. Moreover, unlike in English, pitch movement and durational effects play an unimportant role. On the whole, a loudness peak seems to be the best correlate of focus in the speech data discussed. Despite comparing his results in detail with the ones reported in the previous study of English, Toledo oflers no explanation for the cross-linguistic difference found.

It is clear that the previous studies mentioned above provide many phonetic properties for the ways in which focus is expressed in different languages. However, there is no explanation as to why focus is cued by a certain phonetic manifestation in a certain language, and whether similar/different manifestations really correspond to cross-language similarities/differences. For example, a certain F_0 mark may indicate the presence of a pitch accent, or of a phrasing boundary, or of pitch range manipulation. Issues of this kind can be addressed and clarified if the phonological structure of the language is taken into account.

1.2.3.3 Focus in phonological approach

Study on the phonological component of grammar, particularly from the 1980s onward, held that there are mainly two types of effects induced by focus phenomenon: (i) stress and accent effect and (ii) phrasing effect. The first type of effect is clearly shown in the highlighted discussion of the relation between focus and nucleus placement on English and Dutch by Ladd (1980; 1990; 1996) and Gussenhoven (1983; 1984; 1994). To this relation, Ladd adds the role played by abstract prominence patterns: the nucleus signals the focus of the utterance, and the nucleus is assigned to the element that bears the sentence stress in the sentence-level prominence pattern. In English, the final prominence pattern (w(eak)-s(trong)), that is usually the neutral/unmarked pattern is considered by Ladd to be ambiguous between a *broad* or a *narrow* focus reading, whereas early prominence (s-w) usually conveys narrow focus, as illustrated in (1) (the examples are taken from Ladd 1996):

(1) a. five FRANCES   (broad/narrow)

b. Five frances (narrow)   (narrow)

From the perceptional experiment of the accent pattern in English by Gussenhoven (1983), the ambiguity illustrated in (1) is partially confirmed. He finds that the final accent pattern is easy to interpret on the part of listeners, but it tends to be more ambiguous than the non-final one (as in (1)). However, his findings show that listeners are able to disambiguate between the "narrow" and "full" focus readings of the final accent pattern in cases where pre-focal accents may occur. According to Gussenhoven (1983; 1994), and although de-accenting of unfocused constituents is more consistent after focus than before focus, the absence of pre-focal pitch accents may only convey the narrow focus reading of the final accent pattern, as shown below (Gussenhoven 1983[1]).

(2)   a. He <u>teaches</u> in Chana.   (broad focus: 'what does he do?')

b. He teaches in Chana.   (narrow focus: 'where does he teach?')

According to Féry (1992; 1993), as in English and Dutch, a focused constituent in German is also signaled by a pitch accent: late nucleus (the neutral accent pattern) is ambiguous between the broad and narrow readings, whereas early nucleus usually has a narrow focus reading and involves de-accenting.

The previous studies clearly show that the accent location signals focus in English, Dutch, and German, but the specific features of the intonational nucleus (paralinguistic emphasis aside, Ladd 1996) do not seem to cue whether focus is broad or narrow.

Now let's turn to some languages in which the specific features of the nucleus (also) have a role to play.

According to Hayes and Lahiri (1991), focus in Bengali is signaled by phrasal relative prominence. Broad focus is conveyed by (rightmost) final prominence or late nucleus and, more importantly, narrow focus is marked by a special tune type, wherever it appears. Therefore, the final

---

[1] The nucleus is capitalized: a pre-focal accent is underlined.

nucleus pattern is not ambiguous due to the difference in tune type (i.e. H*L$_I$, the neutral declarative nucleus, contrasts with L* Hp L$_I$, the focus nucleus).

Palermo Italian stands as another example of focus marking by means of a tune type difference. According to Grice (1995), the final neutral focus has the unmarked tonal form used to signal broad focus (HL*). However, a final nucleus conveying narrow focus has a different tonal form (H*L). On the other hand, an early nucleus can be realized with either of the tonal forms (and is not followed by de-accenting). This distinguishes Palermo Italian from Standard Italian, as in the latter variety the same tonal form (H*L) signals narrow focus whether in early or late position within an utterance (Grice 1995).

As mentioned in the previous part, not only *stress* and *accent* effects of focus have been reported in the literature. Focus phenomena may also be cured by *phrasing* effects. This has been claimed for languages such as Hungarian, Huausa, and Korean.

Vogel and Kenesei (1987) demonstrated that focus (and scope) determines phrasing at the intonational phrase level in Hungarian. A similar analysis, but at the phonological phrase level, has been proposed for Hausa. According to Zec and Inkelas (1990), the role played by "prominence" in phrasing in this language is manifested by the fact that "prominent" elements are necessarily mapped into their own phonological phrase. Consequently, this information has to be accessed by the phonological phrase mapping algorithm. Korean seems to be another language in which focus determines phrasing at the phonological phrase (Cho 1990). It should be further noted that in Jun (1996), a study that presents an analysis of Korean prosody that is in disagreement with the prosodic phonology approach to phrasing represented by works such as Cho's, focus is also assigned a crucial role in determining phrasing. In fact, Jun contends that non-syntactic factors (such as weight and speech rate) may influence phrasing, but are realized as tendencies, only syntactic constraints and narrow focus have a *fixed* effect on the phrasing.

There are languages, however, in which the focus effects on phonological phrasing do not appear to be as clear as those already described. Selkirk and Shen (1990) analyzed the domain of phrasal tone deletion in Shanghai Chinese. They claim that this rule applies after focus (and focus here refers to "contrast" or "emphasis"). It is observed that although focus is followed by a considerable lowering of pitch register (or pitch range compression), that is sometimes associated with a phrasing change, a distinction can still be seen in the phrasing that accounts for the application of post-focus tone deletion.

Selkirk and Chen (1990) relate the post-focus pitch range compression in Shanghai Chinese to what they take to be a similar phenomenon of tonal implementation in Japanese, as described in Beckman and Pierrehumbert (1986) and Pierrehumbert and Beckman (1988). In fact, according to Beckman and Pierrehumbert, the phonetic effects after a focused word in Japanese may be interpreted either as a consequence of accent subordination to the focused word (i.e., pitch range compression). However, another fact about Japanese has to be noted: regardless of what is the best interpretation for post-focal phenomenon, it seems clear that in Japanese a focused word has a raised H tone. This is interpreted in Pierrehumbert and Beckman as being due to the blocking of catechesis triggered by focus.

By contrast, English is a well-known example of a language in which focus can restructure phrasing. Beckman and Pierrehumbert note that it is possible to introduce an intonational phrase boundary next to a focused constituent. In fact, this is an instance of their statement that (intonation-based) phrasing in English is highly facultative. However, it is in the work on the rhyme rule that a more common effect of focus on phonological phrasing has been described. The rhythm is an optional process bounded by a phonological phrase and is generally taken to be a strategy of clash resolution in which either there is a stress shift or a stress reduction (Nespor and Vogel 1989, and Vogel et al 1995, among others). Focus has been described to trigger a phrasing restructuring that blocks this rule: if the target word is focused, the trigger word no longer leads to a stress shift/reduction on the target word, and this is interpreted as being due to the placement of a phonological phrase.

It has been shown that the focus phenomenon may be phonologically expressed in terms of *stress* and *accent* effects, and *phrasing* effects. Among the former, prominence patterns, nucleus placement and general pitch accent distribution seem to be prevalent in some languages (e.g., English and Dutch), while a special tune type is crucially used in others (e.g., Bengali and Palermo Italian). Among the latter, in some languages, focus seems to determine phrasing algorithms (e.g., Hungarian and Korean), in others whether it determines phrasing or not appears to be unclear (e.g., Shanghai Chinese and Japanese), and still in others the focus effect on phrasing seems to be best expressed by restricting conditions that affect, and therefore presuppose, 'default' phrasing (e.g., English and Italian). Whether these *effects* are arbitrary choices to follow in a principled way from some linguistic properties is a question that this study will address. The properties of the prosody of information induced focus in SC will be shown to favor the hypothesis that phonological focus effects are not arbitrary.

1.3 Significance of the research

With respet to the studies reviewed, it is important to note the following considerations: (i) all the views of focus have been discussed mainly on the basis of English and other Germanic languages (such as German and Dutch); (ii) the semantic/pragmatic and syntactic studies are not entirely supported by concrete phonetic evidences; and (iii) the phonetic and phonological investigations on focus phenomena have scarcely taken the syntactic structure into consideration. Therefore, this study takes up the issues of how the focus, syntactic structure, and intonation structure are modeled to account for prosodic variances in SC. Specifically, it employs the evidence of *focus* marked by both *wh*-operators induced information variations (theme focus, rheme focus, different numbers of rheme focus) and syntactic markers (*lian*-marked focus or *shi*-marked focus), through which to explore the underlying causes for the accent distribution of the focused constituents in the sentential surface form.

To go a step further, understanding the linguistic strategies speakers employ to express *focus* is of fundamental significance. Firstly, it can present the acoustic cues that speakers adopt to express their intended information categories. Secondly, it can provide categorical representations of focus driven variances of prominence and boundary patterns. Thirdly, it can reveal the underlying forces motivating intonation reorganization. Fourthly, it can clear up disagreement and confusion in the components of intonation structures. Fifthly, it contributes greatly to the overall description and explanation of Chinese grammar. Finally, it can help improve the naturalness of speech synthesis and speech recognition.

The basic hypothesis of this study is that languages employ universal prosodic parameters such as fundamental frequency (F_0) and duration to signal prosodic differences. In particular, in SC, F_0 and duration are adopted to transmit phonetic variations of focus conditions. The study discusses the following questions: i) What characterizes the F_0 and durational patterns for the constituents dwelling in different focus conditions in unmarked structures? ii) How is *syntax*-marked (i.e., *lian*-marked or *shi*-marked) focus acoustically realized? iii) How are the syntactic structures and focus structures modified for unification in the expression of intonation structure? iv) What is the phonological description and explanation of accent patterns and accent distribution? v) What constitutes the grammar for restricting the surface distribution of accent in SC? vi) What is the corresponding relation between *focus* and *accent* in SC?

1.4　Basic concepts in this study

An integrated view of phonetics and phonology with respect to 'Focus-to-Accent[1] of SC, the goal of the study, concentrates on the examination of *accents* conveyed by different numbers and various kinds of focuses. It is therefore appropriate at this point to define the terms *focus*, *nuclear accent*, *pre-nuclear accent*, and *relative prominence* for the purpose of delimiting the research topic. One of the implicit goals of the study is to show that the area so defined is a coherent object of study.

1.4.1　Definition of focus

The definition of the term *focus* that I adopt in this study follows Steedman (2000). Steedman draws a primary distinction between *theme* and *rheme*[2] and a secondary distinction between *focus* and *background*. The point is to show a theory of grammar in which phrasal intonation and information structure are reunited. Specifically, the first dimension corresponds to the contrast between the *theme* of an utterance and the *rheme* that the utterance contributes to the theme. Also, Steedman defines them more formally in terms of both "structured meanings" and "alternative semantics." Informally, it is to be thought of as *that part of an utterance that connects it to the rest of the discourse*, a notion that is most unambiguously determined when the preceding utterance is itself a *wh*-question[3]. In English, this dimension of information

---

[1] This term is taken from Gussenhoven (1983).
[2] The terms theme and rheme are taken from Mathesius (1929), Firbas (1964; 1966), and Halliday (1967; 1970).
[3] In particular, Steedman follows and Bolinger (1989) in reverting to Mathesius and rejecting Halliday's requirement that the theme be sentence-initial. The theme of an utterance in this sense is sometimes called the "topic" or the "presupposition".

structure contributes, among other things, to the determination of the overall shape of the intonational phrasal tune or tunes imposed on an utterance.

The second dimension concerns the distinction between words whose interpretations contribute to distinguishing the theme or rheme of the utterance from other alternatives that the context makes available, and words whose interpretations do not. Halliday (1967), who was probably the first to identify the orthogonal nature of these two dimensions, called it *new information*, in contrast to *given information*. Whereas, Steedman (2000) follows the phonological perspective in calling the information marked by prominence as the "focus"[1], distinguishing *theme-focus* and *rheme-focus* where necessary, as in example (3):

(3)   I   know   who   proved   soundness.   But   who   proved COMPLETENESS?

(MARCEL) (proved COMPLETENESS)[2].

The effect of the *wh*-question in (3) is to encourage a hearer to regard the theme linking the answer to the discourse as something that might informally be thought of as *proving completeness*. The subject MARCEL is the rheme, the part of the answer that advances the discussion by contributing novel information.

Steedman (2000) mentions that the position of prominences in the phrase has to do with the further information structural dimension that is called "focus." Within both theme and rheme, those words that contribute to distinguishing the theme and the rheme of an utterance from other alternatives made available by the context may be marked visa prominences. The following example (4) shows how this works:

(4)   I know that Marcel likes the man who wrote the musical.

---

[1] The term *focus*, like the term *topic*, is used in the literature in several conflicting ways. The present use of the term is common among phonologists who adopt it simply to denote the material marked by prominence.

[2] This example is taken from Mark Steedman (2000) and is adopted to illustrate the differences between theme and rheme.

But who does he ADMIRE?

(Marcel ADMIRES) (the woman who DIRECTED the musical)

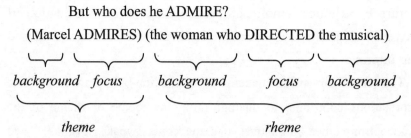

The significance of the presence or absence of primary prominence within a theme such as *Marcel ADMIRES* seems to lie in the prior existence or accommodatability of a theme differing in its translation only in those elements corresponding to accented items such as ADMIRES. Within the rheme, which is *the woman who* DIRECTED *the musical*, only the word DIRECTED is contrasted.

As is mentioned in the previous part on the focus studies from the phonetic and phonological perspective, these two areas mainly adopt the definition of *broad focus* and *narrow focus* to mark the different status of information. With regard to the proper implications of these two focuses, broad focus is the carrier of new information, i.e., it introduces some new information into the discourse. Narrow focus expresses identification in the sense that it operates on a set of contextually relevant entities present in the domain of discourse, and identifies a subset of this set. Naturally, broad and narrow focus relate differently to the preceding discourse. As pointed out in Leusen and Kálmán (1993), each can only occur felicitously in specific contexts such as the following: for broad focus, in narratives, list structures, answers to "what happened"; for narrow focus, in answers or replies. In (1) and (2) below illustrative examples of the two types of focus are given using the classic question-answer pair, in which the question functions as a licensing context (the capitalized words are the narrow focus bearing units):[1]

(1) Broad focus: What happened?

---

[1] For the relevance of these pairs in relation to focus, see Chomsky (1971) and Jackendoff (1972), among others.

JIM is going to visit us.

(2) Narrow focus: a. Who is going to visit us?

JIM is going to visit us.

b. So Rob is going to visit us?

No, JIM is going to visit us.

Language can not only have different ways of encoding each type of focus, but the semantic contents of (especially narrow) focus may also vary from language to language (as shown in Szabolcsi 1981 and Kiss 1996).

A comparison of the *broad vs. narrow focus* classifications and Steedman's (2000) concept of *rheme focus* with other constituents dwelling within a theme background shares identical implications with *narrow focus*. Also, the information status described by *broad focus* is equal to the rheme focus with other constituents distributed under the rheme background. Therefore, the information status expressed by the broad and narrow focus is included in Steedman's definition. Crucially, the classifications of *theme* or *rheme* and *focus* or *background* provide a more explicit description of the information status; the primary information is marked by rheme focus and the secondary information is marked described by theme focus in one target sentence. Thereafter, the hierarchical levels of accents can be examined based on this conception.

1.4.2   Nuclear accent and pre-nuclear accent

The terms *nuclear accent* and *pre-nucler accent* are defined by Ladd (1996) according to the intonation structure of the British School (Palmer 1922, O' Connor and Arnold 1973, Kingdon 1958, Crystal 1969). In the founding work of the British school, e.g., Palmer (1922), the contour is divided into three parts, called *head*, *nucleus*, and *tail*. Only the *nucleus* is obligatory and associated with the most prominent stressed syllable in the utterance. *Head*, an independent choice, refers to the stretch of the contour preceding the nuclear syllable, and the *tail* is adopted to describe the stretch of contour following the nuclear syllable. With some variation, this basic plan has been part of the British approach to describing intonation ever since. Probably the most significant widely agreed upon change to the structure outlined by Palmer has been the idea that the head begins with a major stressed syllable (see Kingdon 1958). Based on these arguments, Ladd (1996) proposes that accent can be classified as *nuclear accent* and *pre-nuclear accent*, with the former one deserving the obligatory and primary nature and the latter having optional and secondary characteristics. Acoustic evidence of SC is provided to further support the levels of accents at the sentence level.

1.4.3　Relative prominence

In previous literature, two prominence patterns are usually distinguished. The first, *weak-strong*, is the 'normal' stress pattern, used when there is no particular reason for emphasis, or when the focus is on the phrase as a whole. The second pattern of prominence 'strong-weak' focuses on a given constituent for contextual reasons. The distinctions of relative prominence in this research are for the following reasons: (i) the features under discussion are obvious supra-segmental; (ii) the meanings conveyed are clearly not lexical, since relative prominence can affect the implications of the utterance; (iii) the distinctions are linguistically structured, in the sense that we are dealing with *categories* such as rising vs. falling or *weak-strong* vs. *strong-weak*.

1.5　Outline of this research

Several steps were taken in this study in the examination of evidences of prosodic effects induced by variations in focus conditions. These involve a series of production experiments using controlled speech materials that were designed so that the various sources of evidence for the relevant categories of phonological structure could be assessed. The speech materials used, the procedures followed, and the results obtained, are described in Chapters Two to Six.

Chapter Two presents the methodology employed to identify the prosodic patterns induced by various focus conditions. Specifically, the chapter is a detailed description of the experimental design, data extraction and recording procedures, and data analysis, through which to explore the acoustic property of the *syntax*-marked focus and *wh*-elicited information focus.

Chapter Three presents an investigation of how F_0 and duration are employed by SC speakers to convey various kinds of information in unmarked structures. The data from the production experiment are examined in detail: (i) the fundamental frequency contours and durational lengthening of the constituents dwelling in the information categories such as 'rheme focus' , 'theme focus' , 'rheme background' , and 'theme background'; (ii) F_0 prominence induced by double or multiple rheme focus. Based on the acoustic results from the data analysis, the study argues that different levels of information can generate different levels of accents and the same level of information also triggers different levels of accents. Therefore, the study proposes that the accents have both obligatory and optional characteristics in SC, i.e., the *nuclear accent* are the *unique* and *primary* tone, while the *pre-nuclear tone* is *optional* and the *secondary* tone.

Chapter Four mainly provides evidences for the interaction of *syntax*-marked focus and *wh*-operators induced information focus on the formation of F_0 and duration patterns. Results of experiments further support the observations of the accent level differences in SC, i.e., *nulcear tone* and *pre-nulcear tone*. There are at least two intonation properties that unambiguously place SC into the category of languages with two levels of accents: (i) the information induced focus and the *syntax*-marked focus can convey accent simultaneously; (ii) the rightmost focus (*syntax*-marked or information induced focus) can always realize accent.

Chapter Five deals with the phonological representation and analysis of the accent patterns as defined in Chapter Three and Chapter Four. An account of the intonation structure is presented, making crucial use of the intonational grammar from Pierrehumbert (1980), Ladd (1996), the ToBI labeling system, the IViE labeling system, and Gussenhoven (2004). As for explanation of the underlying causes for restricting the distribution of accents in surface form, the study adopted a series of ranked constraints.

Chapter Six presents a discussion of the accent pattern and distribution under the theoretical model of OT. A series of ranked constraints are adopted to analyze the accent pattern, accent distribution, and phonological phrasing in SC.

Chapter Seven is the concluding part of this research that summarizes the major finding of this study and proposes related issues for future research.

Chapter Two

Methodology

2.1 Background and claims

In many languages, F_0 raising and durational lengthening are crucial to the expression of focus and phonological events in an utterance (refer to Ladd 1996, Xu 1999, Gussenhoven 2004, Chen 2006). However, the exact role played by these parameters in phonetic and phonological aspects within a specific language and across languages is still elusive (refer to, among others, Venditti et al 1996). This is most probably due to a wide range of intricate questions that need to be considered and involved, in particular, (i) a rigorous inspection of *accent pattern variations* induced by various kinds and different numbers of *focuses*; and (ii) the implications of hierarchical levels of accents. Leaving the cross-linguistic considerations for later, the experimental design is a contribution to both (i) and (ii), as far as SC is concerned.

Previous findings on the relation between *focus* and *accent* support the following claims: (a) focus does induce F_0 and durational variations; (b) the crucial phonological means for the expression of focus is *accent patterns* and *tonal events*. The utterances of the present experiment are designed to have various *kinds* and different *numbers* of focuses through which to explore the factors behind previous results and also provide a further test for these claims. An *accent* pattern can be assessed by comparison of the effect of *different* kinds and numbers of *focuses* on F_0 and durational variations. Further, the precise nature of the phonological means associated with the expression of focus can be examined in detail by comparisons with segments identical utterances in various focus conditions. Thereafter, the results of the present experiment may also contribute to the understanding of the relation between *prosodic phrasing* (assessed by pause phenomena), and *intonational structure* (assessed by the selection, distribution and status of tonal events). Acoustical and perceptual experiments are adopted to achieve the research goals, with the former one being the primary means.

2.2 Design of acoustic experiment

2.2.1 Materials selection

With regard to the research aim of the acoustic experiment, the following factors were considered: word order, tonal combinations, segmental combinations, syntactic structure, and focus categories. Since the effect of segments on the change in F_0 and duration has been reported by many researchers (Lehiste 1970, among others), the influence imposed by the segments should be controlled; otherwise, the validity of the experimental results might be impaired. The means of offsetting the segmental effect is to select syllables with zero and voiced initials[8] to compose the target words. In this regard, the following segments, which fall into four sets, were selected: Subject = {Wu1Yin1(Wuyin); Liu2Min2(Liumin); Mai4Li4(Maili)}; Verb = {Wei1Bi1 (intimidate); Ti2Ba2(elevate); Nüe4Dai4(maltreat)}; Adverb = {Jin1Tian1(today); Ling2Chen2(early morning); Ban4Ye4(midnight)}; Object = {Wen1Yin1(Wenyin); Mao2Lan2(Maolan); Lu4Na4(Luna)}[9]. The reasons that the tonal combinations of "tone1+tone1", "tone2+tone2" , and "tone4+tone4" are employed in each syntactic constituent is that it facilitates the observation of the entire range of F_0 change for one tonal feature and the

---

[8] The classifications of the initials are based on Duanmu (2000).
[9] The words in sets 'Subject' and 'Object' are Chinese names. The selection of all the words in sets 'verb' and 'Adverb' are common dictionary vocabulary to ensure the naturalness of the target sentences.

pitch performance of the '*H-L*' tone permutation in one sentence type. The 'Subject' and 'Object' serve as the major target words that are systematically investigated in various syntactic and information structures. Therefore the selection of other syntactic elements such as 'Verb' and 'Adverb' are merely required to meet the needs of tonal combinations. A sentence is thus constituted respectively by combining each member from the four sets with corresponding identical tonal combinations, specifically, each sentence is only allowed to contain one kind of tone, e.g. tone1, tone2, or tone4.

2.2.2   Syntactic structure of target sentence

All the above components are merged into the following syntactic patterns of sentences that are classified into three types, i.e., unmarked structure, *lian...dou* structure, and *shi...de* structure, all of which are taken, in one way or another, as the classical structures to represent focus status in SC (refer to, among others, Fang 1995, Liu and Xu 1998, and Xu 2004).

2.2.2.1   Unmarked structure

There is still a great deal of debate on the unmarked structure in SC; i.e., Tai (1973) proposes that it is appropriate to classify SC as an 'SVO' (Subject+Verb+Object) language, whereas the word order processes the change from 'SVO' to 'SOV'(Li and Thompson, 1979). Xu (2004) points out that word order is relatively flexible in Chinese, the canonical form of the Chinese sentence is 'SVO', though 'SOV' is also found as an alternative. Liu (2004; 2004) also claims that the topic (marked as "T") in Chinese should be treated as a syntactic component to distinguish subject. Therefore, he proposes that besides "SVO", the word sequence "TSV(O)" and "STV(O)" are also common in Chinese. This study adopts the "SVO" order as the basic unmarked structure in SC following Tai (1973) and Xu (2004), and studies by different authors (e.g., Frota 1993 and Xu 1999) that examined the phonetic aspect, the intonation of the neutral sentence with the word order of 'SVO.' Thus, the syntactic items are put into the structure "Subject Verb Object Le0."[10] Further, the basic target sentences are extended to four syntactic constituents: "Subject+Aderb+Verb+Object+Le0." The reason for the increase in the number of the syntactic constituents in the unmarked structure is due to the research of Gussenhoven (1983), and Faber (1987), all of whom suggest that in the short one-phrase pattern the subject and predicate in some sense form a single unit of new information, while in the two-phrase pattern the subject is in some sense separated out and presented as a reference point in the discourse with the really new information in the predicate. Therefore, the relation between focus and accent can be addressed within both short and long unmarked sentences that are also taken as the basis for a comparison with the '*lian...dou*' and '*shi...de*' construction. All the target sentences are listed in (i)-(ii) as follows:

(i)   Unmarked short sentence:

a.   Wu1 Yin1 Wei1 Bi1 Wen1 Yin1 Le0.

    wu   yin   intimidate wen yin   le

    (Wuyin intimidated Wenyin).

b.   Liu Min2 Ti2 Ba2 Mao2 Lan2 Le0.

    liu min   elevate   mao   lan   le

    (Liumin elevated Maolan).

c.   Mai4 Li4 Nüe4 Dai4 Lu4 Na4 Le0.

    mai   li   maltreat   lu   na   le

    (Maili maltreated Luna).

(ii)   Unmarked long sentence:

a.   Wu1 Yin1 Jin1 Tian1 Wei1 Bi1 Wen1 Yin1 Le0.

    wu   yin   today   intimidate   wen yin   le

    (Wuyin intimidated Wenyin today).

---

[10] The insertion of the perfective *le* in sentence final position is to counterbalance the phonetic nature of the final syllable of the sentence, since we also have the '*shi...de*' construction with *de* located in sentence final position in certain circumstances in chapter four.

b.   Liu Min2 Ling2 Chen2 Ti2 Ba2 Mao2 Lan2 Le0.

liu min   early morning elevate   mao   lan   le

(Liumin elevated Maolan on the early morning).

c.   Mai4 Li4 Ban4 Ye4 Nüe4 Dai4 Lu4 Na4 Le0.

mai li   midnight   maltreat   lu   na   le

(Maili maltreated Luna at midnight).

2.2.2.2   *Lian...dou* structure

A production experiment is carried out on the '*lian...dou*' structure with the aim of examining whether F_0 prominence and durational lengthening are the property of *lian*-marked focus in SC and a reflection of the relation between *focus placement* and *accents distribution*. As in the previous part, the basic structure selected is: "Subject+Verb+Object+Le0", and the unmarked target sentence is composed of the three sets of syntactic components placed onto the given positions in the sentence. Thus, it is possible to examine the '*lian...dou*' construction by using similar methods through which the basic word order can be kept the same and further contrastive examination can be conducted among the components in different syntactic structures. Additionally, Fang (1995), Liu and Xu (1998), and Cai (2004) also adopt the same method for generating the '*lian...dou*' formula. Therefore, the basic word order can be expressed as: "*Lian*+Subject+*Dou*+Verb+Object+Le0." Since the unmarked sentence ends with the particle *le* and the '*shi...de*' construction is finalized by *de*, the sentence final particle *le* is utilized so as to maintain a phonetic balance. The variation in the *lian*-marked focus is realized through changes in the word order of '*lian...dou*;' e.g., "Subject+Lian+Object+*Dou*+Verb+Le0." The same elements occurring in part 2.2.2.1 above are also assessed. Specifically, {Liu2Min2(Liumin) and Mai4Li4(Maili)}; {Ti2Ba2(elevate) and Nüe4Dai4(maltreat)}; {Mao2Lan2(Maolan) and Lu4Na4(Luna)} for subject, verb and object items, respectively[11]. Each the target sentences is presented below:

(i) *Lian* **marked subject:**

    a.   Lian2 **Liu2 Min2**$^{[+LianF]12}$ Dou1 Ti2 Ba2 Mao2 Lan2 Le0.

        even   liu   min   all   elevate   mao lan   le

        (Even Liumin elevated Maolan).

    b.   Lian2 **Mai4 Li4**$^{[+LianF]}$ Dou1 Nüe Dai4 Lu4 Na4 Le0.

        even   mai4 li   all   maltreat   mao lan   le

        (Even Maili maltreated Luna).

(ii) *Lian* **marked object:**

    a.   Liu2 Min2 Lian2 **Mao2 Lan2**$^{[+LianF]}$ Dou Ti2 Ba2 Le0.

        liu   min   even   mao   lan   all   elevate   le

        (Liumin even elevated Maolan).

    b.   Mai4 Li4 Lian2 **Lu4 Na4**$^{[+LianF]}$ Dou1 Nüe Dai4 Le0.

        mai   li   even   lu   na   all   maltreat le

        (Maili even maltreated Luna).

2.2.2.3 *Shi…de* structure

The aim of the experiment is to investigate the co-existences and conflicts in the *shi*-induced focus, *lian*-marked focus, and the information triggered focus. The core set of the test-sentences is formed by the "Subject+Verb+Object" word order as the unmarked sentence following part 2.2.2.2, and the '*shi…de*' sentence is composed by '*shi…de*' being inserted in the unmarked sentence in accordance with Fang (1995), Cai (2004), Xu (2001), and Yuan (2003). Also, based on the definition from Fang (1995), *shi* can only be taken to mark the contrastive focus on the nominal constituent in the position proceeding the verb. Two central

---

[11] The tone1 constituent is excluded in the discussion in this part due to the limitations of the spaces.

[12] The feature [+LianF] is adopted to mean the proceeding subject is *lian*-marked focus.

concerns determine the choice of syntactic components for the target sentence for the 'shi...de' structure: (i) the attempt to allow for the most informative comparisons with the 'lian...dou' and the unmarked structure; and (ii) the effort to construct natural sentences that could occur in many conversations, while involving as little phonetic repetition as possible, and including varied lexical tones. To accomplish (i) and (ii), the following target sentences were selected as the samples with the sets {Liu2Min2(Liumin) and Mai4Li4(Maili)}; {Ti2Ba2(elevate) and Nüe4Dai4(maltreat)}; {Mao2Lan2(Maolan) and Lu4Na4(Luna)} serving as subject, verb, and object, respectively:

(i) *Shi* marked subject:

    a.   Shi4 **Liu2 Min2**[+ShiF]13 Ti2 Ba2 Mao2 Lan2 De0.

        is liu min   elevate mao lan de

        (It is Liumin that elevated Maolan).

    b.   Shi4 **Mai4 Li4**[+ShiF] Nüe4 Dai4 Lu4 Na4 De0.

        is mai4 li4   maltreat lu na de

        (It is Maili that maltreated Luna).

2.2.3   Focus identification

2.2.3.1   Focus in unmarked structure

As the research interest lies in the description and analysis of how information induced focus is expressed by *phonological* means, the following possibilities may be expected: (i) different ways of encoding each type of focus in SC, i.e., there are phonological differences between focused and unfocused constituents; (ii) there is a three-way phonological distinction, i.e., not only focused and unfocused differ, but different levels of focuses are realized in a particular way; (iii) different types of focuses

---

[13] The feature [+ShiF] is taken to indicate that the proceeding constituent is a *shi*-marked focus.

are unambiguously expressed by phonological means, i.e., *syntax*-marked focus and information induced focus[14]. Based on the concept of the *broad* vs. *narrow* focus and theme vs. rheme focus, although the terms in these systems are different, the phonological implication of the narrow focus resembles that of the rheme focus with other constituents serving as the theme background bearing unit, and the phonological meaning of rheme focus with all the other items in the rheme scope being conveyed by virtue of the broad focus. However, the "theme vs. rheme" system can provide a better classification of information and focus status variation through which the inventory of tone types conveyed by various kinds of focuses can be further addressed.

2.2.3.1.1　Different kinds of focuses

In the experiment, the focus conditions are achieved by the use of *wh*-question equivalents preceding the target sentence in order to elicit the production of utterances with *a rheme background reading*, *a rheme focus reading*, *a theme background reading*, or *a theme focus reading*. For clarity, these four categories, together with the context that trigger them, are presented in examples "a-d" in type (i) sentences. In "a" and "b", the syntactic item 'Subject' is a rhematic item, the background in "a", and the focus in "b"; whereas, in "c" and "d", the 'Subject' bears thematic information, either background in "c" or focus in "d". In contrast with the four information categories of 'Subject', the 'Object' only occurs in two kinds of focuses categories: rheme focus and theme background; however, differences within these rheme focuses are due to the corresponding thematic status.

---

[14] The detailed discussion of the acoustic manifestations of the syntax-marked focus is presented in chapter four.

(i)   Subject   Verb   Object   Le0

a.   Fa1 Sheng1 Le0 Shen2 Me0 Shi4? (What happened?)

Subject   Verb   **Object**[+RF]15   Le0

S   V   O   Le0

background   focus

rheme

b.   Shei2   Verb   Object   Le0? (Who   Verb   Object?)

Subject[+RF]   Verb   Object   Le0

S   V   O   Le0

focus   background

rheme   theme

c.   Subject   Verb   Shei2   Le0 ? (Subject Verb whom?)

Subject   Verb   **Object**[+RF]   Le0

S   V   O   Le0

background   focus

theme   rheme

d.   Subject   Verb   Shei2 Le0 ?   Shei2   Verb   Shei2   Le0?

(Subject Verb whom ? Who Verb whom?)

Subject[+TF]   Verb   **Object**[+RF]   Le0

S   V   O   Le0

focus   background   focus

theme   rheme

---

15 The feature [+RF] denotes the rheme focus bearing unit.

2.2.3.1.2 Different numbers of rheme focuses

Chen (2006) states that the rhematic focus statuses induce the greatest magnitude of F_0 raising and durational lengthening. Therefore, different numbers of rheme focuses, i.e., two rheme focuses in short target sentences or three rheme focuses in long target sentences, are designed into the target sentences in order to further explore the corresponding relationships between the positions of the focuses and the distribution of the prominences (accents). In the dual focus condition, both short sentences and long sentences are adopted in order to compare the F_0 differences between the two rhematic focuses. For the multiple rheme focuses, only the long sentence is adopted as the research anchor.

(i) Short sentence:

    Subject   Verb   Object Le0.

    Shei2   Verb   Shei2   Le0 ? (Who Verb whom?)

    Subject[+RF]   Verb   **Object[+RF]** Le0

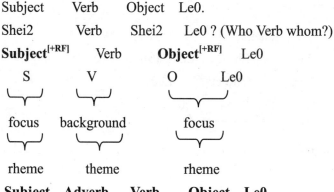

(ii) **Subject Adverb   Verb   Object Le0**

    a. Fa1 Sheng1 Le0 Shen2 Me0 Shi4?[16](What happened?)

    Subject Adverb   Verb   **Object[+RF]** Le0

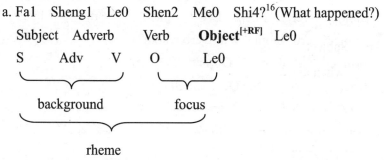

---

[16] The design of the context here is to obtain a target sentence with a rheme scope that can be used as the basis for comparing the prominence realizations in dual and multiple focus conditions.

b.   Shei2   Adverb   Verb   Shei2 Le0?(Adverb, who Verb whom?)

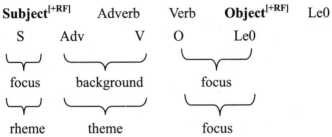

c.   Shei2 Shen2 Me0 Shi2 Hou0 Verb Shei2 Le0? (Who when verb what?)

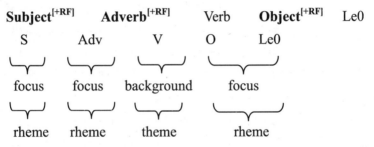

d.   Shei2 Aderb Zen3 Me0 Shei2 Le0? (Adverb, who did whom?)

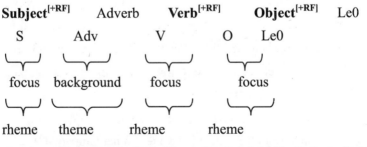

e.   Subject Shen2 Me0 Shi2 Hou0 Zen3 Me0 Shei2 Le0 (Subject when did what?)

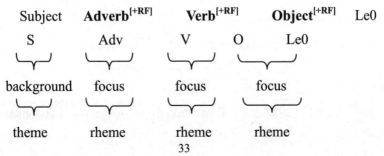

f. Shei2 Shen2 Me0 Shi2 Hou0 Zen3 Me0 Object Le0?

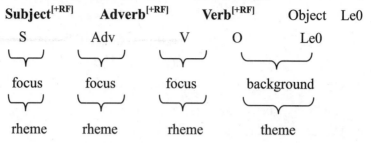

2.2.3.2 Focus conditions in the *lian…dou* structure

Previous designs of the focus conditions in an unmarked structure can provide comprehensive evidence of accent distribution induced by information of a different status. Information induced focus is also designed into the '*lian…dou*' structure to observe both the phonetic and phonological properties of the *lian*-marked focus. In particular, the intent is to answer the following questions: (i) what is the acoustic similarity and difference between *lian*-marked focus and rheme focus? (ii) what constitutes the co-existing and conflicting relations between the *lian*-marked focus and *wh*-operator elicited information induced focus? (iii) what is the relation between the nuclear tone distribution and *lian*-marked focus? The experiment selects the following asking-answering pairs:

(i) *Lian* marked subject:

  lian Subject *dou* Verb Object Le0.

  a. Fa1 Sheng1 Le0 Shen2 Me0 Shi4? (What happened?)

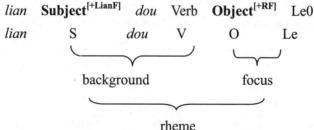

  b. Lian2 Shei2 Dou1 Verb Object Le0?(Even who

34

verb Maolan?)

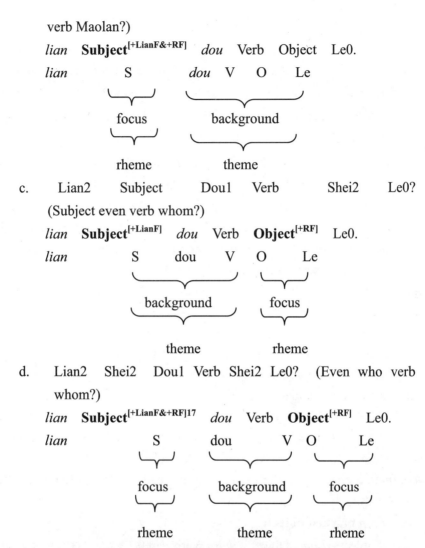

lian **Subject**[+LianF&+RF] *dou* Verb Object Le0.

lian   S   *dou* V O Le

focus   background

rheme   theme

c.   Lian2   Subject   Dou1   Verb   Shei2   Le0?

(Subject even verb whom?)

lian **Subject**[+LianF] *dou* Verb **Object**[+RF] Le0.

lian   S   dou V O Le

background   focus

theme   rheme

d.   Lian2 Shei2 Dou1 Verb Shei2 Le0? (Even who verb whom?)

lian **Subject**[+LianF&+RF]17 *dou* Verb **Object**[+RF] Le0.

lian   S   dou   V O Le

focus   background   focus

rheme   theme   rheme

Apart from the desired focus environment and the question asked in the above part, another crucial issue is the grammatical form of the information focus in the *lian*-marked sentence. In a study of the nature of the focus marked by *lian*, Liu and Xu (1998) maintain that the *lian*-marked focus can form a contrastive relation with other constituents. Based on this statement, context "b" is a grammatical *asking-answering* pair. Also based

---

17 The feature [+LianF&+RF] denotes the addition of the *lian*-marked focus and the rheme focus.

on the argument from Liu and Xu (1998) that the major information within a *lian*-marked sentence is distributed on the constituents after the *lian*-marked focus, context "c" is a well-formness asking-answering pair. As for context "d", a similar context can be obtained from Zubizarreta (1998) who adopts the example: a. Who ate what? b. there is an <x, y>, such that *x* ate *y*, through which the study supports the argument of *uniqueness* of the nuclear tone. The explanation of the form of type (ii) in the following paragraph also comes from these statements.

In the above four target sentences, the *lian*-marked focus always locates on the 'Subject' items as marked by the bold characters. Due to the variations in context, the subject components exhibit the following information statuses: (i) rheme backgournd, (ii) rheme focus, (iii) theme background, and (iv) rheme focus. Correspondingly, the object constituents exhibit information focus statuses as: (a) rheme focus, (b) theme background, (c) rheme focus, and (d) rheme focus. Crucially, the *lian*-marked focus combines with the information induced focus in context "b", and the *lian*-marked focus locates on a different position than the information focus under the conditions of (a) and (c). Further, the rhematic focus realizes the same position with the *lian*-marked focus under condition (d) and the rheme focus also locates on the object item within the same sentence. Therefore, we can observe the co-existing and conflicting effect upon the F_0 and duration patterns from these two kinds of focuses.

(ii)   *Lian* marked object:

Subject *lian* Object *dou* Verb Le0.

b.   Fa1 Sheng1 Le0 Shen2 Me0 Shi4? (What happened?)

Subject   *lian*   **Object**[+LianF]   *dou*   **Verb**[+RF]   Le0.

S   *lian*   O   *dou*   V   Le

background   focus

rheme

36

b.   Shei2   Lian2   Object   Dou1   Verb   Le0? (Even who verb object?)

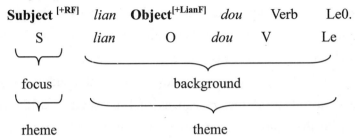

c.   Subject   Lian2   Shei2   Dou1   Verb   Le0? (Subject even verb whom?)

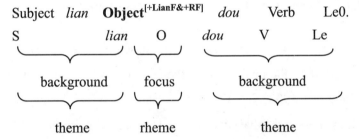

e.   Shei2   Lian2   Shei2   Dou1 Verb Le0? (Even who verb whom?)

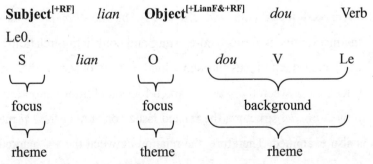

Under the construction of "Subject+*lian* +Object +*Dou* +Verb +Le", the *lian*-marked focus distributes in the object item. Through the four given contexts, the 'Subject' and 'Object' elements also exhibit four focus statuses of (i)-(iv) in the above paragraph, since the relationships between the *lian*-marked focus and the information induced focus are varied. Specifically, under condition "a" in type (ii), the *lian*-marked focus locates

37

in the position following the rhematic focus that forms the conflicting relationships, and under "b", the 'Subject' and the 'Object' also exhibit conflicting relationships with the *wh*-elicited focus in the proceeding position. However, an additive effect can be obtained from condition "c" in which the rhematic focus and the *lian*-marked focus locate on the same entity: 'Object'. More interestingly, the "d" condition displays a different case than the rhematic focus, and the addition of the rhematic focus with the *lian*-marked focus results in conflict between the two focuses.

2.2.3.3   Focus conditions in the *shi...de* structure

Different from the '*lian...dou*' structure, the focused constituent symbolized by the marker *shi*, is the contrastive focus (refer to Fang 1995, Liu and Xu 1998, and Cai 2004). Thus, it bears the characteristics of exclusiveness and exhaustiveness, and the information marked by *shi* is the most prominent part within the clause. With regard to the *asking-answering* pair in the '*shi...de*' construction, the answer should be related to the *shi*-marked focus (Liu and Xu 1998). In the '*lian...dou*' structure, the *lian*-marked focus forms a co-existing and conflicting relationship with the *wh*-elicited rheme focus through which may be observed the similarity and difference between the *syntax*-marked focus and information induced focus. In the '*shi...de*' structure, the related issue concerning the *shi*-marked focus is also examined. Therefore, the relation between the *shi*-marked focus and the nuclear tone distribution can be explored. The following sentences were adopted based on the research aim and the comparative needs with the unmarked and '*lian...dou*' structures:

(i)   *Shi* marked subject:

    shi   Subject Verb   Object   De0.

    a.   Fa1 Sheng1 Le0 Shen2 Me0 Shi4? (What happened?)

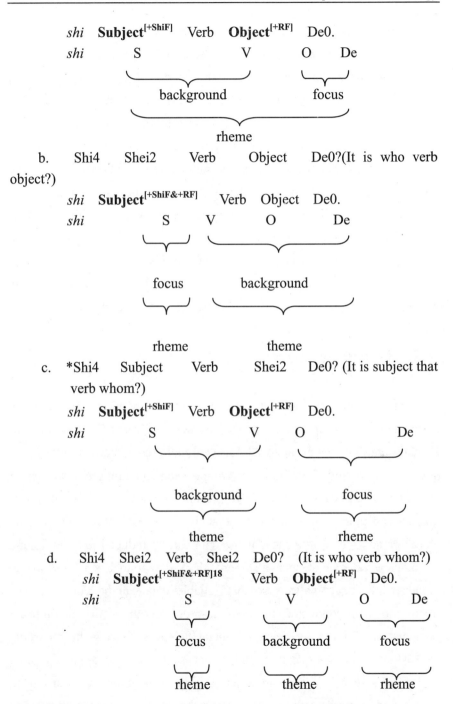

b.   Shi4   Shei2   Verb   Object   De0?(It is who verb object?)

c.   *Shi4   Subject   Verb   Shei2   De0? (It is subject that verb whom?)

d.   Shi4   Shei2   Verb   Shei2   De0?   (It is who verb whom?)

---

[18] The feature [+LianF&+RF] is adopted to denotes the addition of the *lian*-marked focus and the rheme focus.

As for the four contexts in the above examples, 'a', 'b', and 'd' are the grammatical well-formness samples based on the arguments from Liu and Xu (1998) and Zubizarreta (1998). The context of 'c' is ungrammatical due to the location of the rheme focus on the object constituent. Under the 'Unique Strong Focus Principle' (Xu 2001), when a simple clause includes multiple focuses, the strong focus marker can only mark one of them. Therefore, the focus marked by the strong marker should coincide with the major focus of the clause. Thus, the asking-answering pair '*Shi4 Zhang1 San Da3 Le0 Shei2? (It is Zhangsan that beat whom?)' (Xu 2001), is ungrammatical due to the variations of the *'Unique Strong Focus Principle.'* A similar case can be obtained from context 'c', and the selection of this sentence is designed to investigate whether an ungrammatical question can trigger systematic prosodic variations.

2.3 Recording procedure

All the above-mentioned sentences are contained in the recording schema with two repetitions for each sentence. Eight SC speakers, four females and four males, aged 20-45, were recruited as participants. These participants were divided into four groups, each containing two women or two men. The advantage of collecting sound samples from more than one person and more than one time is that the individual differences among speakers and the contingency of the data can be reduced to a minimum. Another advantage of such an approach is that it makes it possible to conduct statistical analyses so that reliable data can be obtained. The recording was conducted in a sound-proof booth at the Institute of Linguistics, Chinese Academy of Social Sciences. During the recording procedure, each *wh*-question and target sentence pair appeared on a computer screen in a random order. Within each group, one participant was asked to read the *wh*-questions and the other the target sentences as the answer to the questions at a normal speech rate without any irregular pauses. The participants were instructed to read the sentences as naturally as possible according to the context given, and were free to repeat them in case they considered their reading to be unnatural or not fluent. Each target sentence was typed on a separate sheet to avoid a list-reading effect and was read twice. After the presentation of the materials, the participants were asked to change their *asking-answering* roles. The analysis was performed on the tokens produced by all eight participants. Utterances that sounded unnatural or that were not fluent were not used for measurement.

2.4   Data processing

2.4.1   Data annotation

All the sound files were annotated. The annotation is based on the following system: i) All '*wav*' files were segmented by automatic segmentation software, and then the syllable boundaries of each syllable were modified by hand; ii) the four levels of prosodic boundaries were labeled based on perception of the prosodic boundaries, i.e. '1' stands for prosodic word boundary, '2' designates the intermediate phrase boundary, '3' is the intonation phrase boundary, and '4' is for a sentential boundary; iii) the information induced focus condition was labeled as theme focus, theme background, rheme focus, or rheme background for each clause based on the definition of Steedman (2000); and, 4) the *syntax*-marked focus was labeled according to the types of focus markers, i.e., *lian* or *shi*.

Following Figure 2.4.1.1 is the labeling results for the target sentences. Within the figure, the left side is the *wh*-operator while the right side presents the target sentences. And as for the target sentence, the first tier presents the content of each syllable and its boundaries, the second tier describes the word content, the third tire states the prosodic boundaries and the fourth tier accounts for the focus condition of the target sentences.

2.4.2 Data extraction

Research data were extracted and analyzed. The following steps were utilized: i) the "PitchTier" file for each target sentence was modified automatically by praat script; ii) the extraction of F_0 data was based on PitchTier with the range of ten points being assigned to each syllable in the target sentence for purposes of F_0 data collection; iii) duration data was extracted according to the syllabic boundaries labeled in the TextGrid files; iv) the SPSS software program was adopted for obtaining the F_0 and duration means from the eight participants; and v) the information category was obtained directly from the annotated text files.

2.5 Measurement of parameters

For the overall stretch of each test-sentence, F_0 and duration patterns were systematically measured.

2.5.1 Measurement of F_0

F_0 was measured from F_0 contours plotted using the pitch tracker feature of the PitchTier files. F_0 values for the following set of points in the contour were obtained for each test-sentence: (i) F_0 contour (the overall F_0 movements), (ii) onset (the minimum and maximum pitch values), (iii) maximum (the highest F_0 point in the sentence), and (iv) final low (the lowest F_0 point in the last vowel). Additionally, the following points were also measured: (i) the H and L targets of the prominent element and (ii) the H or L target of the post-prominent and pre-prominent element. In every case, the H target was measured at the highest F_0 point. If an L target also existed, it was measured at the lowest F_0 point. The F_0

points of measurement were the basis for the computation of (i) each test sentence's global range, defined as the difference between maximum and final low; and, (ii) the local range of every tonal sequence event, defined as the difference between the values of the H and L targets.

2.5.2 Measurement of Duration

In addition to the F_0 measurements, duration was also measured. The durations of the following aspects were obtained: (i) the duration of the prominent word, (ii) the duration of the post-prominent word, (iii) the duration of the pre-prominent word[19], and (iv) the duration of the interval between the prominent and the post-prominent constituents. These particular measurements were taken for two main reasons: on the one hand, they are consistent with the F_0 measurements obtained for prominent items; on the other hand, the durations in both the proceeding and following prominent positions permits addressing issues related to the prosodic domain induced by various focus conditions.

2.6 Perceptual experiment

2.6.1 Aim of the perceptual experiment

This part reports on a perceptual study with the aim of testing how the systematic prosodic differences that characterize a read utterance with different numbers of focuses[20], as they are produced by SC speakers, are perceived by subjects that are not speakers of the same variety of SC. In various production tasks described in the previous parts, contexts are given to elicit the production of utterances with a double information focus on

---

[19] The duration data for each prominence bearing unit is measured in each sentence. The other two measurements, (ii) and (iii), are optional when it is necessary.
[20] In the perceptual study of the single focus condition, Jia (2006) proposed that single focus can be unambiguously perceived by subjects.

unmarked short sentences, and also *syntax*-marked focus vs. rheme focus. The prosody and intonation of these utterances were analyzed, and a group of systematically occurring patterns associated with the four information category bearing units was established. The perceptual experiment in the present part only employs a small number of samples of the utterances produced that are representative of the prosodic and intonation patterns that the previous analysis isolated as crucial for the expression of the hierarchical structure of tunes. It is thus predicted that utterances of different 'categories' will be systematically perceived as distinct, and that listeners will be able to identify the 'category' to which an utterance belongs.

It is known that the intonation system for signaling linguistically meaningful contrasts has been shown by perceptual studies of 'pitch accent' languages and of 'intonation' languages. Examples of the former language type are Swedish and Serbo-Croatian, which rely on timing differences for the distinction between accent types (refer to, respectively, Bruce 1977 and Purcell 1976). As for the latter, English, German, Dutch, and Italian have been demonstrated to use tonal alignment to manifest contrasts in intonation (e.g., Pierrehumbert and Steele's 1989). Focus identification has also been shown, under certain circumstances, to rely on accent pattern differences in Swedish, Greek, and Neapolitan Italian (refer to Botinis and Bannert 1997). In order to put forward an analysis of accent alignment, focus identification, and the hierarchical patterns of accents in SC, the following need to be ascertained according to the double focus and multiple focus view, i.e., dual rheme focus: whether the theme focus vs. rheme focus, *syntax*-marked focus vs. rheme focus, and multiple focus are categorically distinct in accent patterns in SC. Utterances with these readings are expected to be perceived as distinct from broad rheme readings. Specifically, two questions need to be answered: (i) is the accent is early, final or at both places? (ii) is there any status difference between two accents?

2.6.2   Stimuli selection

The stimuli consisted of a set of sentences that were uttered to convey double or multiple focus readings; i.e., theme focus vs. rheme focus, double rheme-focus, and *syntax*-marked focus (*lian*-marked or *sh*-marked) vs. rheme focus or multiple focuses. The sample utterances used in the perceptual test are assumed to be representative of the set of features that are found to systematically reflect the prosodic manifestations of the aforementioned focus status. The utterances used in the perceptual experiment contain no *wh*-operators and have a reasonable spread over the eight different participants that took part in all the production tasks described in this study. As has been mentioned above, each target sentence exhibits three kinds of tonal combinations, only tone2 was collected for each target sentence so as to reduce the amount of data. The test stimuli consists of the following pairs:

a. **Liu2 Min2**$^{[+TF]}$ **Ti2 Ba2 Mao2 Lan2**$^{[+RF]}$ Le0.

  liu   min   elevate   mao   lan   le

  (Liumin elevated Maolan).

b. **Liu2 Min2**$^{[+RF]}$ **Ti2 Ba2 Mao2 Lan2**$^{[+RF]}$ Le0.

c. **Liu2 Min2**$^{[+RF]}$ **Ling2 Chen2 Ti2 Ba2**$^{[+RF]}$ **Mao2 Lan2**$^{[+RF]}$ Le0.

  liu   min   early morning elevate   mao   lan

  (Liumin elevated Maolan on the early morning).

d. *Lian* **Liu2 Min2**$^{[+LianF]}$ *Dou1* **Ti2 Ba2 Mao2 Lan2**$^{[+RF]}$ Le0.

  even liu   min   all   elevate   mao   lan   le

  (Even Liumin elevated Maolan).

d. *Lian* **Liu2 Min2**$^{[+LianF\&+RF]}$ *Dou1* **Ti2 Ba2 Mao2 Lan2**$^{[+RF]}$ Le0.

f. **Liu2 Min2**$^{[+RF]}$ *Lian* **Mao2 Lan2**$^{[+LianF]}$ *Dou1* Ti2 Ba2 Le0.

  liu   min   even mao   lan   dou   elevate   le

  (Liumin even elevated Maolan).

g. **Liu2 Min2**[+RF] *Lian* **Mao2 Lan2**[+LianF&+RF] *Dou1* Ti2 Ba2 Le0.

h. Shi4 **Liu2 Min2**[+ShiF&+RF] Ti2 Ba2 **Mao2 Lan2**[+RF] De0.

    is liu min   elevate mao lan   de

(It is Liumin that elevated Maolan).

The utterances in 'a-c' were taken from the data provided by the production experiment involving unmarked structure on theme focus vs. rheme focus readings, double rheme focus readings, and multiple focus readings. In utterances 'd-g', the *lian*-marked focus forms various co-existing relations with rheme focus, and in 'g', the sentence provides for the occurrence of the *shi*-marked focus and the rheme focus.

2.6.3 Procedure

A forced choice response experiment was carried out in order to answer questions (i) and (ii) of part 2.6.1. In order to minimize the negative analogical effect，the sentences involved were arranged in random order using perceptual software, and each sentence could be repeated as required by the participants to confirm their judgment. Eight SC participants were invited to participate in the experiment, and all the participants have a similar linguistic and educational background. None of the participants had any known hearing problems, and they were all naive as to the purpose of the experiment. During the procedure, each participant was asked to finish the experiment individually, without any interpersonal consultation. During the course of the experiment, the options for each syntactic component, such as 'Liu2Min2 (Liumin)', 'Ling2Chen2 (early morning)', 'Ti2Ba2 (elevate)' and 'Mao2Lan2 (Maolan)' in the target sentence appeared in a window of the software. The participants were expected to choose from among the options according to their decisive judgment of the position of the intonation prominence in the target sentences. There was no restriction on the number of options that could be chosen. The results of the test were measured through the computation of several item scores (expressed in '%'), and the consistency score. The consistency score is a measure of the degree of consistency with which the participants made their choices for each of the syntactic elements. The item score constitutes a step in the computation of a specific syntactic item.

Chapter Three

Phonetic Realization of Accent Patterns in

Unmarked Structure

3.1 Introduction

This chapter provides a unified description of the essential acoustic correlates of accent manifestation in various focus categories in unmarked structures in SC. Previous studies on the focus status of unmarked structures of SC mainly discuss the default position of the focus distribution, e.g., LaPolla (1995) identifies the focus position as sentence-final in modern Chinese. Zhang and Fang (1996), on the basis of their observations of the relative order of the verbal object, the directional expression, the order of the object, and the verbal classifier propose that the focus tends to locate near the ending position of an utterance. Xu (2004) also claims that informational focus is always grammatically realized in natural language, but in different ways across languages. Compared with the focus in European languages that have a systematic manifestation in pitch accents, SC is a language in which there is a reverse relationship between syntactic positioning and phonological prominence of focus. Xu further points out that it is the sentence-final position, and usually the most deeply embedded position on the recursive side of branching, where the informational focus is located, that is the default position in SC. With regard to the relation among negation, focus and scope, Xiong (2005) proposes that the negative focus is sensitive to different rankings of constrains. If the syntactic rule is higher than the prominent rule, which is in turn higher than the default rule, then the negation is associated with focus, and the negative operator does not have to be adjacent with the negative focus. However, if the syntactic rule is higher than the default rule, which is in turn higher than the prominent rule, then the focus in negative sentences might be isolatable from the negative focus. Hu (2007) investigates the scope of negation, the interaction between negation and focus, and the syntax of the negative marker "bu" in Mandarin Chinese. It claims that "bu(no)" syntactically negates the VP, it adjoins to and may not negate any focus element beyond its VP scope.

Phonetic investigation of the focus in an unmarked structure of SC mainly deals with the focus-induced influence on F_0 and durational changes with the focus position being identified through the *wh*-operators. An example can be drawn from Xu (1999) who adopts F_0 and duration as two parameters and examines how lexical tones and focus contribute to the formation and alignment of F_0 contours in speech. Results of his experiment indicate that (a) while the lexical tone of a syllable is the most determining factor for the local F_0 contour of the syllable, focus extensively modulates the global shape of the F_0 curve, which in turn affects the height and even the shape of local structure; (b) the tones of adjacent syllables also extensively influence both the shape and height of the F_0 contour of a syllable, with the preceding tone exerting more influence than the following tone; (c) despite extensive variations in shape and height, the F_0 contour of a tone remains closely aligned with the associated syllable; and (d) both focus and tonal interaction may generate substantial F_0 decline over the course of an utterance. Chen (2006) selects duration as the parameter and examines the patterns of durational adjustment of mono-morphemic four-syllable words in SC when different constituents of the words are focused for corrections. She points out that when the word is in utterance medial position, corrective focus induces robust lengthening. The domain of lengthening is best characterized as the constituent that is under focus. When a focus domain is *multi*-syllabic, the distribution of lengthening is non-uniform; i.e., there is a strong tendency for an edge effect with the last syllable being lengthened the most. There is also *spill-over* lengthening on the neighboring syllables outside the focused constituent. The magnitude of such lengthening is conditioned by prosodic boundaries in that word boundaries attenuate lengthening more than syllable boundaries. When a word is in utterance-final position, focus does not introduce significant lengthening effects on any of the syllables. Final lengthening, however, is observed in the rhyme of the final syllable when the word is focused, and the lengthening extends to the onset of the final syllable when the word is not focused. Jia et al (2006; 2008) investigated the phonetic and phonological properties of the focus conveyed by disyllabic focused words with exhausive tonal combinations in SC.

Major findings demonstrate that (a) the F_0 ranges of focused words are expanded as the "H" tones of both focused syllables are raised; (b) the F_0 of the post-focus syllables are obviously compressed in the way that the "H" tones of Tone1 and Tone2 are lowered, and this effect can extend to the very end of the sentence; (c) the realization of accents is closely related to the tonal target of the focused words in that accents influence the acoustic performances of tones; furthermore; (d) the combination of H/L determines the distribution of accents. Further, Jia et al (2008) extended the focused constituents to five-syllable words and investigated the effect triggered by five-syllable focused constituents upon the pitch and durational patterns in SC. Results of the experiment demonstrate that focus raises the "H" tones of each focused syllable and the magnitude of such rising is largest in the final syllable. Focus does not induce influence upon tone sandhi at the phonological level, although it restricts the phonetic co-articulation to some extent. For the durational adjustment of the constituents, although all the syllables observe lengthening, the greatest change lies in the final syllable. Based on the pitch and durational patterns of the five-syllable words, Jia et al propose that the effect of focus in SC is sensitive to the metrical structure of the focused constituents; specifically, the metrically strongest position undergoes the greatest pitch risings and durational changes.

Following the path suggested by previous findings, this chapter describes the general F_0 and durational patterns of single rheme focus, double rheme focus, and multiple rheme focus in the unmarked sentence in SC. There are three basic questions in this chapter: i) what is the basic F_0 and durational patterns (accent patterns) of single focus in the unmarked structure in SC? ii) what characterizes the differences of accent patterns of double focus, theme focus vs. rheme focus, and double rheme focus? iii) how is the accent distributed when multiple constituents bear focus? iv) what constituents the corresponding relationship between *focus distribution* and *accent distribution* in SC? and v) what is the underlying cause for restricting the distribution of *accent* in the surface form? In section 3.2, an account of the intonation of the unmarked target sentence under four kinds of information induced focuses (as defined in part 1.4.1 of Chapter One) is presented. Within this account, the phonological means of *nuclear accent* and *pre-nuclear accent* (as defined in part 1.4.2 of Chapter One) involved in the expression of different information induced focus in SC is presented. In section 3.3, the results of the production experiment contrasting utterances with double rheme focus and single focus are shown not only to corroborate the analysis presented in section 3.2, but also to provide evidence for the asymmetric relation between focus status and accent level. In section 3.4, the SC data are shown to support the *structure-based approach*: once the focused part of an utterance is specified, the accent distribution follows language-specific structural rules. Finally, the accent pattern in SC and the relation between focus and accent are summarized in section 3.5.

3.2 Phonetic realization of constituents in four information categories in unmarked structure

This section deals with the acoustic manifestations of accent realization at the post-lexical[21] level in the unmarked structure in SC. As described in part 2.2.2, the target sentences are designed as 'Subject Verb Object Le0' and various information-induced focuses are placed onto the unmarked structure. In particular, the 'subject' constituents attain the statuses of *rheme background, rheme focus, theme background,* and *theme focus.* With regard to the 'object' components, they exhibit *rheme focus, theme background, rheme focus,* and *rheme focus,* respectively. Within the account of the sentential level accents in this section, it is important to consider the following aspects: (i) the physical correlates of the *nuclear accent,* the *pre-nuclear,* and the *post-nuclear constituents*; (ii) the specific manner of realization of *nuclear accent* with different tonal combinations; (iii) the hierarchical level of accents induced by different levels of focus, and (iv) the phonological nature of accents. The universal prosodic parameters F_0 and duration[22] are adopted to identify the position and levels of the accents.

3.2.1　F_0 contour of tone1 utterances in four information categories

The description of the F_0 pattern of the four target sentences given in this part is tone1 utterances in four information categories. As mentioned in Chapter Two, the short tone1 target sentence is always 'Wu1 Yin1 Wei1 Bi1 Wen1 Yin1 Le0 (Wuyin intimidated Wenyin)', and four kinds of *wh*-operators are inserted into the sentence to obtain the intended focus status. The corresponding relation between *wh*-question and the focus conditions of the utterance is described as follows:

(i)　　Fa1 Sheng1 Le0 Shen2 Me0 Shi4?(What happened?)

---

[21] By this definition, intonation excludes features of stress that are determined in the lexicon. There remains much debate on the existence of word stress in Standard Chinese (Duanmu 2000).

[22] The F_0 (fundamental frequency) and duration are known to be major acoustic manifestations of suprasegmental structures such as tone, pitch accent, and intonation in cross-language perspective (Cambier-Langeveld and Turk 1999, Xu 1999).

Wu1 Yin1   Wei1 Bi1   **Wen1 Yin1**[+RF][24]   Le0.
   ↓   ↓   ↓

{Rheme background} {Rheme background} {Rheme focus}

(ii)   Shei2 Wei1 Bi1 Wen Yin1 Le0? (Who intimidated Wenyin?)

Wu1 Yin1[+RF]   Wei1 Bi1   Wen1 Yin1   Le0.
   ↓   ↓   ↓

{Rheme focus}   {Theme background}   {Theme background}

(iii)   Wu1 Yin1 Wei1 Bi1 Wei Bi1 Shei2 Le0? (Wuyin intimidated whom?)

Wu1 Yin1   Wei1 Bi1   **Wen1 Yin1**[+RF]   Le0.
   ↓   ↓   ↓

{Theme background}   {Theme background} {Rheme focus}

(iv)   Wu1 Yin1 Wei1 Bi1 Shei2 Le0? Shei2 Wei1 Bi1 Shei2 Le0?
        (Wuyin intimidated whom? Who intimidated whom?)

Wu1 Yin1[+TF]   Wei1 Bi1   **Wen1 Yin1**[+RF]   Le0.
   ↓   ↓   ↓

{Theme focus}   {Theme background} {Rheme background}

3.2.1.1   Overall F_0 contour

The F_0 patterns of the previous four sentences are illustrated in Figure 3.2.1.1. Within this figure, the top part of the X-coordinate describes the content of each syllable in the sentence, while the bottom part displays the information category of each utterance. Within each sentence, the focus condition of each word is described by capitalized abbreviations. Specifically, 'RB-RB-RF' stands for the condition that the subject and verb item locate in the rheme background environment, and the object locates in the rheme focus condition; 'RF-TB-TB' indicates the rheme focus, theme background, and theme background distributing on subject,

---

[23] The bold characters stand for the focus-bearing unit.
[24] Following Chapter Two, [+RF] and [+TF] denote the focus bearing unit with the focus status of 'rheme focus' and 'theme focus', respectively.

verb, and object constituents, respectively; as for 'TB-TB-RF', it is taken to mean the theme background, theme background, and rheme focus are placed onto the corresponding syntactic components; finally, 'TF-TB-RF' implies that the focus status for each element in the sentence is theme focus, theme background, and rheme focus. The Y-Coordinate illustrates the F_0 range measured in Hz. Since each of the sentences is produced four times by eight participants, the F_0 means of each contour is obtained from 32 tokens. The pitch range of all the graphs are designed as 110Hz-260Hz[25] based on the pitch range of the eight participants. In the analysis of the pitch contour, the study adopts the methods of Jia et al (2008) who discuss two aspects of the effect of focal accents upon F_0: (i) the manner of effect, specifically taken to mean *rising* or *lowering* of F_0, and (ii) the condition of effect, which means whether the lowering or rising imposes the effect on H or L tones. The fundamental unit applied to describe these effects is the underlying tonal target, H or L; specifically, each focused syllable is rendered separately to divide it into its original tones and in this manner to observe the phonetic performance, rather than deal with a single syllable as a descriptive unit.

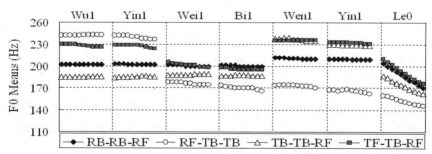

Figure 3.2.1.1 Mean F_0 for "Wu1 Yin1 Wei1 Bi1 Wen1 Yin1 Le0" in various focus conditions

In Figure 3.2.1.1, all the utterances deserve tone1, thus all the syllables

---

[25] The pitch range of the F_0 figures are selected as 110Hz-260Hz based on the pitch ranges from all the participants.

bear the tonal feature *"HH."* Examination of the above contour 'RB-RB-RF', demonstrates that there is no obvious declination phenomenon; whereas, the pitch register of "wen1yin1" is *lifted* to some extent. As for the pitch performances of the syllables "wen1yin1 wei1bi1" that are locating before "wen1yin1", they perform as a line and show no obvious raising or lowering on the tonal target. Taking into consideration the F_0 contour of 'RF-TB-TB', the intonation prominence of the sentence locates at the initial word "wu1yin1" that serves as the rhematic focus. Although we identify the focus status here as the *rhematic* focus based on the classification of Steedman (2000), it bears the same implication as the definition of *narrow* focus (Kiss 1995, King 1995). As for the study of the narrow focus conveyed by a disyllabic word upon the sentential level, Jia et al (2008) point out that when the narrow focus distributes at the clause-initial position, the pitch of the under-focus is obviously raised, and the pitch registers of the following syllables are compressed. This phenomenon can extend to the very end of the sentence. Here, the rhematic focus has a similar effect upon the F_0 contour with the narrow focus in the way that the *H* tones are *raised* and the pitch-registers of the post-focus are obviously compressed with the last syllable being down to the bottom. As for the thematic background bearing units "wei1bi1" and "wen1yin1", their pitch register shows a greater magnitude of lowering than the corresponding rheme focus. Under the environment of 'TB-TB-RF', the F_0 contour of the subject constituent "wu1yin1" shows a much lower pitch than the rhematic focus bearing unit "wen1yin1" that is considered to be the prominence bearing element in this sentence. Comparing the present contour with 'RF-TB-TB', the only difference lies in the position of the rheme focus; whereas, the specific realization of the rheme focus shows an identical pattern. With regard to the dual focus F_0 contour 'TF-TB-RF', the pitch registers of the words "wu1yin1" and "wen1yin1" are higher than the verb constituent "wei1bi1" and the sentence-final syllable "le0." Thus, the present target sentence contains two F_0 prominences, one locates on the subject induced by secondary information and the other on the object triggered by primary information. Owing to the existence of *declination*[26] in F_0 contour, it is proposed that the prominence induced by primary information gets the primary prominence. The status of the prominence level can be determined by the status of information. Further, we provide the maximum pitch values of each word under all the focus statuses, e.g., 'RB-RB-RF': [wu1yin1: 202Hz, wei1bi1: 202Hz, and wu1yin: 210Hz], 'RF-TB-TB': [wu1yin1: 243Hz, wei1bi1: 178Hz, and wen1yin1: 173Hz] 'TB-TB-RF': [wu1yin1: 187Hz, wei1bi1: 189Hz, and wen1yin1:239Hz], and 'TF-TB-RF': [wu1yin1: 230Hz, wei1bi1: 206Hz, and wen1yin1: 236Hz].

3.2.1.2 Statistical analysis

A One-Way ANOVA[27] was performed to compare the significance of the same words in different information statuses, i.e., subject, verb, and object constituent. As is mentioned in the introduction, the target word "Subject" exhibits four information categories, i.e., rheme background, rheme focus, theme background, and theme focus. As for the verb constituent, it observes only a background condition; specifically, theme background and rheme background. The object items have rhematic focus and thematic background statuses. In the statistical analysis, the Bonfrroni post hoc test is adopted to examine the differences in the maximum pitch values for each syntactic component.

As already stated, the subject constituent exhibits four information categories, i.e., rheme background, rheme focus, theme background, and theme focus. Examination of the above figure shows that the rhematic focus exhibits the highest pitch register, and the thematic focus occupies the secondary position; the rhematic background is in ternary position, and

---

[26] The phenomenon of declination was first proposed by Cohen and Hart (1967).
[27] The description of the statistical results is also based on the F_0 contours shown in Figure 3.2.1.1.

the thematic background display the lowest pitch registers. A One-Way ANOVA shows that the highest points of this word are significantly different from each other. Specifically, rhematic focus vs. thematic focus (P=0.012), rhematic focus vs. rhematic background (P=0.00), rhematic focus vs. thematic background (P=0.00), thematic focus vs. thematic background (P=0.00), and rhematic background vs. thematic background (0.004).

The verb-item observes only two information statuses: rheme background and theme background. In Figure 3.2.1.1, the F_0 contour of the verb items are affected by the proceeding and following focus condition of the subject and object constituents. The information status exerts no obvious influence on the F_0 contour of the verb constituents. Results of the Bonfrroni post hoc test shows that the verb constituent of 'RB-RB-RF' and 'TF-TB-RB' shows no obvious differences (P>0.05), and 'TB-TB-RF' and 'TF-TB-RB' significantly differ from 'RF-TB-TB' and 'TF-TB-RB' (P=0.035 and P=0.036). Further, 'TB-TB-RF' and 'TB-TB-RF' also differ from each other.

Different from the subject constituents, the object constituents only exhibit two focus statuses: rheme focus and theme background. It can be seen from Figure 3.2.1.1 that there are no obvious differences in the two rhematic focuses 'TF-TB-RF' and 'TB-TB-RF', with the subject constituents serving as thematic focus and thematic background, separately. Moreover, the pitch register of the other rhematic focus bearing unit in 'RB-RB-RF' distributes lower than the former two constituents when its corresponding subject exhibits rhematic background status. A further One-Way ANOVA was conducted and results of the Bonfrroni post hoc test shows that in contour 'RB-RB-RF' the maximum pitch value of the word "wen1yin1" is different from the other three conditions, i.e., 'RB-RB-RF' vs. 'TB-TB-RF' (P=0.001), 'RB-RB-RF' vs. 'TF-TB-RF' (P=0.002), and 'RB-RB-RF' vs. 'RF-RF-TB' (P=0.00). When the subject word "wu1yin1" exhibits both thematic background and thematic focus, i.e., 'TB-TB-RF' and 'TF-TB-RF', the maximum pitch values of the object items display no significant differences, i.e., 'TB-TB-RF' vs. 'TF-TB-RF' (P=0.065>0.05) and these two items are significantly different from the object constituent bearing a thematic background condition, e.g., 'RF-TB-TB', (P=0.00 and P=0.00). Thus, the thematic focus exerts no effect upon the realization of the prominence induced by rhematic focus.

On the whole, in the tone1 target sentence, under a single focus condition, the prominence corresponds with the focus. When the focus distributes in the initial position, the focus-induced prominence exerts a compressive effect on the constituents immediately following the prominence. When it is located in the object position of the utterance, the prominence exerts no obvious effect upon the pitch registers in the proceeding positions. Under double focus conditions, it is known that two prominences can co-exist with each other in one sentence and the scale differences are determined by the focus statuses, i.e., the primary information focus triggers primary F_0 prominence. The phenomenon of a dual prominences pattern in one sentence induced by *wh*-questions has already been reported in English (Eady and Cooper 1986): F_0 of the dual focus can achieve a prominence similar to the single focus with the difference between dual focus and single focus being that the post-focus constituent in dual focus exhibits no F_0 lowering[28].

3.2.2 F_0 contour of tone2 utterances in four information categories

The major aim of this section is two-fold: (i) to investigate the specific manner of the realization of tone2 utterances and (ii) to explore

---

[28] Note that, there is no focus status difference in the study of Eady and Cooper (1986). This part concentrates on the discussion of the levels of prominences induced by different levels of focus conditions. The dual rheme focus induced prominence realizations will be dealt with in part 3.3.

whether tonal variation can affect the distribution of prominence. The target sentence in this part is: 'Liu2 Min2 Ti2 Ba2 Mao2 Lan2 Le0 (Liumin elevated Maolan)'. Similar to the previous part, the *wh*-operators and the corresponding focus conditions are described as:

(i)   Fa1 Sheng1 Le0 Shen2 Me0 Shi4?(What happened?)

Liu2 Min2   Ti2 Ba2   **Mao2 Lan2**[+RF]   Le0.

{Rheme background} {Rheme background} {Rheme focus}

(ii)   Shei2 Ti2 Ba2 Mao2 Lan2 Le0? (Who elevated Maolan?)

Liu2 Min2[+RF]   Ti2 Ba2   Mao2 Lan2   Le0.

{Rheme focus}   {Theme background} {Theme background}

(iii)   Liu2 Min2Ti2 Ba2 Shei2 Le0? (Maolan elevated whom?)

Liu2 Min2   Ti2 Ba2   **Mao2 Lan2**[+RF]   Le0.

{Theme background} {Theme background} {Rheme focus}

(iv)   Liu2 Min2 Ti2 Ba2 Shei2 Le0? Shei2 Ti2 Ba2 Shei2 Le0? (Wuyin elevate dwhom? Who elevated whom?)

Liu2 Min2[+TF]   Ti2 Ba2   **Mao2 Lan2**[+RF]   Le0.

{Theme focus}   {Theme background} {Rheme background}

3.2.2.1   Overall F_0 contour

The overall F_0 patterns of the utterances in various information categories are presented in Figure 3.2.2.1. The implications of the content of the coordinate are identical to Figure 3.2.1.1.

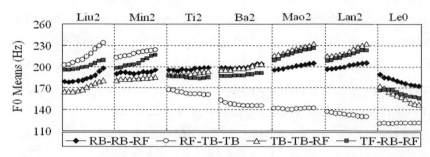

Figure 3.2.2.1   Mean F₀ for "Liu2 Min2 Ti2 Ba2 Mao2 Lan2 Le0" in various focus conditions

Apparently, the general pattern of the tone2 target sentence maintains an identical distribution with tone1 utterances. However, the difference lies in the specific realization of the syntactic component induced by variation in tonal combination. Specifically, it can be seen from contour 'RB-RB-RF' in the figure that there exists no obvious intonation prominence in the contour; whereas, the *declination* phenomenon is restricted by the rheme focus on the object item. What constitutes an interesting phenomenon here is that the syllables "min2", "ti2", and "ba2" nearly lose their *L* tone features due to tonal co-articulation. It has been reported by Yip (1980) that when a tone2 syllable is preceded by a tone1 or tone2 syllable, it obtains tonal change, i.e., tone2→tone1. It is also proposed by Jia et al (2008) that focus exerts an effect on the restriction of tonal changes at the phonetic level to some extent specifically, it helps a tone2 item maintain an *L* tone feature. Therefore, in the above figure, the three mentioned syllables are not affected completely by the tonal co-articulation rule. As for the contour 'RF-TB-TB,' the rhematic focus exerts an obvious *lifting* effect on the pitch register under focus, and the pitch registers of the post-focus elements exhibit similar performances with the previous tone1 sentence in that they are significantly compressed. Moreover, the tone2 syllables in the post-focus positions nearly lose their original tonal target of "*LH*" and perform like the level tones[29]. Such *post-focus* pitch range compression is not an uncommon phenomenon cross-linguistically, and different languages such as Danish, and Chinese or Japanese are among those that have been reported to reduce post-focal material (Beckman and Pierrehumbert 1986, Xu 1999, and Jia et al 2008). Within contour 'TB-TB-RF', the prominence locates on the object-position with the whole pitch register of the object being obviously raised. Under a double focus condition, for example, contour 'TF-TB-RF' the two prominences also correspond with the theme focus and the rheme focus, however, the primary one associates with the primary information focus and the secondary one with the secondary information. Thus, the concrete distribution position of the contour is identical to the tone1 sentence with the difference being caused by the tonal combinations.

3.2.2.2   Statistical analysis

The tonal target of the tone2 component is *LH*, and a One-Way ANOVA analysis was conducted on the minimum and maximum pitch values of each syntactic word in the sentence. With regard to the subject, verb, and object constituents, they observe an identical information status with the tone1 constituents. As can be seen from Figure 3.2.2.1, in the subject position, the low point and high point of the rhematic focus constituent shows the highest value, and the difference in the *H* tone is more obvious than the *L* tone. Thematic focus occupies secondary position, then the rhematic background bearing unit and the thematic background bearing unit. As for the tone2 constituents in the mentioned focus conditions, the maximum pitch values also show significantly differences[30].

---

[29] The prominent unit shows a much higher pitch register. The specific comparisons of the pitch values for each item are not listed due to space limitations.
[30] The specific values are: RF vs. TF (P=0.002), RF vs. RB (P=0.00), RF vs. TB (P=0.00), TF vs. TB (P=0.001), RB vs. TB (P=0.003). With regard to the minimum pitch value differences of subject item "liu2min2" , RF vs. TF (P=0.003), RF vs. RB (P=0.00), RF vs. TB (P=0.00), TF vs. TB (P=0.002), RB vs. TB (P=0.004).

These indicate that variation in information statuses can determine F_0 performances, i.e., the existence or absence of prominence and the height of the pitch registers.

In the positions of the verb constituents, the contours 'RB-RB-RF', 'TB-TB-RF', and 'TF-TB-RF' exhibit similar performances that demonstrate that the double-focus triggers have no compressive effect on the pitch register between the two focuses. This result also demonstrates that the rheme focus on the object position is not affected by the pitch register of the proceeding constituents. It is worth noting that the rheme focus on the subject position exerts an obvious compressive effect on the following constituents with the pitch register of the verb items lower than the other three contours[31]. The results of the statistical analysis support the above observations.

In the object positions, although the object item "mao2lan2" exhibits two kinds of focus statuses, there exists two rheme focuses that exhibit no obvious differences in contour performance with their corresponding subject constituents serving as *thematic background* and *thematic focus*. However, when the subject unit is located in the rhematic background, the highest and lowest points of the constituents exhibit a difference from the other three conditions. In addition to that, the thematic background constituent shows the lowest pitch registers[32]. Thus, the prominence on the

---

[31] Results of a One-Way AVONA shows that the lowest and highest of the verb constituents in contours of 'RB-RB-RF', 'TB-TB-RF', and 'TF-TB-RF' are not different from each other (P_{min}>0.05 and P_{max}>0.05). As for 'RF-TB-TB', its maximum pitch and minimum pitch values are different from the previous three contours (P_{min}<0.05 and P_{max}<0.05).

[32] Further, results of the Bonfrroni post hoc test shows that the minimum pitch values of the words "mao2lan2" in the following conditions are difference from each other: $RF_{rhematic\ background}$ vs. $RF_{thematic\ background}$, $RF_{rhematic\ background}$ vs. $RF_{thematic\ focus}$, $RF_{rhematic\ backgroud}$ vs. TB (P<0.05). However, $RF_{thematic\ background}$ vs. $RF_{thematic\ focus}$ (P=0.095) displays no obvious differences. They are significantly different from the object constituent in thematic backgrond condition, e.g., $RF_{thematic\ background}$ vs. TB (P=0.00), $RF_{thematic\ focus}$ vs. TB (P=0.00). As for the maximum pitch value of the object word "mao2lan2", they show similar results. The specific values are: $RF_{rhematic\ backgroud}$ vs. $RF_{thematic\ background}$ (P=0.001), $RF_{rhematic\ background}$ vs. $RF_{thematic\ focus}$ (P=0.001), $RF_{rhematic\ backgroud}$ vs. TB (P=0.00), $RF_{thematic\ background}$ vs. $RF_{thematic\ focus}$ (P=0.074), $RF_{thematic\ background}$ vs. TB (P=0.00), and $RF_{thematic\ focus}$ vs. TB (P=0.00).

object constituent is not affected by the preceding theme status on the subject and verb components; whereas, the status of rheme shows the opposite effect.

In summary, the effect of the four information categories upon the tone2 constituents is similar to the tone1 sentences in the way that the contour in each information-status exhibits the same prominence distribution. However, the specific realization of the constituent is the tonal combinations. In the tone2 sentence, the maximum and minimum point of the prominent element shows higher, with the major manifestation on the H tone.

3.2.3   F$_0$ contour of tone4 utterances in four information categories

Tone4 target sentences are applied in this part to further support the relation between prominence and the variation of the tonal combinations of the target sentences. The *wh*-questions and the focus status of the target sentence are expressed as:

(i)   Fa1 Sheng1 Le0 Shen2 Me0 Shi4? (What happened?)

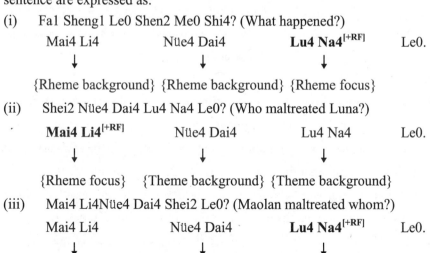

(i)   Mai4 Li4   Nüe4 Dai4   **Lu4 Na4**[+RF]   Le0.
                 ↓   ↓   ↓
       {Rheme background} {Rheme background} {Rheme focus}

(ii)   Shei2 Nüe4 Dai4 Lu4 Na4 Le0? (Who maltreated Luna?)
       Mai4 Li4[+RF]   Nüe4 Dai4   Lu4 Na4   Le0.
                 ↓   ↓   ↓
       {Rheme focus}   {Theme background} {Theme background}

(iii) Mai4 Li4Nüe4 Dai4 Shei2 Le0? (Maolan maltreated whom?)
       Mai4 Li4   Nüe4 Dai4   **Lu4 Na4**[+RF]   Le0.
                 ↓   ↓   ↓
       {Theme background} {Theme background} {Rheme focus}

(iv)   Mai4 Li4 Nüe4 Dai4 Shei2 Le0? Shei2 Nüe4 Dai4 Shei2 Le0?
       (Wuyin maltreated whom? Who maltreated whom?)

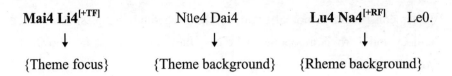

Mai4 Li4[+TF]   Nüe4 Dai4   **Lu4 Na4[+RF]**   Le0.

↓   ↓   ↓

{Theme focus}   {Theme background}   {Rheme background}

3.2.3.1 Overall F_0 contour

Figure 3.2.3.1 below is the F_0 contours for the tone4 sentences adopted to further observe the F_0 patterns triggered by various information categories. The content of the coordinates also bear consistent implications with the tone1 sentences.

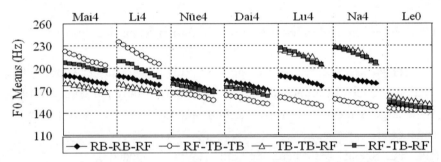

Figure 3.2.3.1 Mean F_0 for "Mai4 Li4 Nüe4 Dai4 Lu4 Na4 Le0" in various focus conditions

Closer examination of the above figure reveals that the tone4 target sentences also exhibit the same patterns as the tone1 and tone2 utterances. Under a single focus condition, the contours of 'RF-TB-TB' and 'TB-TB-RF' show that the rheme focus can induce prominence with the H and L tone of the words being obviously *lifted*. Between these two tonal targets, the acoustic realization mainly manifests on the H tones. As for the contour 'RB-RB-RF', the effect of the rheme focus is mainly manifesting on the blocking of the declination. Further, dual focus can trigger double prominences with one distributing near the ending position serving as the primary one. The level difference of the prominence is mainly caused by the information status; i.e., the primary one corresponds with the primary information.

3.2.3.2   Statistical analysis

As for the subject constituents, it can be seen from the above figure that the low point and high point of the rhematic focus constituent shows highest value, thematic focus occupies secondary position, then the rhematic background bearing unit and the thematic background bearing unit. As for the tone2 constituents in the mentioned focus conditions, the maximum pitch values also show significantly differences [33]. These indicate that the variation of information statuses can determine F_0 performances, i.e., the existence or absence of prominence and the height of the pitch registers.

The verb constituents of the contours 'RB-RB-RF', 'TB-TB-RF', and 'TF-TB-RF' also resemble each other. This indicates that there is no compressive effect from single focus on the object and double focus on both the subject and object positions. The lowest F_0 contour is due to the compressive effect of the subject rheme focus [34].

Under object-positions, examination of the above figure reveals similar F_0 patterns for the tone1 and tone2 constituents in that the two rhematic focuses have obvious differences in minimum and maximum pitch values when they have thematic background and thematic focus serving as the subject constituents. When the subject unit is put into the rhematic background condition, the corresponding object constituent displays a lower pitch register compared to the previously mentioned two rhematic focuses. However, the object constituent that displays the lowest pitch register among the four pitch contours is the theme background

---

[33] The specific values are: RF vs. TF (P=0.002), RF vs. RB (P=0.00), RF vs. TB (P=0.00), TF vs. TB (P=0.001), RB vs. TB (P=0.003). With regard to the minimum pitch value differences of subject item "liu2min2", RF vs. TF (P=0.003), RF vs. RB (P=0.00), RF vs. TB (P=0.00), TF vs. TB (P=0.002), RB vs. TB (P=0.004).

[34] Minimum and maximum pitch values of 'RB-RB-RF,' 'TB-TB-RF,' and 'TF-TB-RF' are not different from each other ($P_{min}>0.05$ and $P_{max}>0.05$).

bearing unit with the rheme focus as the subject item[35].

Thus, it can be concluded that tonal combinations do not have an effect on the distribution of the prominences. It only contributes to the specific realization of the prominences.

3.2.4 Durational patterns of constituents in four information categories

The results of the experiments in parts 3.2.1-3.2.3 on utterances with a rheme background, rheme focus, theme background, or a theme focus reading on the subject constituents have shown that F_0 prominence yields a coherent picture of the focused constituents. However, tonal combinations of the focused constituents did not signal the appearance of the prominence. Cross-language studies have shown that F_0 excursion is the primary cue to mark accent (refer to Beckman and Pierrehumbert 1986, Frota 1993). However, studies have also shown that the secondary cue, duration, is also associated with sentential accents (Eefting 1991). Therefore, the major aim of this part is to deal with lengthening phenomena, particularly with durational changes of the target words induced by various information statuses through which to provide the secondary cue, *duration,* to mark the distribution and levels of *accents* in SC. Based on the aim, it is therefore important to consider the following questions: (i) duration pattern variations induced by different information categories and (ii) the corresponding relationship between the *lengthening* and *prominence.*

With regard to focus-induced lengthening in SC, many researchers take the position that when a mono-syllabic word is focused, both onset and rhyme are lengthened significantly (for example, Chen 2003); and

---

[35] Due to space limitations, the specific supporting statistical analysis data obtained for the above analysis is omitted.

when a disyllabic word is focused, both syllables are lengthened; however, the distribution of the two syllables is not symmetric (Xu 1999). For the poly-syllabic focused constituents, e.g., a four-syllable word, although all the syllables become lengthened under focus, the distribution of lengthening within the focus domain is not uniform (Chen 2006). Chen further points out that the pattern of lengthening within the focused words is determined together by two principals.

One is that the increase in duration is sensitive to the metrically stronger syllables that exhibit more lengthening than the metrically weaker ones. The other is the edge-effect of lengthening that requires the edges of a focused constituent lengthen more than the rest of the constituent. Jia et al (2007) further investigates the focus-induced lengthening of a *five-syllable constituent.*

Results of the experiment demonstrate that when the focused constituents are set in the beginning and middle positions of the target sentences, the final syllables exhibit the greatest lengthening and the first syllables exhibit secondary lengthening. When the focused constituents are treated in the final position of the target sentences, focus-induced lengthening on the final syllable is not obvious. This illustrates that the effect of final lengthening and focus on durational change is not additive.

As for the factors affecting durational change, focus (within-word syllable position and within-sentence position), and subjects are considered together in determining the durational patterns of the target constituents. From the typological perspective of durational patterns of SC, it is the language that is sensitive to a metrically stronger position, i.e., a metrically stronger position exhibits greater lengthening. Based on the classification of the theme vs. rheme and background vs. focus as in the present study, Chen (2006) investigated the prosodic differences among the four focus categories, and proposes that rhematic items are consistently realized with a longer duration than thematic items. Focused elements, in general, also show a longer duration than background constituents, but their effects are smaller than those between theme and rheme.

3.2.4.1 Duration of subject constituents

Since the important constituents related to the distribution of *prominence* are the subject and object constituents, duration data needs to be provided to further identify the levels and distributions of the *accents*. Thus, only these two syntactic components are selected as the research anchors. Only the tone2 and tone4 items are adopted due to space limitations. Figures 3.2.4.1 and 3.2.4.2 illustrate the durational patterns induced by various information statuses. The abscissa axis describes the focus statuses of each target word in the sentence, specifically, "RB" denotes rheme background; "RF" denotes rheme focus; "TB" denotes theme background, and "TF" denotes theme focus. The ordinate axis illustrates the durational distribution in milliseconds (ms). The range of durational changes in the ordinate axis is chosen as 30-50ms based on all the durational data.

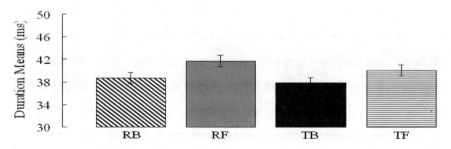

Figure 3.2.4.1 Mean duration for "Liu2 Min2" in different focus conditions

Examination of figure 3.2.4.1 shows that the rhematic focus constituent exhibits the greatest magnitude of lengthening. This phenomenon is illustrated by the second rectangle in figure 3.2.4.1. The thematic focus induced lengthening occupies the secondary position, the rhematic background constituent occupies the ternary position, and the thematic background constituent shows the least magnitude of durational change. Specific values of duration lengthening are: liu2min2$_{RF}$: 41.77ms, liu2min2$_{TF}$: 40.1ms, liu2min2$_{RB}$: 38.7ms, and liu2min2$_{TB}$: 37.8ms. A further One-Way ANOVA was conducted to test the significance of the differences in the durational distribution among the four focus categories. Results of the Bonfrroni post hoc test demonstrates that the lengthening of the word "liu2min2" in various information categories are different from each other: RF vs. TF (P=0.001), RF vs. RB (P=0.00), RF vs. TB (P=0.00), TF vs. RB (P=0.002), TF vs. RB (P=0.002), RB vs. TB (P=0.004)[36].

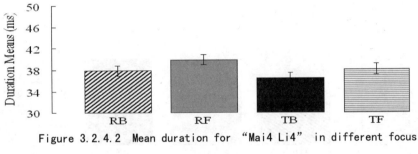

Figure 3.2.4.2 Mean duration for "Mai4 Li4" in different focus conditions

The tone4 subject constituents exhibit a similar durational distribution as the tone2 item; specifically, the rhematic focus bearing unit lengthens most, and the thematic focus constituent exhibits a secondary magnitude of lengthening. Then, the rhemtic focus occupies the third position and the thematic background item undergoes the least magnitude of lengthening. Specific values of the duration distribution are: mai4li4$_{RF}$: 39.91ms,

---

[36] 'RF', 'TF', 'RB', and 'TB' denote rheme focus, theme focus, rheme background, and theme background, respectively.

mai4li4$_{TF}$: 38.11ms, mai4li4$_{RB}$: 37.83ms, and mai4li4$_{TB}$: 36.42ms[37].

The lengthening results of subject constituents show regular patterns. As is the case with the F_0 evidence, the *rheme focus* exerts the most obvious effect upon lengthening, and the *theme focus* exhibits a secondary effect on durational change. The *rheme background* and *theme background* also exhibit different pattern characteristics.

3.2.4.2　Duration of object constituents

In the following paragraph, the duration distribution of the object target words "mao2lan2" and "lu4na4" in two kinds of focus statuses is discussed; i.e., rheme focus and theme background. These results are illustrated in Figures 3.2.4.2.1 and 3.2.4.2.2.

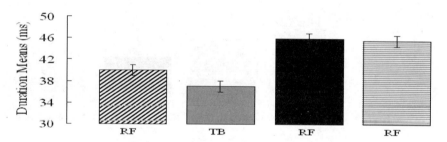

Figure 3.2.4.2.1　Mean duration for "Mao2 Lan2" in different focus conditions

From the F_0 analysis, it can be observed that although the object constituent "mao2lan2" has two information statuses, the F_0 patterns display differences among the rhematic focus due to the corresponding information condition on the subject items. It can also be determined from Figure 3.2.4.2.1 that the three rhematic focus bearing units exhibit

---

[37] Results of the Bonfrroni post hoc test shows that the durational distribution of the words in different focus statuses are significantly different from each other, i.e., RF vs. TF (P=0.002), RF vs. RB (P=0.00), RF vs. TB (P=0.00), TF vs. RB (P=0.012), TF vs. RB (P=0.001), RB vs. TB (P=0.003).

unsymmetrical distribution. Apparently, the last two constituents get the first and secondary duration lengthening and the difference is not obvious. The first rhematic unit exhibits ternary lengthening while the thematic background constituent exhibits the least magnitude of lengthening. Specific durational distribution values are: rheme focus$_{\text{Theme background}}$[38]: 45.87ms, rheme focus$_{\text{Theme focus}}$: 45.56ms, rheme focus$_{\text{Rheme background}}$: 39.98ms, and theme background: 37.07ms. Results of the Bonfrroni post hoc test shows that RF$_{\text{Theme background}}$ vs. RF$_{\text{Theme focus}}$ are not significantly different from each other (P=0.23>0.005). However, these two rhematic focuses exhibit obvious differences with other constituents; specifically, RF$_{\text{Theme background}}$ vs. RF$_{\text{Rheme background}}$ (P=0.001), RF$_{\text{Theme background}}$ vs. TB (P=0.00), RF$_{\text{Theme focus}}$ vs. RF$_{\text{Rheme background}}$ (P=0.002), and RF$_{\text{Rheme background}}$ vs. TB (P=0.00).

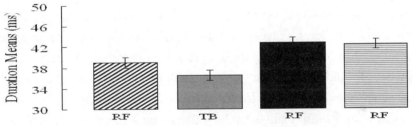

Figure 3.2.4.2.2 Mean duration for "Lu4 Na4" in different focus conditions

The tone4 object constituent has a similar durational distribution with the tone2 constituent. The two columns located at the right side in figure 3.2.4.2.2 have the greatest magnitude of lengthening, while the rheme focus on the left side occupies the third place, and the thematic background constituent gets the least magnitude of lengthening. The specific durational values are: rheme focus$_{\text{Theme background}}$: 42.77 ms, rheme focus$_{\text{Theme focus}}$: 42.48ms, rheme focus$_{\text{Rheme background}}$: 39.01ms, and theme

---

[38] The subscript describes the corresponding information status on subject constituents.

background: 36.57ms[39].

Thus, both the graph and the specific values show that when the subject constituents are put into four kinds of information statuses, they are significantly different from each other. The object constituents are not different from each other although they exhibit two kinds of focus categories: rheme focus$_{theme\ background}$ and the rheme focus$_{theme\ focus}$; whereas, they are quite different from another rheme focus with the subject constituent as rheme background.

3.2.5 Summary

Therefore, the durational data, in conjunction with the F_0 patterns, provides consistent evidence that the rheme focus that is also the newest information in the sentence can induce the most obvious sentential accentuation. Following Ladd (1996), the term adopted to describe this phenomenon is *accent*. It is generally accepted that *sentential accent* reflects, in some way, the intended *focus* of an utterance. However, there remains a number of disagreements about *how* focus is conveyed by accent, and in many ways these disagreements represent the continuation of a decades-old debate about the relationship between *focus* and *accent*[40]. The acoustic manifestations in SC observed in the above parts has shown that the status of information can be reflected by different levels of accents i.e., the most important information is marked by primary accent and the subordinated information is symbolized by secondary accent. Consequently, the rheme focus is marked by primary accent and the theme focus is related with secondary accent. The two kinds of accents can co-exist with each other in one sentence with the secondary one locating in the proceeding position. The following paragraph presents an examination of the levels of accents induced by identical information status; particularly, it mainly deals with the relationships between *rheme focus*

---

[39] Results of the Bonfrroni post hoc test also shows that RF$_{Theme\ background}$ vs. RF$_{Theme\ focus}$ exhibits no statistical differences (P=0.21), and they both differ significantly with other constituents: RF$_{Theme\ background}$ vs. RF$_{Rheme\ background}$ (P=0.002), RF$_{Theme\ background}$ vs. TB (P=0.00), and RF$_{Theme\ focus}$ vs. RF$_{Rheme\ background}$ (P=0.003), RF$_{Rheme\ background}$ vs. TB (P=0.00).
[40] The relationship between *focus* and *accent* is systematically discussed in chapter five.

and *levels of accents*.

3.3   Phonetic realization of double rheme focuses

Previous analysis demonstrates that rhematic focus exerts the greatest magnitude of F_0 and durational change. This part is concerned with evidence for an acoustically defined accent nature induced by a double rheme focus. Additionally, the effect of the relationships between the status of rheme focus and level of accent are further addressed. Therefore, the phonological means for the expression of focus status can be explored. To investigate whether the same status of information produces identical levels of accent in SC, parallel target settings were chosen so that the relevant observations could be made. Specifically, the basic word order is 'Subject Verb Object Le0', and, through the effect from the *wh*-operator 'Shei2 Verb Shei2 Le0 (Who Verb whom?)', the two rheme focuses locate on the *subject* and *object* positions. The tonal combinations for each syntactic component are designed to have tone2 and tone4 to reduce the amount of data.

3.3.1 F_0 contour of tone2 utterances in double rheme focuses

This section is mainly concerned with the *prominence distribution* and the *manner* in which *prominence* in double focus utterances with the syntactic components bearing tonal combinations of tone2 is realized. In order to reveal the phonological nature of the *accents* conveyed by a double focus, the target sentences with single rheme focus in the previous part are also adopted for comparisons with double focus constituents. They are illustrated as follows, with the asking-answering pairs (ii)-(iv) taken from part 3.2.2:

(i)   Shei2 Ti2 Ba2 Shei2 Le0? (Who elevated whom?)

Liu2 Min2[+RF]   Ti2 Ba2   **Mao2 Lan2**[+RF]   Le0.

↓   ↓   ↓

{Rheme focus}   {Theme background}   {Rheme focus}

73

(ii)   Shei2 Ti2 Ba2 Mao2 Lan2 Le0? (Who elevated Maolan?)

Liu2 Min2 [+RF]   Ti2 Ba2   Mao2 Lan2   Le0.

↓   ↓   ↓

{Rheme focus}   {Theme background} {Theme background}

(iii)   Liu2 Min2Ti2 Ba2 Shei2 Le0? (Liumin elevated whom?)

Liu2 Min2   Ti2 Ba2   **Mao2 Lan2** [+RF]   Le0.

↓   ↓   ↓

{Theme background} {Theme background} {Rheme focus}

(iv)   Fa1 Sheng1 Le0 Shen2 Me0 Shi4? (What happened?)

Liu2 Min2   Ti2 Ba2   **Mao2 Lan2**   Le0.

↓   ↓   ↓

{Rheme background} {Rheme background}   {Rheme focus}

Figure 3.3.1.1 is concerned with evidence for the prominence pattern under a double rheme focus in SC. Additionally, the prominences in double focus environments are also compared with the single rheme focus on both subject and object positions.

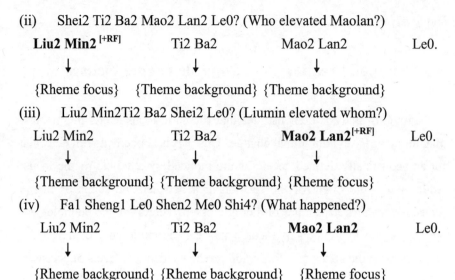

Figure 3.3.1.1 Mean F₀ for "Liu2 Min2 Ti2 Ba2 Mao2 Lan2 Le0" in dual and single focus conditions

With regard to the 'RF-TB-RF' contour, the sentence consists of two F_0 prominences. One distributes on the subject, the other on the object. With regard to the phonetic realization of these two constituents, the '*H*' and '*L*' tones of these two constituents are raised by the rheme focus. In order to investigate whether these two prominences can be realized so as to resemble in manner the F_0 pattern with a single focus status, the 'RF-TB-TB', 'TB-TB-RF', and 'RB-RB-RF' contours were also selected so that the relevant comparisons could be conducted.

A comparison between the intonation of 'RF-TB-RF' and the intonation of 'RF-TB-TB' shows a similar F_0 movement on the subject positions. A clear difference exists in the constituents after the subject positions: in the former, the verb item exhibits no F_0 lowering, while the latter exhibits a compressive effect upon F_0 register from the subject rheme focus. It is important to note that the prominence in the 'RF-TB-RF' contour can also resemble contours with the single rheme focus on the object position. Further, there is no obvious pitch register difference between subject and object constituents. The minimum and maximum pitch values of each syntactic component of the 'RF-TB-RF' contour are: $liu2min2_{min}=205Hz$, $ti2ba2_{min}=175Hz$, and $mao2lan2_{min}=205Hz$; and, $liu2min2_{max}=221Hz$, $ti2ba2_{max}=183Hz$, and $mao2lan2_{max}=222Hz$. In cases such as 'RF-TB-RF', the second prominence does not show a lower pitch register than the previous one. *Declination*[41], or the tendency of pitch to drift downwards over the course of an intonation group, has been observed in many languages. For example, it is known to occur in French (Vaissère 1971), Finish (Hirvonen 1970), and in a large number of African languages (Silverstein 1976 and Welmers 1973). Pierrehumbert (1979) also mentioned that when two accented syllables sound equal in pitch, the second was actually lower, and when accented syllables perform equal in pitch, the second one sounds more accented. Perceptual experiment results have shown that the accented constituents are unambiguously perceived: the primary accents are the object item and the secondary one is the subject.

This kind of phenomenon displays cross-language features; i.e., Jaeggli (1982) in a study of prominence patterns within one phrase, proposed that although the first focused constituent begins with a high

---

[41] This term was coined by Cohen and 't Hart (1967).

pitch, the main prominence falls at the end of the phrase. Thus, the two rheme focuses can not convey an identical level of accent; the primary one also locates in the right position.

A further One-Way ANOVA was conducted in order to compare significant differences among the words in the positions of subject, verb, and object in the 'RF-TB-RF', 'RF-TB-TB', 'TB-TB-RF', and 'RB-RB-RF contours.' The Bonfrroni post hoc test was adopted in order to examine the differences in the minimum and maximum pitch-values of each syntactic component. As for the subject constituents in the previous mentioned four contours, although the dual focus sentence contains both the subject and object rhematic focuses, the subject rheme focus shows no obvious F_0 difference with the single rheme focus sentence. Moreover, it also exhibits a higher pitch-register than the rhematic background and thematic background bearing unit. Results of a One-Way ANOVA shows that the item in dual rheme focus, e.g., 'RF-TB-RF', exhibits significant differences in the minimum and maximum pitch values in the rhematic background and thematic background conditions ($P_{min}=0.023$ and $P_{min}=0.00$; $P_{max}=0.019$ and $P_{max}=0.00$). Further, no obvious minimum and maximum pitch value differences exist between the single rhematic focus and dual rhematic focus ($P>0.05$).

It has been proposed by Eady et al (1986) that regardless of whether a sentence contains one or two foci in English, the main difference between single focus and dual focus sentences is due to the F_0 performances of the word following the initial focused item. A dual-focus sentence does not exhibit a low F_0 value characteristic of words that follow the focused item. Eady et al further state that the lack of a low post-focus F_0 in dual-focus sentences represents an anticipatory influence of the additional focus at the end of the sentence. This observation also applies to SC in which the double rheme focus exhibits no compressive effect on the constituents between the two focuses. This phenomenon can be seen under the verb positions. Specifically, 'RF-TB-RF' shows no obvious difference with

'RB-RB-RF' and 'TB-TB-RF' (P_{min}>0.05 and P_{max}>0.05 [42]). The 'RF-TB-TB' contour differs from the previous three contours in the verb positions (P_{min}<0.05 and P_{max}<0.05). These results show that only the single rhematic focus exerts a compressive effect upon the F_0 of the post focus item.

In the object positions, 'RF-TB-RF' and 'TB-TB-RF' exhibits similar F_0 contours. Specifically, the Bonfrroni post hoc test demonstrated that these are not significantly different from each other in minimum and maximum pitch values (P_{min}>0.05 and P_{max}>0.05). However, they are obviously different from the 'RB-RB-RF' and 'RF-TB-TB' contours (P_{min}<0.05 and P_{max}<0.05).

Therefore, the dual rheme focus on the subject and object positions can realize an identical F_0 pitch register with the single rheme focus without compressing the pitch registers between these two focuses.

3.3.2 F_0 contour of tone4 utterances in double rheme focuses

Figure 3.3.2.1 is adopted to further examine the F_0 prominences under a double focus condition in tone4 utterances.

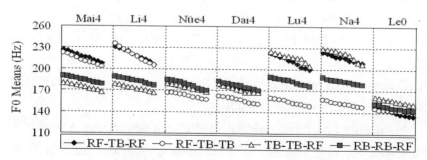

Figure 3.3.2.1   Mean F_0 for "Mai4 Li4 Nüe4 Dai4 Lu4 Na4 Le0" in dual and single focus conditions

A detailed examination of the intonation pattern of the tone4 utterances

---

[42] Specific values are not listed here due to space limitations.

reveals that they maintain a similar distributing pattern with the tone2 sentences. Within the 'RF-TB-RF' contour, the two rhematic focus induce obvious intonation prominences in both the subject and objects positions. Specifically, the "H" and "L" tones of "mai4li4" and "Lu4Na4" are obviously raised when compared with the verb constituent. Specific minimum and maximum pitch values of the subject, verb, and object constituents are: mai4li4$_{min}$: 206Hz, nüe4dai4$_{min}$:158Hz, and lu4na4 $_{min}$:200Hz; and, mai4li4$_{max}$: 231Hz, nüe4dai4$_{max}$:174Hz, and lu4na4$_{max}$:224Hz, respectively. These numbers also demonstrate that the subject and object exhibit equal height in pitch register and also display a much higher F_0 register than the verb item.

In the subject positions, results of a One-Way ANOVA show that the item in dual rheme focus exhibits significant differences in minimum and maximum pitch values in the rhematic background and thematic background conditions (P_{min}=0.00 and P_{min}=0.019; P_{max}=0.00 and P_{max}=0.00). Further, no obvious minimum and maximum pitch value differences exist between the single rhematic focus and dual rhematic focus (P_{min}>0.05 and P_{max}>0.05).

With regard to the tone4 verb constituent, the dual rhematic focus triggers no obvious compression effect on the verb items. A One-Way ANOVA demonstrates that the minimum and maximum pitch values of the 'RF-TB-RF', 'TB-TB-RF', and 'RB-RB-RF' contours are not significantly different from each other (P_{min}>0.05 and P_{max}>0.05). However, they are significantly different from the 'RF-TB-TB' contour that exhibits a compressive effect from rheme focus.

In the object positions, the 'RF-TB-RF' contour imposes a similar F_0 contour on the object positions. It exhibits no obvious differences in minimum and maximum pitch values with the 'TB-TB-RF' contour (P_{min}>0.05 and P_{max}>0.05). However, they are higher than the 'RB-RB-RF' and 'RF-TB-TB' contours (P_{min}<0.05 and P_{max}<0.05).

Therefore, the dual rheme focus on the subject and object can realize identical F_0 pitch register with the single rheme focus regardless of the tonal combinations of the utterances.

3.3.3   Duration patterns of words in double rheme focuses

In parts 3.3.1 and 3.3.2, the study mainly discusses the F_0 differences induced by dual and single focus conditions. It is pointed out that the two rhematic focuses on both the subject and object constituents can realize similar intonation prominence with the single subject and object constituents regardless of the tones of the target words. Here, *dual* and *single* focus induced lengthening is compared to provide further evidence for the distinction between focus status and accent level.

3.3.3.1   Duration patterns of subject constituents

Figure 3.3.3.1.1 illustrates the durational differences of the subject constituent "liu2min2" in *single* and *dual* focus environments. The designation "D-RF" denotes the subject rhematic focus bearing unit that also gets object rhematic focus; "S-RF" denotes a single focus condition with the subject serving as the only focus in the sentence; "S-TB" denotes that the subject constituent is the only thematic background in the sentence although it contains rhematic focus on the object; and "S-RB" denotes that the subject is under a rhematic background circumstance. The abscissa axis describes the focus conditions of each target word in the sentence, while the ordinate axis illustrates the durational distribution in milliseconds (ms). The range of durational changes in the ordinate axis is chosen as 30-50ms.

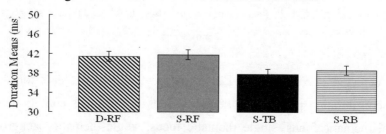

Figure 3.3.3.1.1 Mean duration for "Liu2 Min2" in dual and single

focus conditions

As can be seen from figure 3.3.3.1.1, the single rhematic focus induces the greatest magnitude of lengthening, and the dual rhematic focus exerts secondary lengthening; however, the magnitude of this kind of difference is not obvious. The durational distribution of the rhematic background bearing item exhibits ternary lengthening, and the rhematic background bearing unit exhibits the least magnitude of lengthening. Specific values of the durational distribution of these four constituents are: liu2min2$_{D-RF}$: 41.42ms, liu2min2$_{S-RF}$: 41.77ms, liu2min2$_{S-TB}$: 38.7ms, and liu2min2$_{S-RB}$: 38.7ms. A further One-Way ANOVA was adopted in order to compare the significant differences among the word "liu2min2" in four conditions. It is shown that Liu2Min2$_{S-RF}$ is different from Liu2Min2$_{S-TB}$ and Liu2Min2$_{S-RB}$ (P=0.024 and P=0.011, respectively). The results for Liu2Min2$_{D-RF}$ resemble the results for Liu2Min2$_{S-RF}$ in that it exhibits a significant difference from Liu2Min2$_{S-TB}$ and Liu2Min2$_{S-RB}$ (P=0.031 and P=0.015). Additionly, Liu2Min2$_{S-TF}$ is different from Liu2Min2$_{S-RB}$ (P=0.035). However, there are no durational difference between the dual and single subject rhematic focus (P>0.05).

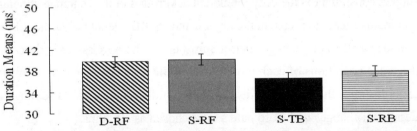

Figure 3.3.3.1.2 Mean duration for "Mai4 Li4" in dual and single focus conditions

As depicted in Figure 3.3.3.1.2, when the target word bears tone4, the general duration patterns of the four words in the focus conditions (i.e., dual rhematic focus, single rhematic focus, single thematic background, and single rhematic background) are consistent with the tone2 target words. Specifically, the single rhematic focus bearing unit shows the longest duration, the dual rhematic focus occupies the secondary position, and the rhematic background item exhibits a ternary position. Further, the rhematic focus exerts a slight effect among these four conditions, with the duration being of the smallest magnitude. Specific duration values of these four constituents are: $mai4li4_{D-RF}$: 39.74ms, $mai4li4_{S-RF}$: 39.99ms, $mai4li4_{S-TB}$: 36.42ms, and $mai4li4_{S-RB}$: 37.63ms. These values show that the magnitude of lengthening of tone4 items is less than for the corresponding tone2 words[43].

The present focus lengthening results corroborate the F_0 data results obtained in that the dual rheme focus results resemble the duration elongation on the subject constituent that is also longer than the theme focus induced lengthening.

3.3.3.2   Duration patterns of object constituents

Similar to the previous part which deals with the analysis of the duration adjustment by various focus statuses, this part is devoted to investigating the durational patterns of object constituents[44] in the rhematic focus and thematic background positions where there are various focus conditions on the subject constituents within one sentence. In the following two figures, 3.3.3.2.1 and 3.3.3.2.2, "D-RF" denotes that the sentences contain two rhematic focuses with one distributing on subject and the other on object constituents; "S-RF" denotes that the sentence contains one rhematic focus on the object constituent; "S-TB" denotes the sentence has the thematic background on the object constituent; and "RB-RF" denotes the case where the subject is the rhematic background bearing unit and the object is the rhematic focus containing entity. The axises are identical to those of Figure 3.3.3.1.1.

---

[43] Statistical analysis demonstrates that the durations of $Mai4Li4_{S-RF}$ and $Mai4Li4_{D-RF}$ are different from $Liu2Min2_{S-TB}$ and $Liu2Min2_{S-RB}$ ($P < 0.05$). Also, no obvious differences exist between $Mai4Li4_{S-RF}$ and $Mai4Li4_{D-RF}$($P > 0.05$).
[44] The duration of verb constituents exhibits a   prominence related feature in lengthening. The specific data is abbreviated.

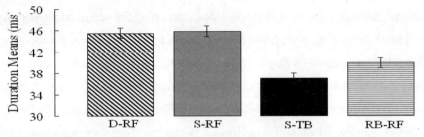

Figure 3.3.3.2.1　Mean duration for "Mao2 Lan2" in dual and single focus conditions

Although the target words are placed into the rhematic focus environment, the duration distributions do not show symmetric distribution. The left two columns display similar durational lengthening while the third column exhibits a shorter duration distribution than the proceeding two. The reasons are due to the focus statuses of the subject constituents. The last column exhibits a rhematic background on the subject constituents. Specific duration values of these four items are: $mao2lan2_{D-RF}$: 45.5ms, $mao2lan2_{S-RF}$: 45.87ms, $mao2lan2_{S-TB}$: 45.56ms, and $mao2lan2_{RB-RF}$: 39.98ms. Results of the Bonfrroni post hoc test demonstrates that the duration of $Mao2Lan2_{RB-RF}$ is significantly different from that of $Mao2Lan2_{D-RF}$, $Mao2Lan2_{S-RF}$, and $Mao2Lan2_{S-TB}$ ($P<0.05$). Also, the duration distribution of $Mao2Lan2_{D-RF}$ and $Mao2Lan2_{S-RF}$ exhibits obvious differences ($P>0.05$).

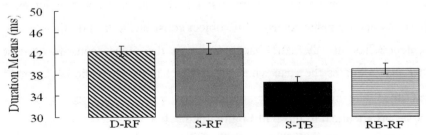

Figure 3.3.3.2.2　Mean duration for "Lu4 Na4" in dual and single focus conditions

The durational adjustment of the tone4 items exhibit patterns similar to the tone2 object word "mao2lan2" in that the left two conditions resemble each other in durational distribution; i.e., Lu4Na4$_{D-RF}$ and Lu4Na4$_{S-RF}$. Among the four constituents, the word "lu4na4" in the thematic background condition exhibits the least magnitude of lengthening. Specific values for these four words are: Lu4Na4$_{D-RF}$: 42.41ms, Lu4Na4$_{S-RF}$: 42.77ms, Lu4Na4$_{S-TB}$: 36.57ms, and Lu4Na4$_{RB-RF}$: 39.01ms[45].

The general lengthening pattern related to *dual* and *single* rheme focuses shows consistent results with F$_0$ prominence in that the dual and single rheme focuses exert a similar effect on the magnitude of lengthening.

3.3.4 Summary

In summary,the *dual rheme focus* induced F$_0$ prominence and durational lengthening results obtained in the above part have two implications: (i) dual rheme focus can realize double accents in the surface form, and (ii) the two accents have hierarchical distinctions. Therefore, it is reasonable to suggest that the level difference of accent in SC is related to the classification of *nuclear tone* and *pre-nuclear tone*, with the former referring to the *obligatory* and *unique* accent in a contour and the latter indicating *optional* and *secondary* accent according to the intonation tradition from the British School (Palmer 1922, Crystal 1969, Cruttenden 1992, Ladd 1996, Gussenhoven 2004, to list just a few). According to the founding work in the British school, Palmer (1922) proposes that the contour is divided into three parts, called *head, nucleus* and *tail.* Only the nuclear part is obligatory, so that in a mono-syllabic utterance, the contour consists of the nucleus alone. In an utterance with more syllables, the

---

[45] Results of the Bonfrroni post hoc test exhibits similar results in that no obvious differences exist in the duration of Lu4Na4$_{D-RF}$ and Lu4Na4$_{S-RF}$ (P<0.05). However, significant differences lie in Lu4Na4$_{RB-RF}$ and Lu4Na4$_{T-TB}$ with the former two words (P>0.05).

nuclear occurs on the most prominent stressed syllable. In English grammar, Ladd (1996) and Gussenhoven (2004) also state that contours obligatorily consist of one accent that corresponds to the nucleus. They also state that the nuclear part may be preceded by one or more accents that are defined as *pre-nuclear accents*. This grammar gives us something corresponding to the term *head* in the British tradition.

Evidence from acoustic manifestations have shown that SC exhibits the phonological entities of *nuclear accent* and *pre-nuclear accent* at the sentential level. The two kinds of accents can co-exist with each other in one target sentence, and the information status can determine the distribution of the nuclear and pre-nuclear parts: *nuclear accent* is always related to the most important information that is here described as *rheme focus*. The secondary information, i.e., theme focus, can be suggested to determine the appearance of pre-nuclear tone. However, of interest in the above analysis is that identical status of information can not lead to the same level of accent with the *right accent serving as the nuclear tone* and *the left one the pre-nuclear tone*. This provides important evidences for the *unique* and *obligatory nature* of the unclear tone; however, the underlying cause for the restriction of the distribution of the nuclear tone needs to be further tested when multiple syntactic components observe identical important status of information.

3.4   Phonetic realization of multiple rheme focuses

The previous section discusses the acoustic realizations of *nuclear accents* and *pre-nuclear accents* induced by dual rhematic focus, and also by theme focus vs. rheme focus. Additionally, this part concentrates on the analysis of the phonetic realization of nuclear tone triggered by multiple rhematic focuses; specifically, the basic syntactic items are enlarged to four constituents of which three are designed to generate a rhematic focus through which to observe the co-existence or conflicts of multiple focuses on the formation of F_0 in the surface form. Thus, the underlying causes for restricting the distribution of nuclear tone and the hierarchical levels of accents can be further explored.

The basic target sentence in this part is "Subject+Adverb+Verb+Object+Le0." The syntactic constituent "adverb" is inserted into the basic pattern "Subject+Verb+Object+Le0" so as to place three syntactic items into rhematic focus status in order to investigate the conflicts from three rhematic focuses on the realization of sentential level accents. As for the composition of the syntactic items in the target sentences, the subject, verb, and object elements retain the same content as in part 3.3. The previous discussion has demonstrated that accent distribution exhibits no corresponding relationships with tonal combinations, and the tone2 constituent is selected as the research anchor to reveal the phonological nature for the distribution of the *nuclear accent*. Therefore, the target sentence adopted in this part is "Liu2 Min2 Ling2 Chen2 Ti2 Ba2 Mao2 Lan2 Le0 (Liumin elevated Maolan in the early morning)." Since the durational data in the above analysis always exhibits a consistent pattern with F_0, the major aim in this part is to identify the position of the *nuclear accent*, while the F_0 is taken as the only acoustic parameter. The *wh*-operators and the focus distribution are delineated in (i)-(v):

(i)   Shei2 Shen2 Me0 Shi2 Hou0 Ti2 Ba2 Shei2 Le0?(Who and when elevated whom?)

Liu2 Min2[+RF]   **Ling2 Chen2**[+RF]   Ti2 Ba2   **Mao2 Lan2**[+RF]   Le0.

　　↓　　　　　　　　↓　　　　　　　↓　　　　　　　↓

{Rheme focus} {Rheme focus} {Theme background} {Rheme focus}

(ii)   Shei2 Ling2 Chen2 Zen3 Me0 Shei2 Le0?(Who did what to whom on the early morning?)

Liu2 Min2[+RF]   Ling2 Chen2   **Ti2 Ba2**[+RF]   **Mao2 Lan2**[+RF]   Le0.

　　↓　　　　　　　　↓　　　　　　↓　　　　　　　↓

{Rheme focus} {Theme background} {Rheme focus}   {Rheme focus}

(iii)   Liu2 Min2 Shen2 Me0 Shi2 Hou0 Zen3 Me0 Shei2 Le0?(Liu Min when did what to whom?)

Liu2 Min2　　**Ling2 Chen2**[+RF]　　**Ti2 Ba2**[+RF]　　**Mao2 Lan2**[+RF] Le0.

　↓　　　　　　↓　　　　　　↓　　　　　　↓

{Theme background} {Rheme focus} {Rheme focus}　{Rheme focus}

(iv)　Shei2 Shen2 Me0 Shi2 Hou0 Zen3 Me0 Mao2 Lan2 Le0?(Who and
　　　when did what to Maolan?)

Liu2 Min2[+RF] **Ling2 Chen2**[+RF]　　**Ti2 Ba2**[+RF]　　Mao2 Lan2　Le0.

　↓　　　　　　↓　　　　　　↓　　　　　　↓

{Rheme focus} {Rheme focus}　{Rheme focus}　{Theme background}

(v)　Fa1 Sheng1 Le0 Shen2 Me0 Shi4? (What happened?)

Liu2 Min2　　Ling2 Chen2　　Ti2 Ba2　　**Mao2 Lan2**　Le0.

　↓　　　　　　↓　　　　　　↓　　　　　　↓

{Rheme background} {Rheme background} {Rheme background} {Rheme focus}

3.4.1　F_0 patterns of rheme focus on "S+Ad+O" and "S+V+O"[46]

In this section, the rhematic focuses are placed on three syntactic components. The three syntactic components are: subject, adverb and object constituents and subject, verb and object components as described in (i) and (ii) in the previous part. In comparison with the previous two sentences, (v) is also adopted in order to put the rheme focus on the object constituent and the rheme background on the other components in the sentence. It is mentioned in part 3.3 that the subject rhematic focus and the object rhematic focus can simultaneously exerted F_0 and duration prominences, and here, the emphasis is on the following questions: (i) can three F_0 prominences be realized within one sentence? (ii) which constituent exhibits *nuclear accent* in the surface form? and (iii) what is the underlying cause for restricting the distribution of the *nuclear accent*?

Figure3.4.1.1 displays the mean for three F_0 sentences: "Liu2 Min2

---

[46] S, V and O denote subjct, verb and object, respectively.

Ling2 Chen2 Ti2 Ba2Mao2Lan2 Le0 (Liumin elevated Maolan in the early morning)." The symbol 'RB-RB-RB-RF' denotes that the object is the only rheme focus bearing unit and the other components in the sentences are the rheme background bearing units. 'S+Ad+O' denotes that rheme focus locates on subject, adverb, and object constituents, while 'S+V+O' denotes that the rheme focus distributing on the subject, verb, and object components. The abscissa axis describes the content of each syllable in the sentence while the ordinate axis illustrates the F_0 range with the unit of measurement in Hz.

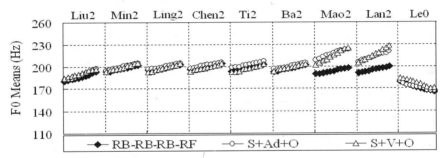

Figure 3.4.1.1   Mean F_0 for "Liu2 Min2 Ling2 Chen2 Ti2 Ba2 Mao2 Lan2 Le0"

In comparison with the 'RB-RB-RB-RF' contour, it is obvious in the 'S+Ad+O' contour that the F_0 prominence locates on the object constituents that exhibit higher pitch registers than for the corresponding 'RB-RB-RB-RF' contour; i.e., both the L tone and H tone show higher pitch than the other syntactic items; specifically, the pitch register of "liu2min2", "ling2chen2", and "ti2ba2" are obviously lower than the corresponding object. The minimum pitch values of each syntactic items are: liu2min2: 182Hz, ling2chen2: 197Hz, ti2ba2:197Hz, and mao2lan2: 206Hz, and the maximum pitch values of these words are: liu2min2: 205Hz, ling2chen2: 206Hz, ti2ba2: 207Hz, and mao2lan2: 223Hz. It can be seen that although there are three rhematic focuses, subject, adverb, and object, only the object that is the right most rheme focus in the utterance exhibits F_0 prominence. As for the 'S+V+O' contour, the subject, adverb, and verb constituents exhibit similar pitch registers, and the object item exhibits a higher pitch register, with both of the L and H tones of the word "mao2lan2" being higher than the other syntactic component. The minimum pitch values of the four items are: liu2min2: 185Hz, ling2chen2: 193Hz, ti2ba2: 193Hz, and mao2lan2: 202Hz. Further, the maximum pitch values of each syntactic entity in the sentence are: liu2min2: 205Hz, ling2chen2: 204Hz, ti2ba2: 203Hz, and mao2lan2: 228Hz; hence, the differences of the maximum values are more obvious. Therefore, the target sentence only contains *one nuclear tone* that is lead by the *right most* rheme focus.

Therefore, when multiple constituents in a sentence are serving as the rheme focus, they can not realize *nuclear accent* simultaneously. In this situation, the right most component is the *nuclear accent* bearing unit.

3.4.2 F_0 patterns of rheme focus on "Ad+V+O"and "S+Ad+V"

Through the analyses in parts 3.4.1 and 3.4.2, the rhematic focuses are placed onto the subject, adverb, and object constituents; and, subject, verb, and object constituents, respectively; and finally, only the object constituent serves as the anchor to lead the nucleus in the surface form. In this part, the rhematic focus is also designed to distribute onto three adjacent constituents: adverb, verb, and object constituents; and subject, adverb, and verb constituents. In this manner, the specific phonetic realization of the *nuclear accent* induced by three adjacent rhematic focuses can be examined.

Figure 3.4.2.1 contains three F_0 contours that have identical syllabic compositions: "Liu2 Min2 Ling2 Chen2 Ti2 Ba2 Mao2 Lan2 Le0." The 'RB-RB-RB-RF' contour is the contour in part 3.4.1 that is also adopted for comparison. The symbols 'Ad+V+O' and 'S+Ad+V' denote the rhematic focus distributing on the adverb, verb, and object; and, subject, adverb, and verb components.

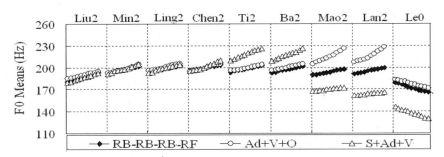

Figure 3.4.2.1   Mean F₀ for "Liu2 Min2 Ling2 Chen2 Ti2 Ba2 Mao2 Lan2 Le0"

Within the 'Ad+V+O' contour, although three positions of rheme focuses of the sentence are placed onto the adverb, verb, and object constituents, the prominence only locates the object item; specifically, the right most rheme focus. The specific phonetic realization of the prominence is due to the raising of the L tone and H tone of the two syllables. The minimum pitch values of each syntactic item are: liu2min2: 185Hz, ling2chen2: 195Hz, ti2ba2: 196Hz, and mao2lan2: 205Hz. The maximum pitch values of the syntactic item are: liu2min2: 205Hz, ling2chen2: 206Hz, ti2ba2: 205Hz; and mao2lan2: 228Hz. These values further support the conclusion that there are intonation prominences on the rightmost rheme focus bearing unit. These results demonstrate that under the three rhematic focus conditions, only the right most constituent can trigger the nuclear tone in the surface form. The 'S+Ad+V' contour in figure 3.4.2.1 illustrates that the verb constituent "ti2ba2" exhibits a higher pitch register than the subject, adverb, and the object constituents. Specifically, both the L tone and the H tone of the verb constituents are raised by the rhematic focus. However, the rhematic focus bearing units of the subject and the adverb constituents exhibit no obvious effect upon pitch rising. In contrast to the former constituents, the object item gets pitch register lowering. The minimum pitch values of all the words in the sentence are: liu2min2: 180Hz, ling2chen2: 193Hz, ti2ba2: 209Hz, and mao2lan2: 162Hz. Additionally, the highest points of the words in the sentences are: liu2min2: 205Hz, ling2chen2: 210Hz, ti2ba2: 226Hz, and mao2lan2: 166Hz. All these results demonstrate that the verb constituent is the prominence bearing unit with the proceeding items remaining much the same, and the post-constituent is compressed significantly. The realization of the nuclear tone in the surface form is lead by the right most rheme focus.

3.4.3 Summary

This part has mainly dealt with accent realization at the surface utterance level with multiple *wh*-phrases. Having thoroughly examined all the possible combinations of the three constituents in four syntactic component sentences, the accent distribution has been shown to exhibit an invariant pattern in which the *right most rheme focus constituent* plays the determining role on the *distribution of nuclear tone* in the surface form. These observations further demonstrate the *unique and obligatory* nature of nuclear tone and the *optionality* of pre-nuclear tone in SC.

3.5 Accent and phrasing

Previous discussions have demonstrated that we have nuclear tone and pre-nuclear tone classifications in a given utterance in SC. A further point that needs to be discussed is the *phonological domain* for the realization of these two kinds of accents; i.e., prosodic word, intermediate phrase, intonation phrase and utterance. The evidence for the phrasing effect of accent can be obtained from the following three aspects: (i) duration of pauses; (ii) internal lengthening of each syllable in the accent word; and (iii) prosodic boundary labeling.

3.5.1 Duration of pauses

The examination of the distribution of pauses is conducted from two aspects. Firstly, the pause distribution is compared for the boundary among each syntactic component position for each target word in one given utterance based on the word order 'Subject+Verb+Object+Le0'[47] in the dual rheme focus sentence. Secondly, the positions that bear obvious pause lengthening are further examined in various information statuses in the post-subject positions. Figure 3.5.1.1 shows the duration of the pauses in the position between subject and verb, verb and object, and object and particle *le*. This relationship is marked by 'S-V' , 'V-O' , and 'O-Le.' The Y-Coordinate indicates the duration of the pauses with a range of 0-10ms.

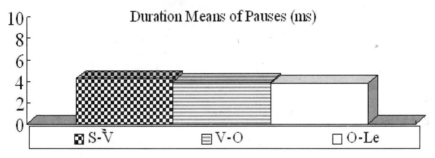

Figure 3. 5. 1. 1   Mean pause distribution among each word in a dual rheme focus

utterance

From Figure 3.5.1.1, it can be clearly seen that the mean duration of the pause in the position between the 'Subject' and 'Object' exhibits a duration that is a little bit longer than for the position between 'Verb' and 'Object' , and 'Object' and 'Le.' Specific duration values are: S-V: 4.35ms, V-O: 3.92ms, and O-Le: 3.78ms. A further One-Way ANOVA was conducted to test the significance of the durational differences among each boundary. Results indicate that there are no obvious differences ($P > 0.05$ for all).

Figure 3.5.1.2 compares the duration pauses in the position after the subject constituents with the aim of exploring whether variations in focus statuses can induce different effects on the pause distribution. The bottom part of the X-Coordinate describes the information status: "RB" , "RF" ,

---

[47] Since there are 32 examples for a target sentence, the pause duration for each position is obtained from 96 samples; thus, the tonal combinations are smoothed.

"TB", and "TF" denote rheme background, rheme focus, theme background, and theme focus, respectively.

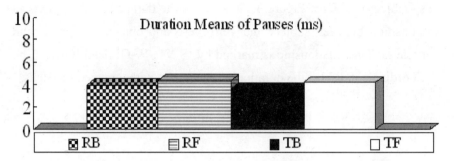

Figure 3.5.1.2 Mean pause distribution of the post-subject position in various focus conditions

From the analysis presented in part 3.5.1 that there is no obvious boundary locating in each boundary among all the syntactic components. Therefore, whether the duration of the pauses would be changed by variations in the information statuses was compared. It can be clearly seen in Figure 3.5.1.2 that although the subject components exhibit the focus statuses of "rheme background", "rhcmc focus", "theme background", and "theme focus", the durational lengthening in the given position exhibit similar lengthening. A further One-Way ANOVA was conducted to test the observations obtained in the above analysis. Results of the Bonferroni post hoc test show that there is no obvious difference among the four constituents (P>0.05). Thus, we may say that the duration of pauses show no corresponding relationships with the focus statuses variations.

On the whole, through the investigation of pause duration in the same utterance and in the same position in various focus statuses, it can be asertained that focus exerts no obvious phrasing effect on the target sentence. Further evidence is provided from the internal lengthening of the focused constituent.

3.5.2 Lengthening

Figure 3.5.2.1 is the mean duration of the target words "Liu2Min2" in the position of subject and object that are both exhibiting a rheme focus status. Within figure 3.5.2.1, each rectangle illustrates the durational distribution of each syllable; i.e., "Liu2" or "Min2." Additionally, the concrete content of each syllable is described in the bottom part of the X-Coordinate, and the top part of the X-Coordinate expresses the focus status and position for each word: the designation "S-RF" denotes the subject constituent in rheme focus and "O-RF" denotes the rheme focus on the object item. The Y-Coordinate marks the range of the variation in durational changes that is fixed as "0-30 ms" based on the range of durational changes.

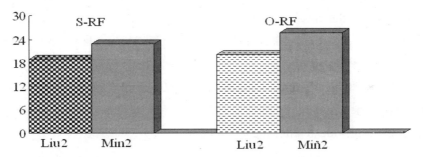

Figure 3.5.2.1 Mean duration for "Liu2" and "Min2" in various focus conditions

For each tone2 target word, "liu2min2", in the rheme focus, the second syllable "min2" exhibits a longer duration than the first syllable in the subject and object positions. Thus, no matter where the rheme focus locates, the second syllable exhibits a longer duration. Specific durational values for each syllable are: $liu2_{S-RF}$: 18.88ms, $min2_{S-RF}$: 22.89ms, $liu2_{O-RF}$: 20.16ms, and $min2_{O-RF}$: 25.71ms. A One-Way ANOVA was conducted to compare the durational differences in one word between each syllable. Results demonstrate that under the subject position, "min2" significantly differs from "liu2" (P=0.023), and the value for the object is P=0.01.

Thus, when the focus status remains identical, the durational lengthening within the word exhibits a non-symmetric distribution, with the second exhibiting a more obvious durational lengthening. Further evidence is obtained from the prosodic labeling result.

3.5.3 Prosodic labeling

This section provides the prosodic boundary labeling results to further test the phonological nature of phrase boundary in the positions among each position. The stimuli selected to label the prosodic boundary is the utterance 'Liu2 Min2 Ti2 Ba2 Mao Lan2 Le0' with the subject word serving as the rheme focus. There are 32 samples for each target sentence. Additionally, 4 skilled participants were invited to provide their subjective judgment on the levels of the prosodic boundary; e.g., prosodic word, intermediate phrase boundary and intonation phrase boundary. Thus, there are 128 labeling results for the position between 'Subject' and 'Verb', 'Verb' and 'Object', and 'Object' and 'Le0.' Table 3.5.3.1 shows the results of the prosodic boundary, syntactic item means that the prosodic labeling results locate after the given item.

Table 3.5.3.1 Labeling results of prosodic boundary

Prosodic boundary/Position	Subject-Verb	Verb-Object
Intonation phrase	7	3
Intermediate phrase	119	10
Prosodic word	2	115

From Table 3.5.3.1, it can be seen that the position after "subject" received the greatest amount of judgments on the intermediate phrase boundary, while the position of 'Verb-Object' received the greatest amount of judgments on the prosodic word boundary.

Therefore, the results of subjective judgments on the prosodic boundary labeling demonstrate that there is an intermediate phrase boundary after the rheme focused constituent. It is pointed out in part 3.5.1 that the rheme focus can not lead the appearance of the rheme focus; whereas, the greater magnitude of lengthening in the second syllable provides the evidence for the intermediate phrase boundary.

3.6   Discussion

This chapter investigates the accent patterns and distributing positions induced by various kinds and numbers of focuses in unmarked structures in SC. The major findings are: (i) accent corresponds with single focus in the same intonation phrase with the specific manner of the accent realization lying in the pitch register raising under focus and the pitch register compression of the post-focus constituents; (ii) the level of information can determine the hierarchical structure of accents with the more informative component triggering a higher level of accent; (iii) the accents have both obligatory and optional characteristics in SC; i.e., the *nuclear accent* is the *obligatory* and *unique* tone, while the *pre-nuclear tone* is *optional* and *secondary*; and (iv) multiple focus can not trigger multiple accents in surface form, only the rightmost focused constituent surfaces as the *nuclear tone*.

As for the relation between *focus* and *accent*, there remains a number of disagreements about how *focus* is conveyed by *accent*, and in many ways the disagreements represent the continuation of a decades-old debate involving the opposing views of accent first or focus first. In the pioneering work on the relation between focus and prosody in English,

Chomsky (1971) and Jackendoff (1972) proposed the well-formedness principle: *The focused constituent (or F-marked constituent) of a phrase must contain the intonation nucleus of that phrase*. This statement reflects the long debated question of 'Focus-to-Accent' (FTA).[48] Within the FTA theory, there are two possible ways of dealing with the relationship between *focus* and *accent*: structure-based or highlighting-based. The first approach was sketched by Ladd (1980) and Gussenhoven (1983). This view deals with the above question by distinguishing between the *distribution of focus* and the *distribution of accent*. That is, the linguistic description of accent patterns involves two complementary, but essentially separate, aspects: a statement about which parts of an utterance are focused, and a statement about how a given pattern of focus is conveyed by the location of the accent. The highlighting-based FTA approach, on the other hand, rejects the distinction between focus distribution and accent distribution and maintains the validity of the bi-directional relation between focus and accent. Thus, in this view, if a word is focused, it is accented. The evidence of the asymmetric relation between focused parts and accented parts in SC supports the observations made by the structure-based approach that the speaker's decision about what to focus is subject to all contextual influences; however, once the focused part of an utterance is specified, the accent pattern follows more or less automatically by language-specific rules[49].

---

[48] The term 'Focus-to-Accent' (FTA) is adopted from Gussenhoven (1983).
[49] The structural rules for restricting the distribution of the accent are discussed in chapter five.

Chapter Four

Accent Patterns in '*lian...dou*' and '*shi...de*' Constructions

4.1 Introduction

In the literature, the '*lian...dou*' and '*shi...de*' constructions are adopted as the typical structures to mark *focus* in SC (refer to Fang 1995, Liu and Xu 1998, Xu 2001, and Liu 2008). Specifically, the general form of the *lian...dou* structure can be presented as: [*lian* Subject *dou* Verb Object] or [Subject *lian* Object *dou* Verb]. In grammatical studies, the structure is adopted to mark *contrast*. Although it bears less contrast in nature than the '*shi...de*' construction, it can be interpreted as highlighting highly informative topics (Chu 1998). The component marked by *lian* has attracted much debate. Tsao (1990) proposes that 'the *lian* constituent is always a topic, and the stress that is associated with it is due to the implicit or explicit contrast associated with the *lian* constituent.' E.g.,

> (1) Lian   Xingqitian Ta Dou Qü Shangban.
>
> *including Sunday he all go work*
>
> 'Even on Sunday, he goes to work.' (Tsao 1990)

Here 'Sunday' is implicitly contrasted with other days of the week. He denies that it carries a focus. His reason for the denial may very well stem from the general belief that focus carries new information and is in direct opposition to topic which carries given information. Therefore, its presence in a topic would be a contradiction in and of itself. However, Ho (1993) treats the '*lian...dou*' construction as a marked focus. E.g.,

(1) Xihuan Chi La de   Lian Zi   Dou Daizhe   Ye   Meiguanxi.

Like   eat hot De   even seed   all   retain   also not matter

'For people who like to eat spicy food, the seeds of the pepper may be retained' (Ho 1993).

Based on this example, Ho proposes that Zi Dou Daizhe 'the seeds of the pepper may be retained' is a marked focus by virtue of the embedded '*lian...ye*' form. A different idea on the scope of the focus can be obtained from Fang (1995) who states that only the constituent immediately following *lian* is the focus bearing unit, and *lian* can be taken as the contrastive focus marker like *shi*. She further explains the nature of the 'NP' after the marker *lian* as: (i) within the *lian* sentence, it contains contrastive meaning and the *NP* marked by *lian* is the most extreme element; (ii) the non-nominal element after *lian* bears the nature of a nominal; (iii) the constituents located after *lian* are equal to the topic elements; and (iv) all the marked items after *lian* bear contrastive accents with *lian* being left out. With regard to the nature of the focus marked by *lian*, Liu and Xu (1998) define it as topic focus with the characteristics of [−Prominence] and [+Contrastive].

These two features are adopted to indicate that the constituents marked by *lian* are not the most informative elements within the sentence, whereas the constituent forms contrastive relationships with the other items. However, Yuan (2006) demonstrates that in the *lian*-construction "*lian*-NP + *ye/dou* VP", the NP is the focus bounded by the focus operator *ye* or *dou*, and it is neither a typical topic nor the so-called 'topical focus.' Then, the arrangement and restriction of the information structure of the *lian*-construction is put forward, and it is proposed that the whole *lian*-construction is a news sentence (broad focus) conveying new information. Additionally, it maintained that the syntactic and semantic mechanism whereby the *lian*-construction extends new construction meaning is through the topic being copied from predicate and   implying the meaning of the predicate.

With regard to the '*shi...de*' sentences, they are generally treated as *shi* sentences, and the *de* sentences are treated as *shi* sentences with *shi* deleted (Zhu 1978). This structure is usually adopted as a device to reverse the normal end-focus pattern in a comment to maintain the basic syntactic structure (Wu 1998). Within this structure, *shi* is the closed equivalent of English copula "be", and *de* is a particle with various functions: modification marker (Ross 1983), nominalizer (Chao 1968, Zhu 1978 and Li and Thompson 1981), and past-tense marker (Song 1981).

Previous grammatical studies on the '*shi...de*' construction concentrate on the following aspects: i) the composition of this structure; e.g., Lü (1983) points out that the *shi...de* structure can be taken as an independent construction to express the past tense and the confirmative mood. Thus, this structure is quite different from the *shi* structure with *shi* and *de* in which *shi* is the major verb and *de* is the object of *shi*. Lisa Cheng (2008) also maintains that there is actually no *shi...de* construction; specifically, *shi* is a copula which selects a small clause (with a subject and a predicate), and *de* marks the presence of two different non-overt operators; i.e., a generalized lamba-operator, and an assertion operator; ii) the semantic and syntactic function of *shi...de* construction; Zhao (1979), for example, based on the syntactic function of *shi* and *de*, classifies it into three types, the "*shi+...de*" serves as the predicate, the *shi* is put before the verb and adverb to express emphasis, the *de* is adopted to express the dynamic state, and "*shi...de*" forms a whole sentence in which *shi* and *de* describe the modality. Shi (2003) points out that the morpheme *shi* in an emphatic sentence is not a copula and the morpheme *de* in the same sentence is not a marker for nominalization; and iii) the focus marking function of *shi...de* structure; Fang (1995), for example, proposes that the *shi...* (*De*) structure is adopted to express the contrastive focus in SC and the focused constituent bears intonation prominence. Yuan (2003) claims that the structure of "Subject+Adverb+Verb+Object+*de*"[50] is an implicitly marked focus structure with focal accent as the focus marker, while the

---

[50] Within this structure, "S","Ad","V", and "O" denote subject, adverb, verb, and object, respectively.

"(*shi*)+S+(*shi*)+Ad+V+O+*de*" structure is an explicitly marked focus structure with the focused constituent de-focusation due to the insertion of the *shi*. Xiong (2007) reckons that *shi* is a focus marker that can be adopted to express broad and narrow focus; whereas, *de* only serves as modality in the "*shi...de*" construction. Liu (2008) lists three kinds of strong focus marking "*shi...de*" structure: "*shi*", "*shi+...+de*", and "*shi+...+de+* NP".

In addition to the grammatical analysis of the 'shi...de' studies of SC, Jia et al (2009) conducted a preliminary study mainly on the accent distribution of the typical focus-marking construction "[shi[...XP...]]" in SC. The study investigates the accent position and the phonetic realization of accent-bearing units in *shi*-sentences through both acoustic and perceptual experiments. Based on the results, the relationships between accent distribution and focus distribution are further discussed. The target sentences adopted in the study are:

(i) Xiao3 Wang2 Shi4 Qü4 Nian2 Chang2 Chang2 Qü4 Tai2 Wan1.

    xiao wang is last year   usually   go Taiwan

    (It was last year that Xiao Wang usually went to Taiwan).

(ii) Jiao4 Ta1 Qü4 Bei3 Jing1 De0 Shi4 Wo3.

    call he go Beijing   de is I

    (It was me who called him to go to Beijing).

(iii) Wo3 Shi4 Zuo2 Tian1 Cai2 Ting1 Shuo1 Shi4 Lao3 Wang2 Tui4 Xiu1 Le0.

    I   is yesterday just   hear   is lao wang retire le

    (It was just yesterday that I heard about the retirement of Lao Wang).

(iv) Shi4 Wo3 Jiao4 Ta1 Qü4 Bei3 Jing1 De0.

    is   I call he go Beijing de

    (It was me who called him to go to Beijing).

(v) Shi4 Wo3 Jiao4 Ta1 Qü4 De0 Bei3 Jing1.

    is   I call he go de Beijing

    (It was me who called him to go to Beijing).

(vi)   Shi4 Xiao3 Wang2 Zhi1 Dao4 Shi4 Xiao3 Liu2 Da3 Sui4 De0 Na4 Ge0 Bei1 Zi0.

is   xiao   wang   know   shi   xiao   liu   break   down   de   that   ge   cup

(It was Xiao Wang who knows that it was Xiao Liu who broken that cup).

Eleven and seven native speakers of SC were invited to participate in the acoustic and perceptual experiments, respectively. All sound files recorded in the acoustic analysis were adopted as the perceptual materials. In the perceptual experiment, all the sentences are broadcast in random order by perceptual software. Each participant was asked to identify the positions of perceived prominences in each target sentence, and there was no constraint in the number of prominences.

Results of the experiments demonstrate that the focus position overtly marked usually has the accent distributed[51] and the accent positions do not necessarily coincide with the loci where the focuses appear. The phonetic realization of the focused constituents can be further stated as: the pitch range is enlarged as a whole and the pitch registers of the following syllables are gradually lowered. According to the result of the experiment, this study further discusses the following highly controversial questions raised among grammarians: i) does focus or accent come first? The study reckons that the focus is identified first through grammatical means after which the accent is assigned; ii) can the accent and intonation variance predicts the focus position? The study points out, on the basis of experiment, that the variance can only be taken as the phonetic performance of the accent-bearing units and by no means predicts the focus distribution; and iii) how does the Chinese grammatical focus perform phonetically? The study indicates that the overtly

[51] In that study, the enlargement of the pitch range and the perceptual results were taken as the cue to identify the accent distribution.

marked focuses are so phonetically demonstrated that the pitch range is obviously enlarged.

Following the path suggested by previous findings on the '*lian...dou*' and '*shi...de*' constructions in SC, the analysis of these two structures mainly covers the expression of the focus, and also their corresponding syntactic function. The phonetic explorations of the '*shi.. .de*' structure mainly deal with the specific manner and position of the phonetic realization of the intonation prominence in the sentential level. Therefore, the purpose of this chapter is to further the study of prominence distribution in both the '*lian...dou*' and '*shi...de*' structures, with the concrete goal of investigating the co-existences and conflicts of *syntax*-marked focus and information induced focus on the formation of the overall pitch and duration patterns in SC.

Within this context, the phonological means involved in the expression of focus in SC are described as hierarchical levels of accent. Further, the association of *pre-nuclear* vs. *nuclear tone* with the *syntax*-marked focus and the information induced focus can be addressed through answering the following questions: i) what constitutes the differences of intonation prominences between the sentences without an overt focus marker and those with '*lian...dou*' and '*shi...de*' as focus marking? ii) how do the positions of prominence vary when different constituents are marked by *lian* and *shi*? iii) what is the co-existing manner of *syntax*-marked focus and information-induced focus in one sentence? iv) when the *syntax*-marked focus and the information focus conflict with each other on the formation of prominence, which kind of focus can be compressed? v) what is the difference in the phonetic nature of the *lian*-marked focus and *shi*-marked focus? vi) what is the corresponding relationship between the nuclear tone distribution and the *syntax*-marked focus? and vii) what composes the difference of levels of the accents conveyed by *lian*-marked focus and *shi*-marked focus? Several sections are adopted to answer the above questions. Section 4.2 presents a discussion of the accent patterns conveyed by the *syntax*-marked focus and the interaction of the *syntax*-marked focus and the information induced focus. It attempts to account for the relations between the *syntax*-marked focus and the information induced focus with the former one always locating in the proceeding position. In section 4.3, the accent patterns conveyed by *syntax*-marked focuses and the information induced focus are further discussed with the information marked focus locating before the *syntax*-marked focus. In section 4.4, the phrasing effect trigger by the *lian...dou* or *shi...de* constructions is of main concern. Finally, the major findings and the phonological pattern of the accents are provided in section 4.5.

4.2   Co-existences and conflicts of *syntax*-marked focus and *information* induced focus in '*lian*+S+*dou*+ V+O+Le' and '*Shi*+S +V+O+De' constructions

This part is concerned with evidence for the F_0 and duration defined acoustic effect of the '*lian...dou*' and '*shi...de*' structures. The basic 'Subject+Verb+Object' word order of the target sentence is retained. The formation of the *syntax*-marked focus is composed by the insertion of the markers '*lian...dou*' and '*shi...de*' into the unmarked order mentioned in sections 2.2.2.2 and 2.2.2.3; i.e., *Lian*+Subject+*Dou*+Verb+Object+Le0' and '*Shi*+Subject+Verb+Object+de0[52]. Within these two structures, the subject items always serve as the *syntax*-marked focus, that is, the *lian* and *shi* marked focus. In order to explore the phonetic and phonological nature of the *lian* and *shi* marked focuses, specific context was designed so that the *syntax*-marked focus and the *wh*-elicited focus can form various relationships; e.g., co-existence on the same constituents to affect the variation of the F_0 and duration patterns or conflict with each other in the

---

[52] A detailed description of the formation of the '*lian...dou*' and '*shi...de*' constructions can be found in part 2.2.2.2 and part 2.2.2.3.

formation of the F_0 and duration patterns. Consequently, the accent patterns conveyed by different kinds of focuses can be defined by phonological means. Further, a consistent correlation between the intonation property and *syntax*-marked focus can be expressed in terms of the phonological categories of intonation and not in terms of variation in physical continua.

4.2.1 Phonetic realization of *syntax*-marked focus

The major aim of this section is to explore the specific manner of the effect from *lian* and *shi* marking upon the F_0 and duration patterns. In particular, if the *syntax*-marked focus (*lian* or *shi* marked) is found to be consistently signaled by specific intonation means in SC, the intonation effect of the focus should be captured in the tonal structure of SC. Additionally, if *syntax*-marked focus is found to induce systematic differences in intonation form, these should be taken as a reflection of distinct phonological means. In contrast, if no such systematic intonation effects associated with the expression of the focus are found, the assumption of any tonal means of phonological focus-marking should be preempted. In order to approach this goal, the following asking-answering pairs are adopted:

(i) Fa1 Sheng1 Le0 Shen2 Me0 Shi4? (What happened?)

     Lian   **Subject**[+LianF]   *Dou*   Verb   **Object**[+RF]   Le0
               ↓   ↓

     {Rheme background & *Lian*-marked focus} {Rheme focus}

(ii) Fa1 Sheng1 Le0 Shen2 Me0 Shi4? (What happened?)

     Shi   **Subject**[+ShiF]   Verb   **Object**[+RF]   De0
               ↓   ↓

     {Rheme background & *Shi*-marked focus} {Rheme focus}

(iii) Fa1 Sheng1 Le0 Shen2 Me0 Shi4? (What happened?)

        Subject   Verb   **Object**[+RF]   Le0
             ↓   ↓

     {Rheme background}   {Rheme focus}

An examination of the effect of the rheme focus upon the overall contour of the syntax unmarked sentence in part 3.2.2 has demonstrated that it can restrict the appearance of the *declination* of the F_0 contour to some extent. Thus, *asking-answering* pair (iii) is adopted as the basic anchor to compare the effect from the *lian* and *shi* marked focuses upon the F_0 and duration patterns. As described in (i)-(iii), each target sentence is expressed by a syntactic component. The specific target sentences are:

(i)   a. Lian2 **Liu Min2**[+LianF] Dou1 Ti2 Ba2 **Mao2 Lan2**[+RF] Le0

(Even Liumin elevated Maolan);

b. Lian2 **Mai4 Li4**[+LianF] Dou1 Nüe4 Dai4 **Lu4 Na4**[+RF] Le0

(Even Maili maltreated Luna).

For *shi*-marked sentences, they are:

(ii)   a.Shi4 **Liu Min2**[+ShiF] Ti2 Ba2 **Mao2Lan2**[+RF] De0 (It is Liumin

that elevated Maolan);

b. Shi4 **Mai4 Li4**[+ShiF] Nüe4 Dai4 **Lu4 Na4**[+RF] Le0 (It is Maili

that maltreated Luna);

The corresponding utterances without the *syntax*-markers are:

(iii)   a.Liu Min2 Ti2 Ba2 **Mao2 Lan2**[+RF] Le0 (Liumin elevated

Maolan).

b.Mai4 Li4 Nüe4 Dai4 **Lu4 Na4**[+RF] Le0 (Maili maltreated Luna).

4.2.1.1   Overall F_0 contour of *syntax*-marked focus

It can be observed that the *lian* and *shi* marked focuses always place on the *subject items* "liu2min2" and "mai4li4" ; and through the selection of the sentence 'Fa1 Sheng1 Le0 Shen2 Me0 Shi4? (What happened?)', the three target sentences exhibit rhematic focus on the words 'mao2lan2' and 'mai4li4.' More importantly, the *syntax*-marked components also exhibit a rheme background condition. Therefore, we can observe the conflict between the *syntax*-marked focus and the information triggered focus on the formation of F_0 prominence with the scope of rheme spreading over the entire utterance.

Figure 4.2.1.1 is adopted to illustrate the mean F_0 for the tone2 sentences in three syntactic structures: Lian **Liu Min2**[+LianF] Dou1 Ti2 Ba2 **Mao2 Lan2**[+RF] Le0, Shi **Liu Min2**[+LianF] Ti2 Ba2 **Mao2 Lan2**[+RF] De0, and Liu Min2 Ti2 Ba2 **Mao2 Lan2**[+RF] Le0. The top part of the X-coordinate describes the contents of each syllable in the sentence as in chapter three, the bottom illustrates the structure and the information status of the utterance, 'LianSB(RB-RB-RF)' denotes an utterance that contains a *lian*-marked focus that distributes on the subject constituent. The symbols in parentheses indicate the information status of each syntactic component, and are the abbreviations of 'rheme background, rheme background and rheme focus' for subject, verb, and object, respectively. The designation 'ShiSB(RB-RB-RF)' denotes a *shi*-marked sentence in which the structure 'Un(RB-RB-RF)' is unmarked. The information status of the other two structures is identical with the *lian*-marked utterance. The Y-coordinate illustrates the pitch range of the graph, and has a range of 110Hz-260Hz as in the previous chapter.

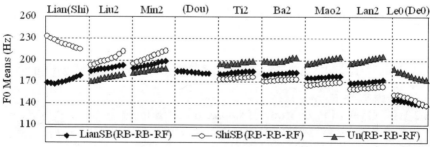

Figure 4.2.1.1.1　Mean F_0 for "Lian(Shi) Liu2 Min2 (Dou) Ti2 Ba2 Mao2 Lan2 Le0(De0)"

In the 'LianSB(RB-RB-RF)' contour, it can be clearly seen that the prominence in the sentence is at the position of *subject constituent*; i.e., the

106

word "liu2min2." The "*H*" tones of the two syllables are obviously higher than the other syntactic elements in the sentence, while the '*L*' tones are a little bit higher. Compared to the 'Un(RB-RB-RF)' contour, the subject constituent in a *lian*-marked sentence also exhibits a higher pitch register than the one in an unmarked sentence. The constituents locating after the *lian*-marked focus undergo compression that exhibits a lower pitch register than the unmarked sentence. With regard to the *shi*-marked sentence, the item that locates immediately after *shi*-marked focus exhibits the most obvious prominence among the three subject constituents. The pitch register distributing after the *shi*-marked subject obtains the lowest pitch register. In the 'LianSB(RB-RB-RF)' contour, the minimum pitch values for each word are: liu2min2$_{min}$:185Hz, ti2ba2$_{min}$: 179Hz, mao2lan2 $_{min}$:168Hz[53]; and, liu2min2$_{max}$:199Hz, ti2ba2$_{max}$: 185Hz, and mao2lan2 $_{max}$: 177Hz. As for the 'ShiSB(RB-RB-RF)' contour, the values are: liu2min2$_{min}$: 185Hz, ti2ba2 $_{min}$: 179Hz, and mao2lan2 $_{min}$: 168Hz[54]: and, liu2min2$_{max}$: 199Hz, ti2ba2$_{max}$: 185Hz, and mao2lan2 $_{max}$:177Hz. Thus, when the '*lian...dou*' and '*shi...de*' structures are inserted into the basic word order, the F$_0$ movement of verb and object displays a declining movement.

A further One-Way ANOVA was conducted to compare the significance of the minimum and maximum pitch value differences induced by various kinds of focuses on the positions of subject, verb, and object. Under the subject position, it can be clearly seen that the highest pitch register is due to the effect of the *shi*-marked focus, and the *lian*-marked focus occupies the secondary position. These two contours are significantly higher than the one in the unmarked structure. Results of the Bonferroni post hoc test demonstrates that the maximum pitch value of

---

[53] Since the effect of the *lian*-marked focus is at the central core of this part, the specific comparisons of the pitch values of the markers *lian* and *dou* are not included.
[54] Since the effect of the *shi*-marked focus is at the central core of this part, the specific comparisons of the pitch values of the marker *shi* is not included.

"liu2min2$_{\text{LianSB(RB-RB-RF)}}$[55]" significantly differs from the other contours; i.e., "liu2min2$_{\text{ShiSB(RB-RB-RF)}}$" and "liu2min2$_{\text{Un(RB-RB-RF)}}$" with $P_{max}=0.023$ and $P_{max}=0.015$. "liu2min2$_{\text{ShiSB(RB-RB-RF)}}$" also differs from "liu2min2$_{\text{Un(RB-RB-RF)}}$" ($P_{max}=0.00$). As for the minimum pitch value difference, "liu2min2$_{\text{LianSB(RB-RB-RF)}}$" shows no obvious difference from the previous two contours ($P_{min}>0.05$). However, "liu2min2$_{\text{ShiSB(RB-RB-RF)}}$" is significantly different from "liu2min2$_{\text{Un(RB-RB-RF)}}$" ($P=0.01$).

In verb position, the contours show exactly the opposite distribution of the subject constituents. The highest pitch register in the subject position exhibits the lowest F_0 register in the object position and vice versa. Results of the Bonferroni post hoc test show that the minimum and maximum pitch values of these three contours are different from each other; specifically, "ti2ba2$_{\text{Lian}}$[56]" vs. "ti2ba2$_{\text{Shi}}$" ($P_{min}=0.032$; $P_{max}=0.021$), "ti2ba2$_{\text{Lian}}$" vs. "ti2ba2$_{\text{Un}}$" ($P_{min}=0.00$; $P_{max}=0.00$), and ti2ba2$_{\text{Shi}}$" vs. "ti2ba2$_{\text{Un}}$" ($P_{min}=0.00$; $P_{max}=0.00$).

The object constituents maintain identical distribution with the verb constituents, with all three contours exhibiting significant contours. Specifically, "mao2lan2$_{\text{Lian}}$" vs. "mao2lan2$_{\text{Shi}}$" ($P_{min}=0.039$ and $P_{max}=0.042$), "mao2lan2$_{\text{Lian}}$" vs. "mao2lan2$_{\text{Un}}$"($P_{min}=0.00$ and $P_{max}=0.00$), and "mao2lan2$_{\text{Shi}}$" vs. "mao2lan2$_{\text{Un}}$" ($P_{min}=0.00$ and $P_{max}=0.00$).

The study of the F_0 pattern in various syntactic structures developed here has produced a set of findings that support the conclusion that the *syntax*-marker can affect the intonation of the constituents immediately following the markers. In comparison with the focus marker *shi*, *lian* shows a slight effect upon F_0 rising under focus and F_0 compression in the positions after the focus.

Figure 4.2.1.2 is the tone4 utterances in three syntactic structures: *Lian*-marked, *Shi*-marked, and unmarked. These three sentences are adapted to further support the observations made in the above analysis.

---

[55] The subscript denotes the syntactic structure of the sentence and the information status.

[56] This subscript denotes the syntactic structure that includes the component.

The designation 'LianSB(RB-RB-RF)' denotes the sentence 'Lian2 **Mai4 Li4**[+LianF] Dou1 Nüe4 Dai4 **Lu4 Na4**[+RF] Le0 (Even Maili maltreated Luna)', 'ShiSB(RB-RB-RF)' denotes the *shi*-marked utterance 'Shi4 **Mai4 Li4**[+ShiF] Nüe4 Dai4 **Lu4 Na4**[+RF] Le0 (It is Maili that maltreated Luna)', and 'Un(RB-RB-RF)' denotes the sentence 'Mai4 Li4 Nüe4 Dai4 **Lu4 Na4**[+RF] Le0 (Maili maltreated Luna).' The content of the coordinates are consistent with those of the previous graph.

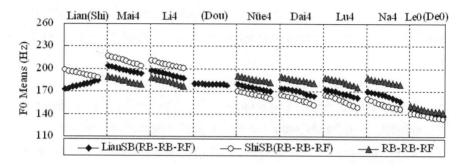

Figure 4.2.1.1.2   Mean F₀ for "Lian(Shi) Mai4 Li4 (Dou) Nüe4 Dai4 Lu4 Na4 Le0(De)"

In the analysis put forward in the above part, the *lian*-marked focus displays an F_0 prominence compared with the other constituents in the 'LianSB(RB-RB-RF)' contour. Supporting evidence is found in the tone4 sentence in that the *lian*-marked subjects show a more obvious prominence phenomenon with both the "*H*" and "*L*" tones being higher than the verb and the object constituents. The subject element marked by *shi* also distributes in the highest position among the three contours. Its corresponding verb and object constituents also locate in the bottom part. In the *Lian*-marked sentence, the specific pitch values of each syntactic component are: mai4li4$_{min}$: 188Hz, nüe4dai4$_{min}$: 164Hz, and lu4na4$_{min}$: 157Hz; and, the maximum pitch values are: mai4li4$_{max}$: 217Hz, nüe4dai4$_{max}$: 170Hz, and lu4na4$_{max}$: 165Hz. Within the *Shi*-marked sentence, the values are: mai4li4$_{min}$: 201Hz, nüe4dai4$_{min}$: 152Hz and lu4na4$_{min}$: 147Hz]. Clearly, the tone4 sentences and the tone2 sentences exhibit similar intonation patterns.

A One-Way ANOVA was conducted to test the significances of the minimum and maximum pitch values for each word in the positions of subject, verb, and object. The tone4 constituents and the tone2 components exhibit similar F_0 patterns. Specifically, the addition of the *shi*-marked focus exhibits the most obvious effect on pitch register rising, and the secondary position is occupied by the *lian*-marked focus. Finally, the lowest position is occupied by the unmarked rhematic background status bearing unit. These observations are supported by the Bonferroni post hoc test[57].

As for the verb constituents, their pitch registers are affected by the proceeding subject items. The relation is that the higher pitch register on the subject corresponds with the lower pitch register on the verb item. Therefore, the lowest pitch register of the verb item lies in the word 'nüe4dai4$_{Shi}$', and the secondary position is occupied by 'nüe4dai4$_{Lian}$'[58].

The object items duplicate the F_0 movements of the verb constituents. While the words 'lu4na4$_{Shi}$' and 'lu4na4$_{Lian}$' exhibit a compressive effect from subject components with the *shi*-marked one distributing in the bottom part. Additionally, the contours in the object positions are significantly different from each other[59].

To sum up, when the scope spreads over the entire sentence, the rhematic focus on the object positions are compressed by both the *lian* and *shi* marked focuses regardless of the tonal combinations of the target sentences.Tonal combinations of the syntactic components mainly

---

[57] In the subject position, the three constituents are different from each in both minimum and maximum pitch values; i.e., 'liu2min2$_{LianSB(RB-RB-RF)}$' vs. 'liu2min2$_{ShiSB(RB-RB-RF)}$' (P_{min}=0.023 and P_{max}=0.18), 'liu2min2$_{LianSB(RB-RB-RF)}$' vs. 'liu2min2$_{Un(RB-RB-RF)}$' (P_{min}=0.027 and P_{max}=0.22), and 'liu2min2$_{ShiSB(RB-RB-RF)}$' vs. 'liu2min2$_{Un(RB-RB-RF)}$' (P_{min}=0.00 and P_{max}=0.00).

[58] As for the verb constituents, the pitch registers are different from each other (P_{min}<0.05; P_{max}<0.05 for all).

[59] The lowest and highest points of the three object constituents are different from each other (P_{min}<0.05 and P_{max}<0.05).

contribute to the specific manner of the *syntax*-marked focus. Based on the study from Ho (1993), when the focus of information is explicitly marked by *shi*, the rest of the sentence is taken as given, and a contrast is inferred with other items. In the structure, the accent is not on *shi*, but on the following element. F_0 data in the tone2 and tone4 sentences support the claim that the sentential *accent* in 'shi...de' construction locates on the subject position. In the *lian...dou* structure, it can also induce prominence in the position of *lian*-marked focus. Xu (2001) takes *lian* as the *focus sensitive operator*, while the constituent marked by *lian* easily becomes the focused constituent in the sentence. In comparing these two *syntax*-marked focuses, the difference lies in the magnitude of the F_0 raising in which they exhibit a similar effect.

4.2.1.2   Durational lengthening of *syntax*-marked focus

This section investigates the durational adjustment induced by the *syntax*-marked, *lian* and *shi* marked, focus[60]. The F_0 contours of Figure 4.2.1.1 and Figure 4.2.1.2 show that *shi* and *lian* can trigger F_0 prominence under the same context. Further evidence is observed from the duration parameter with the aim of exploring the accent level associate with these two *syntax*-marked focuses.

Figure 4.2.2.1 and Figure 4.2.2.2 illustrate the duration distribution of the subject constituents "Liu2Min2" and "Mai4Li4" both of which observe *lian*-marked focus, *shi*-marked focus, or dwell in the unmarked structure. As for the symbols in the bottom part of the X-Coordinate, "LianSB-RB" denotes that the *lian*-marked focus locates on the subject items and the focus status of the subject item is rhematic background. The designation "ShiSB" denotes the *shi*-structure. Further, "Un" denotes that the structure of the target sentence is unmarked. All these constituents

---

[60] Since the focus markers always locate on the subject constituents, the durations of the verb and object constituents are not included.

dwell in the rhematic background condition.

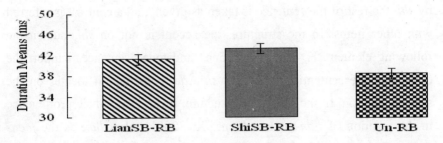

Figure 4.2.2.1 Mean duration for "Liu2 Min2" in different syntactic
structures

Here, the effect of the *lian*-marked focus and *shi*-marked focus on the durational adjustment is examined. Examination of Figure 4.2.2.1 reveals that the greatest magnitude of lengthening lies in the effect of the *shi*-marked focus. The secondary position is occupied by the *lian*-marked focus in the rhematic background condition. Then comes the duration distribution of the constituent bearing the rhematic background condition in the unmarked structure. In comparison with the duration distribution of the unmarked constituent, the *lian*-marked focus and *shi*-marked focus exhibit duration lengthening. There exists a magnitude difference between these two focuses. The specific duration values for each item in the graph are: 41.62ms, 43.65ms, and 38.7ms. A One-Way ANOVA was conducted to test the significance of the differences among each constituent. Results of the Bonferroni post hoc test show that "liu2min2$_{LianSB-RB}$" significantly differs from other constituents: "liu2min2$_{ShiSB-RB}$"(P=0.012) and "liu2min2$_{Un-RB}$"(P=0.01), Moreover, the *shi*-marked constituent also differs from the unmarked element: "liu2min2$_{ShiSB-RB}$" vs. "liu2min2$_{Un-RB}$" (P=0.00). These values further support the observations obtained from the above analysis.

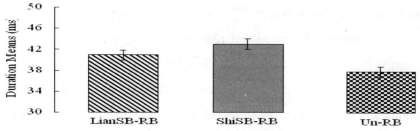

Figure 4. 2. 2. 2   Mean duration for "Mai4 Li4" in different syntactic
structures

Although the tonal combinations are designed as tone4 in the sentence, the manifestation of the effect from the *shi* and *lian* marked focuses on durational lengthening are much the same. Specifically, the most obvious effect is owing to the effect from the *shi*-marked focus in the rheme background condition. This constituent is longer than the *lian*-marked focus bearing unit. These two constituents are longer than the unmarked rhematic background item. This indicates that *lian*-marked focus and *shi*-marked focus can exert durational lengthening on the target words. The specific duration values are: 40.93ms, 43.02ms, and 37.83ms[61].

So far, the *lian*-marked and *shi*-marked focus can induce durational lengthening on the given constituents. Within these two constituents, *shi*-marked focus exerts a more obvious effect than the *lian*-marked focus. The duration data is consistent with the F_0 data in that the *shi*-marked focus triggers a more obvious acoustic effect.

4.2.1.3   Summary

This section has examined the acoustic effect of the *lian*-marked focus and the *shi*-marked focus. The intonation phenomena described in

---

[61] Results of the Bonferroni post hoc test establishes that the duration of the three constituents significantly differs from each other: "mai4li4$_{LianSB-RB}$" vs. "mai4li4$_{ShiSB-RB}$" (P=0.026), "mai4li4$_{LianSB-RB}$" vs. "mai4li4$_{Un-RB}$" (P=0.029), and "mai4li4$_{ShiSB-RB}$" vs. "mai4li4$_{Un-RB}$" (P=0.00).

the structure of '*lian* Subject[+LianF]...*dou*' and '*shi* Subject[+ShiF]' are shown to bear important effects on the reorganization of intonation structure. Specifically, both of the focuses can trigger F_0 rising under focus and exert compressive effect on the constituents following the focus. Duration lengthening is also observed in the under-focused position. Although the *shi*-marked focus and the *lian*-marked focus are treated to bear different grammatical characteristics (Liu and Xu 1998 and Cai 2004), they exhibit similar acoustic effects on the F_0 and duration variation. The only difference lies in the magnitude of the effect that is more obvious in the *shi*-marked focus than in the *lian*-marked focus. Therefore, these observations support the claim of Xu (2004) that different kinds of focus in SC can be expressed in similar ways. Further, we have proposed in chapter three that the most obvious acoustic effect is expressed by the *nuclear accent* at the sentential level. With respect to the *lian* and *shi* marked sentence, we can also propose that the *nuclear accent* associates with the *syntax*-marked constituents with a slightly different phonetic realization after a different focus marker.

4.2.2 Addition of the *syntax*-marked focus with the rheme focus on the same constituent

This section was concerned with the *additive effect* from the *syntax*-marked focus and the information induced focus on the formation of the accent patterns in SC. A marked focus always implies some kind of contrast that usually refers to a situation where one piece of information, say *X*, is explicitly or implicitly opposed to some other piece of information, say *Y*, that stands in some specific relation in opposition to *X* in the given setting (Dik et al 1981). It is thus important to investigate the prosodic mechanism employed by the same constituent to express two kinds of focuses: *syntax*-marked focus and information induced focus. In a study of the additive effect from different kinds of focus, this section is concerned with the following issues: (i) the physical correlates of the effect from the addition of *lian*-marked focus or *shi*-marked focus with the information induced focus; (ii) the domain over which the focused constituents may extend; and (iii) the phonological means to represent the additive focus in the surface form. Previous analysis has demonstrated that tonal combination difference only contributes to the specific manner of the focus realization, whereas it triggers no effect upon the distribution of the accent pattern. Thereafter, the target sentences adopted in this section are confined to tone2 utterances[62]. These sentences are:

(i)   Lian2 Shei2 Dou1 Ti2   Ba2   Mao2   Lan2 Le0? (Even who elevated Maolan?)

   Lian **Liu2 Min2**[+LianF&+RF]63   Dou1   Ti2Ba2   MaoLan2   Le0.

              ↓   ↓

   {Rheme focus & *Lian*-marked focus}   {Theme background}

(ii)   Shi4 Shei2 Ti2 Ba2 Mao2 Lan2 De0?(It is who that elevated Maolan?)

   Shi   **Liu2 Min2**[+ShiF&+RF]   Ti Ba2   Mao2 Lan2   De0.

              ↓   ↓

   {Rheme focus & *Shi*-marked focus}   {Theme background}

(iii) Fa1 Sheng1 Le0 Shen2 Me0 Shi4?(What happened?)

   Lian **Liu2 Min2**[+LianF] *Dou* Ti2Ba2   **Mao2Lan2**[+RF] Le0.

              ↓   ↓

   {Rheme background & *Lian*-marked focus}   {Rheme focus}

---

[62] The specific realization of the tone4 utterances is displayed in the Appendix.
[63] Features [+LianF&+RF] and [+ShiF&+RF] denote the focus status of the addition of *lian*-marked focus and rheme focus, and the addition of *shi*-marked focus and information induced focus, respectively.

(iv) Fa1 Sheng1 Le0 Shen2 Me0 Shi4?(What happened?)

Shi   **Liu2 Min2**[+ShiF]   Ti2Ba2   **Mao2Lan2**[+RF] De0.

         ↓   ↓

    {Rheme background & *Shi*-marked focus}   {Rheme focus}

Asking-answering pairs (iii) and (iv) are taken from section 4.2.1 to serve as the basic anchor to explore the additive effect from different kinds of focuses. In regard to type (i), Xu (2001) treats *lian* as the 'Focus-Sensitive Operator' and the constituent marked by *lian* exhibits a strong tendency to attract focus. Therefore, the constituent in the interrogative environment is easily distributed in the center of the interrogative. Thus, the type (i) *asking-answering* pair meets the grammatical needs of this study. As for the *asking-answering* pair of the *shi*-marked structure, Ho (1993) proposes that if the '*shi...de*' construction is used in a sentence that contains an interrogative mood (inherent focus), this word is to be included in the *shi...de* structure as an explicitly indicated focus. Xu (2001) also maintains this observation based on the 'Unique Strong Focus Principle' that can be explained as: 'When a simple clause contains more than one focus, the specific grammatical marker can only be taken to emphasize one of them.' He argues that in the interrogative sentence, the interrogative pronoun may locate closely to the focus marker *shi*. Thus, the utterance 'Shi4 Shei2 Fa1 Ming2 De0 Fei1 Ji1 (It is who that invented the plane) ?' is a grammatical sentence, and so is the type (ii) sentence.

4.2.2.1 Overall F_0 contour of additive focus

The present section desribes the F_0 realization of the above mentioned focus status. Figure 4.2.2.1.1 is the mean F_0 for the utterances that exhibit various influences on the subject constituents: the addition of *lian*-marked focus and information induced focus; the addition of *shi*-marked focus and information induced focus; and the addition of *lian* and *shi* marked focuses

116

in the rheme background condition. These focus statuses are described by the symbols in the bottom part of the graph. Specifically, 'LianSB(RF-TB-TB)' and 'ShiSB(RF-TB-TB)' denote the case in which the *lian* and *shi* marked focuses combine with the rheme focus. The designations 'LianSB(RB-RB-RF)' and 'ShiSB(RB-RB-RF)' denote the identical content as in the previous part. The content of the coordinates are the same as the prior F_0 graph.

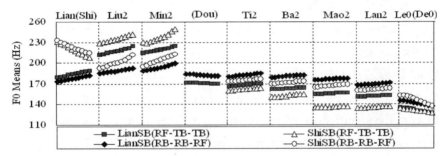

Figure 4.2.2.1.1 Mean F_0 for "Lian(Shi) Liu2 Min2 (Dou) Ti2 Ba2 Mao2 Lan2 Le0(De0)"

The mean F_0 contour 'LianSB(RF-TB-TB)' shows that the subject bearing units clearly exhibit pitch register raising that is more obviously than that in the context of 'LianSB(RB-RB-RF).' Moreover, the pitch registers of the successive syllables, which are significantly compressed, indicate a compressive effect triggered by the subject items. Further evidence for the 'LianSB(RF-TB-TB)' contour are found through the minimum and maximum pitch values among each syntactic component. Specifically, the values are: $liu2min2_{min}$: 212Hz, $ti2ba2_{min}$: 162Hz, $mao2lan2_{min}$: 150Hz; and, $liu2min2_{max}$: 224Hz, $ti2ba2_{min}$: 170Hz, and $mao2lan2_{min}$: 156Hz. Further, the mean F_0 for 'ShiSB(RB-RB-RF)' replicates the effect of the focus in 'LianSB(RF-TB-TB)' in that the sentential prominence locates on the word "liu2min2" and the pitch registers of the following syllables are compressed. The difference found between the two F_0 contours lies in the overall pitch range values. The additive focus from the rheme focus and the *shi*-marked focus leads to more expansion in the prominence position and more reduction of the post prominence items. The minimum and maximum pitch values of each syntactic item in the sentences are: $liu2min2_{min}$: 229Hz, $ti2ba2_{min}$: 150Hz, and $mao2lan2_{min}$: 134Hz; and, $liu2min2_{max}$: 249Hz, $ti2ba2_{max}$: 164Hz, and $mao2lan2_{max}$:137Hz. These two additive focuses exhibit more a obvious F_0 raising under the focus position and F_0 compression after the focused items than the 'LianSB(RB-RB-RF)' and 'ShiSB(RB-RB-RF)' contours.

A One-Way ANOVA was conducted to investigate the F_0 differences of the same constituents that are put into various focus statues; i.e., LianSB(RF-TB-TB), ShiSB(RF-TB-TB), LianSB(RB-RB-RF), and ShiSB(RB-RB-RF). The Bonferroni post hoc values are also used to explore the significance of the minimum and maximum pitch values. The four contours in the subject positions clearly exhibit the highest pitch register due to the effect from the addition of the *shi*-marked focus and the rheme focus. The pitch contour under the addition of the *lian*-marked focus and rheme focus performs immediately lower than the previous contour. These two contours are higher than the single focus environment; i.e., *lian*-marked focus or *shi*-marked focus. These results demonstrate that different kinds of focuses can combine together on the same constituent to exert a more obvious F_0 raising in the position under focus. Further evidence is found from the Bonferroni post hoc test in which the pitch registers of the constituents under the additive focus are significantly different from the single focus status, specifically, '$liu2min2_{LianSB(RF-TB-TB)}$' vs. '$liu2min2_{LianSB(RB-RB-RF)}$' ($P_{min}$=0.00 and P_{max}=0.00), '$liu2min2_{LianSB(RF-TB-TB)}$' vs. '$liu2min2_{ShiSB(RB-RB-RF)}$' ($P_{min}$=0.00 and P_{max}=0.00), '$liu2min2_{ShiSB(RF-TB-TB)}$' vs. '$liu2min2_{LianSB(RB-RB-RF)}$' ($P_{min}$=0.00 and P_{max}=0.00), and '$liu2min2_{ShiSB(RF-TB-TB)}$' vs. '$liu2min2_{ShiSB(RB-RB-RF)}$' ($P_{min}$=0.00 and P_{max}=0.00). Furthermore, the two additive effects from the addition of the *lian* and *shi* marked focuses are also significantly different from each other in terms of minimum and maximum pitch values; i.e., 'liu2min2$_{\text{LianSB(RF-TB-TB)}}$' vs. 'liu2min2$_{\text{ShiSB(RF-TB-TB)}}$' ($P_{\text{min}}$=0.011 and P_{max}=0.00).

The F_0 of the verb constituents are affected by the proceeding subject items. The higher pitch register on the subject constituents corresponds to the lower pitch registers on the verb constituents. Thus, the word 'ti2ba2$_{\text{ShiSB(RF-TB-TB)}}$' exhibits the lowest pitch register, while the one immediately distributed above 'ti2ba2$_{\text{ShiSB(RF-TB-TB)}}$' is 'ti2ba2$_{\text{LianSB(RF-TB-TB)}}$' . They also exhibit a greater compressive effect from the subject constituents. It is pointed out by Jia et al (2008) that significant effects imposed by the focal accents are found on the H tones of the post-focus constituents. Thereafter, the additive focus from the *syntax*-marked focus and the rheme focus exhibit similar acoustic effects[64].

As for object constituents, it is quite clear in Figure 4.2.2.1.1 that the lowest pitch register lies in the thematic background bearing unit that also exhibits a compression effect from the proceeding additive focus (*shi*-marked focus and rheme focus) of the subject constituent 'mao2lan2$_{\text{ShiSB(RF-TB-TB)}}$' The F_0 contour that locates above 'mao2lan2$_{\text{ShiSB(RF-TB-TB)}}$' is the object constituent of the 'mao2lan2$_{\text{LianSB(RF-TB-TB)}}$' contour. Further, they are both lower than the object elements with single *syntax*-marked focus on the subject position[65].

Thus, the conclusion is that the *lian*-marked focus and *shi*-marked focus can combine with the rheme focus with the result that the entire pitch register is raised higher than for the single *lian* or *shi* marked focus. The post-focus constituents observe more compressive effects from the

---

[64] Results of the Bonferroni post hoc test supports the observations; i.e., the minimum and maximum pitch values of the constituents 'ti2ba2 $_{\text{LianSB(RF-TB-TB)}}$' and 'ti2ba2$_{\text{ShiSB(RF-TB-TB)}}$' are significantly different from 'ti2ba2 $_{\text{LianSB(RB-RB-RF)}}$' and 'ti2ba2$_{\text{ShiSB(RB-RB-RF)}}$' ($P_{\text{min}}$<0.05 and P_{max}<0.05).

[65] Results of the Bonferroni post hoc test illustrates that mao2lan2$_{\text{ShiSB(RF-TB-TB)}}$ and mao2lan2$_{\text{LianSB(RF-TB-TB)}}$ are obviously different from 'mao2lan2 $_{\text{LianSB(RB-RB-RF)}}$' and 'mao2lan2$_{\text{ShiSB(RB-RB-RF)}}$' ($P_{\text{min}}$<0.05and P_{max}<0.05).

additive focus.

4.2.2.2 Durational lengthening induced by additive focus

This section concerns the lengthening phenomena, particularly the lengthening induced by additive focus; i.e., *Lian*-marked focus and the rheme focus or *Shi*-marked focus and rheme focus. Following the path suggested by previous F_0 patterns, the subject constituents are the only anchors employed due to the systematic manifestation of F_0-raising under the influence of the additive focus. As with the F_0 graph, the constituents dwelling in four focus statuses are adopted for examination. The focus status is described in the bottom part of the X-Coordinate. Specifically, 'LianSB-RF' denotes the subject item exhibiting the *lian*-marked focus and the rheme focus, 'ShiSB-RF' denotes the addition of the *shi*-marked focus and the rheme focus, while 'LianSB-RB' and 'ShiSB-RB' denote the *lian* and *shi* marked constituents dwelling in the rheme background condition. The Y-Coordinate illustrates the range of the durational distribution, which is 30ms-50ms.

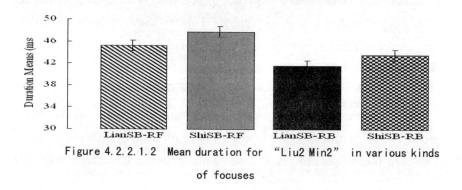

Figure 4.2.2.1.2 Mean duration for "Liu2 Min2" in various kinds of focuses

The duration distribution in Figure 4.2.2.1.2 reveals that the additive focus can induce robust lengthening on the given constituents. Specifically, the greatest magnitude of lengthening is due to the addition of the rhematic focus and the *shi*-marked focus. The secondary lengthening is due to the effect from the addition of the *lian*-marked focus and the rhematic focus. These results are obtained from the comparison of the durational distribution with the subject constituents in the status of 'LianSB-RB' and 'ShiSB-RB.' Although these two constituents observe *lian*-marked focus and *shi*-marked focus, they display a relatively shorter duration distribution with the additive focus status. The specific durational values are: 45.21ms, 47.8ms, 41.62ms, and 43.65ms. A One-Way ANOVA was conducted for the purpose of investigating the significance of the differences in the above constituents. Results of the Bonferroni post hoc test show that the duration distribution of these four constituents are obviously different from each other; i.e., 'liu2min2$_{LianSB-RF}$' vs. 'liu2min2$_{ShiSB-RF}$' (P=0.022), 'liu2min2$_{LianSB-RF}$' vs. 'liu2min2$_{LianSB-RB}$' (P=0.00), and 'liu2min2$_{LianSB-RF}$' vs. 'liu2min2$_{ShiSB-RB}$' (P=0.032). Further, the additive effects from the *shi*-marked constituents are also different from the other single focus marked constituents; i.e., 'liu2min2$_{ShiSB-RF}$' vs. 'liu2min2$_{LianSB-RB}$' (P=0.00) and 'liu2min2$_{ShiSB-RF}$' vs. 'liu2min2$_{ShiSB-RB}$' (P=0.012).

The duration data shows consistent results with the F_0 pattern in that the greatest magnitude of the durational changes is also due to the effect from the addition of the *shi*-marked focus and the rhematic focus. The secondary position is occupied by the addition of the *lian*-marked focus and the rheme focus.

4.2.2.3 Summary

This section extends the investigation of the acoustic manifestations of *nuclear accents* conveyed by the addition of *syntax*-marked focus and information induced focus beyond the existing literature. In comparison with the single focus utterances, a *lian* or *shi* marked sentence, although the *nuclear accent* corresponds with the additive focus (the addition of the *lian*-marked focus and information induced focus or the addition of the *shi*-marked focus and the information induced focus), the additive focus triggers more obvious F_0 raising and durational lengthening in the under focus position and compresses the post-focus constituents to a greater magnitude. In previous grammatical analyses, many scholars proposed that the interrogative pronoun should locate after the focus marker *shi* or *lian* (refer to, for example, Huang 1982). The detailed acoustic evidence for this conjecture has been provided in this section.

4.2.3 Co-existence of two different kinds of focuses on different constituents

In the previous section, the mechanism of the additive effect upon the F_0 and duration pattern was of main concern. This part is concerned with the investigation of the conflicts in the *syntax*-marked focus and the information induced focus on the formation of the accent patterning in the surface form. Thus, the following issues are addressed: (i) the acoustic correlates of two kinds focus in one utterance; i.e., *syntax*-marked and information induced focus; and, (ii) the phonological characteristics of the entities involved in expressing the two kinds of focuses. In order to approach this goal, the following *asking-answering* pairs are adopted:

(i)　Lian2　Liu2　Min2　Dou1　Ti2 Ba2　Shei2　Le0? (Even Liumin elevated whom?)

　　Lian　**Liu2 Min2**[+LianF]　Dou1　Ti2 Ba2　**Object**[+RF]　Le0
　　　　　　　↓　　　　　　　　　　　　　　　↓

　　{Theme background & *Lian*-marked focus }　{Rheme focus}

(ii)　*Shi4　Liu2　Min2　Ti2 Ba2　Shei2　De0? (It is Liumin that elevated whom?)

　　Shi　**Liu2 Min2**[+ShiF]　　Ti2 Ba2　**Object**[+RF]　De0
　　　　　　　↓　　　　　　　　　　　　　　　↓

　　{Theme background & *Shi*-marked focus}　{Rheme focus}

(iii)   Fa1 Sheng1 Le0 Shen2 Me0 Shi4? (What happened?)

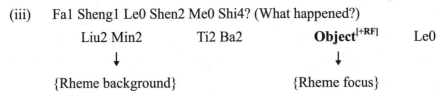

| Liu2 Min2 | Ti2 Ba2 | **Object**[+RF] | Le0 |

{Rheme background}   {Rheme focus}

It is proposed by Xu (2001) that the *lian*-marked component is sensitive to becoming the interrogative or negative center. However, he also accepts the argument from Liu and Xu (1998) that the major information in the *lian*-marked sentence locates in the rheme part. Zubizarreta (1998) adopts an example: a. Who ate what? b. there is an <x, y>, such that *x* ate *y*, through which the study to support the argument of *uniqueness* of the nuclear tone is conducted. Based on the observations from Liu and Xu and also Zubizarreta, *asking-answering* pair (i) is a well-formness example. With regard to the type (ii) utterance, it is ungrammatical according to the *Unique Strong Focus Principle* (hereinafter USFP) that requires multiple strong focuses in one utterance to coincide with each other. Since *shi* is a strong focus marker, the question of 'Shi4 Liu2 Min2 Ti2 Ba2 Shei2 De0? (It is Liumin that elevated whom?)' violates the USFP. Although it is ungrammatical, the selection of this utterance is for the purpose of examining the acoustic mechanism the speakers employ to express two strong focuses in one utterance. The type (iii) utterance is adopted as the basic anchor for comparison with the constituents in type (i) and type (ii).

4.2.3.1   Overall F_0 contour of two different kinds of focuses

Figure 4.2.3.1.1 depicts mean F_0 for the contours with a double focus condition in one utterance: *lian*-marked focus and information induced focus, and *shi*-marked focus and information induced focus. The symbols in the bottom part of the figure illustrate the focus status. Specifically, 'LianSB(TB-TB-RF)' denotes the *syntax*-marked focus also locates on the subject constituent, and the information category in the parentheses states that the utterance also contains a rheme focus on the object position; the *shi*-marked 'ShiSB(TB-TB-RF)' contour denotes that, in addition to the *shi*-marked focus on the subject position, it there is also a rheme focus on the object position; the 'Un(RB-RB-RF)' contour denotes that the sentence has no marked focus and dwells in the condition with all the constituents having rheme background, rheme background, and rheme focus. The top part of the X-Coordinate displays the content of the syllables in the utterances, and the Y-Coordinate provides the pitch-range.

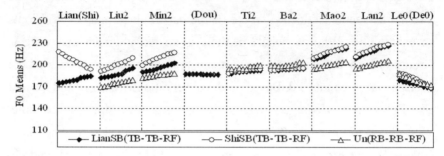

Figure 4.2.3.1.1　Mean F₀ for "Lian(Shi) Liu2 Min2 (Dou) Ti2 Ba2 Mao2 Lan2 Le0(De0)"

It is claimed by Xu (1999) and Jia et al (2008) that *wh*-elicited focus in SC exerts a compressive effect upon the F_0 register after the focus.The discussion in section 4.2.1 has demonstrated that the *syntax*-marked focus can trigger F_0 raising in focus position and compresses the F_0 after the constituents. Different kinds of focus in SC can be manifested in a similar acoustic manner; i.e., *syntax*-marked focus and information-induced focus. Therefore, in a study of the co-existence of *syntax*-marked focus (*lian*-marked focus or *shi*-marked focus) and *wh*-elicited rheme focus, the following aspects need to be considered: (i) whether the *syntax*-marked focus can realize F_0 prominence simultaneously with the *wh*-elicited rheme focus; and (ii) the existence of any variation in pitch register in the position between the two prominences. Therefore, a further question related to the hierarchical structure of accents by *syntax*-marked focus and rheme focus is further addressed. In part 3.3, it was pointed out that dual *wh*-elicited focus can trigger prominences simultaneously and these two prominences exhibit similar F_0 performances. Due to the existence of *declination*, the right one is considered as the primary one.

Further investigation of the phonetic nature of the *lian*-marked focus in the 'LianSB(TB-TB-RF)' contour revealed that the most obvious prominence distributed on the object position with the whole pitch register of the object item being raised. Further, secondary prominence is due to the effect of the *lian*-marked focus that also exerts a prominence that exhibits less magnitude of pitch register rising. Specific minimum and maximum pitch values for each item in the sentence are: liu2min2$_{min}$: 182Hz, ti2ba2$_{min}$: 189Hz, mao2lan2$_{min}$: 208Hz; and, liu2min2$_{min}$: 203Hz, ti2ba2$_{min}$: 195Hz, and mao2lan2$_{min}$: 227Hz. It is apparent in the'ShiSB(TB-TB-RF)' contour, that the F_0 in Figure 4.2.3.1.1 exhibits two prominences, one locates on the subject position, and the other one distributes on the object position.

Although 'Shi4 Liu2 Min2 Ti2 Ba2 Shei2 De0? (It is Liumin elevated whom?)' violates the USFP, the answering sentence can realize two prominences simultaneously that exhibit a similar acoustic mechanism with the *lian*-marked focus. The more obvious one is due to the effect of the *wh*-elicited focus. Specific pitch value evidence supports the conclusion that two prominences are realized in the target sentence: liu2min2$_{min}$: 191Hz, ti2ba2$_{min}$: 189Hz, mao2lan2$_{min}$: 210Hz; and, liu2min2$_{max}$: 217Hz, ti2ba2$_{max}$: 196Hz, and mao2lan2$_{max}$: 229Hz. Thus, the two contours display prominences on both the subject and object positions in comparison with the 'Un(RB-RB-RF)' contour. Perceptual experiment demonstrate that there are two accents in 'LianSB(TB-TB-RF)' and 'ShiSB(TB-TB-RF)' contours. In the former one, the primary accent is on the object constituent, and the secondary one is *lian*-marked one. As for the 'ShiSB(TB-TB-RF)', the primary one is also due to the rheme focus and the secondary one is *shi*-marked one.

A One-Way ANOVA was conducted to investigate significant differences in the minimum and maximum pitch values on specific syntactic components, such as subject, verb, and object in each contour.

Specifically, under subject positions, the general distributing pattern of the *lian*-marked focus and *shi*-marked focus display a similar distribution with the single *lian* or *shi* marked focus. The highest pitch register lies in the effect of the subject focus in the 'ShiSB(TB-TB-RF)' contour, the whole pitch register of the word 'liu2min2$_{ShiSB(TB-TB-RF)}$' is higher than that of 'liu2min2$_{LianSB(TB-TB-RF)}$' and 'liu2min2$_{Un(TB-TB-RF)}$.' The major difference among these three words resides in the *H* tone of the target syllable. The 'liu2min2$_{LianSB(TB-TB-RF)}$' contour also locates lower than the 'liu2min2$_{ShiSB(TB-TB-RF)}$' contour as shown in Figure 4.2.3.1.1, and the lowest pitch register is 'liu2min2$_{Un(RB-RB-RF)}$.' Results of the Bonferroni post hoc test show that the minimum and maximum pitch values of these three constituents are significantly different from each other: i.e., 'liu2min2$_{ShiSB(TB-TB-RF)}$' vs. 'liu2min2$_{LianSB(TB-TB-RF)}$' (P_{min}=0.025 and P_{max}=0.014), 'liu2min2$_{ShiSB(TB-TB-RF)}$' vs. 'liu2min2$_{Un(TB-TB-RF)}$' (P_{min}=0.00 and P_{max}=0.00), and 'liu2min2$_{LianSB(TB-TB-RF)}$' vs. 'liu2min2$_{Un(TB-TB-RF)}$' (P_{min}=0.029 and P_{max}=0.019). These data further support the conclusion that under a double focus condition, the *syntax*-marked focus can also exhibit prominences regardless of the focus status on the object position.

The F_0 contours of the verb constituents suggest that the three constituents exhibit similar performances in the way that all the "*L*" and "*H*" tones are similar with each other; e.g., 'ti2ba2$_{ShiSB(TB-TB-RF)}$', 'ti2ba2$_{LianSB(TB-TB-RF)}$', and 'ti2ba2$_{Un(TB-TB-RF)}$.' Therefore, the pitch registers of the constituents between the two focuses (a *syntax*-marked one and a *wh*-elicited one) do not exhibit a compressive effect from either of the focuses. This effect resembles that of the double focus in an unmarked structure: theme focus vs. rheme focus and double rheme focus. This observation is further supported by the results of the Bonferroni post hoc test (P_{min}>0.05 and P_{max}>0.05 for all).

Among the three constituents 'mao2lan2$_{ShiSB(TB-TB-RF)}$', 'mao2lan2$_{LianSB(TB-TB-RF)}$', and 'mao2lan2 $_{ShiSB(TB-TB-RF)}$' under object positions, the bottom part of Figure 4.2.3.1.1 depicts the distribution of the pitch contour

126

of the element in the condition of rheme focus in an unmarked structure. Further, the highest position in Figure 4.2.3.1.1 contains two similar pitch contours; specifically, the two rhematic focus induced F_0 variations with corresponding *shi*-marked and *lian*-marked focuses on the subjects. These observations indicate that regardless of the focus statuses the subject exhibits, the object can realize the rhematic induced prominence on the object position, and there is no obvious F_0 differences between the rheme focus induced prominence[66].

On the whole, due to the effect from both *syntax*-marked (*lian* or *shi* marked) focus and information induced focus, there appears two prominences in one target sentence. The specific manner of the two prominences is the raising of the pitch registers of the focus bearing units. These two prominences exist level difference with the rheme focus inducing the primary one, and the secondary one is triggered by the *syntax*-marked approach. Within these two *syntax*-marked focuses, the *shi*-marked one exerts a more obvious effect on F_0 raising. Although in the '*shi...de*' construction, the insertion of the rhematic focus on the object constituents is ungrammatical, speakers can manifest the information distinction in terms of a prosodic aspect.

4.2.3.2   Durational lengthening of two different kinds of focuses

In part 4.2.3.1, a systematical examination of the F_0 variations induced by various kinds of focuses in one target utterance was conducted. Results demonstrate that the *syntax*-marked focus can form a co-existing relationship with the information induced focus. When these two focuses co-exist with each other in one target sentence, they can induce prominences simultaneously. Therefore, this part examines further

---

[66] Results of a One-Way ANOVA were found to support the observations made in the above part; that is, 'mao2lan2 $_{ShiSB(TB-TB-RF)}$' vs. 'mao2lan2 $_{LianSB(TB-TB-RF)}$' ($P_{min}>0.05$ and $P_{min}>0.05$). These two constituents are significantly different from 'mao2lan2 $_{Un(TB-TB-RF)}$' ($P_{min}<0.05$ and $P_{max}<0.05$).

evidence for the co-existing effect of different kinds of focuses: *shi*-marked focus or *lian*-marked focus and information induced focus. The findings already presented in this research reinforce the view that there exists *nuclear accent* and *pre-nuclear accent* in SC. Following the path suggested by previous findings, this section investigates whether duration data can provide evidence for the *nuclear* and *pre-nuclear accent classifications* in SC.

Figure 4.2.3.2.1 depicts the durational distribution of the subject constituents that serve as the *lian*-marked focus, *shi*-marked focus, and the unmarked rheme background bearing unit. The abscissa axis describes the focus statuses exhibited by the subject constituents "Liu2Min2." 'LianSB-TB' denotes the condition in which the focus marker *lian* marks the subject, 'TB' denotes the thematic background condition, 'ShiSB-TB' denotes that the shi marked item is subject and the focus condition is thematic background, and 'Un-RB' denotes the constituents in an unmarked structure and dwelling in a rhematic background condition. Therefore, the double symbols for each item in Figure 4.2.3.2.1 indicate the syntactic structure and the information focus statuses. Moreover, the ordinate axis illustrates the durational distribution in ms.

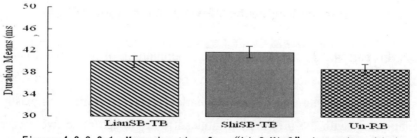

Figure 4.2.3.2.1 Mean duration for "Liu2 Min2" in various kinds of focuses

With regard to the durational adjustment induced by various focus statuses, 'liu2min2$_{LianSB-TB}$', 'liu2min2$_{ShiSB-TB}$', and 'liu2min2$_{Un-RB}$', the subject exhibits the greatest magnitude of lengthening due to the effect of the *shi*-marked focus. The secondary lengthening is due to the effect of the *lian*-marked focus. The least magnitude of lengthening is exhibited in the duration distribution of constituents in the unmarked structure. Specific values of each target word are: 40.01ms, 41.85ms, and 38.7ms[67]. A One-Way ANOVA was performed in order to compare the significance of the differences in the durational distribution among the three items illustrated in Figure 4.2.3.2.1. Statistical results support the observations obtained from the above analysis ($P<0.05$ for all). These results imply that although the *lian* and *shi* marked utterances contain the information induced focus on the object positions, the *syntax*-marked focus can also exert an effect on durational elongation.

The duration data, which is consistent with the F_0 pattern results, supports the conclusion that the *syntax*-marked focus can also exert an effect on durational lengthening under double focus conditions. However, the classification of the levels of accents needs to be further addressed from the aspect of durational lengthening of the object constituents.

The following part deals mainly with the durational adjustment induced by various information statuses on object positions. Except for the unmarked structure item, the other two components contain *syntax*-marked focuses on the subject position in one sentence. Hence, we may investigate the durational distributions of the object constituents that are triggered by *wh*-elicited question information focus statuses.

Figure 4.2.3.2.2 depicts the durational distribution of the object constituents. Specifically, the durational distributions of the target words "mao2lan2" dwelling in the corresponding focus statuses with its subject item are depicted. The abscissa axis shows the focus statuses of the target words. The designation 'LianSB-RF' denotes a *lian*-marked focus locating on the subject item, 'RF denotes rhematic focus, 'TB' denotes thematic background, 'ShiSB-RF' denotes the shi-marked focus locating on subject and rheme focus on object constituent, and 'Un-RF' denotes the rheme

---

[67] The durational values are listed from the left rectangle to right rectangle.

focus bearing unit in the unmarked structure.

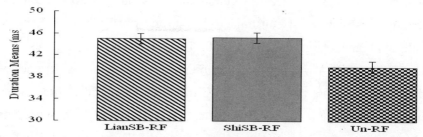

Figure 4.2.3.2.2 Mean duration for "Mao2 Lan2" in various focus conditions

In contrast to the subject items that bear a *syntax*-marked focus, the objects only exhibit an information induced focus. Closer examination of Figure 4.2.3.2.2 shows that the two rhematic focuses trigger the greatest magnitude of lengthening that pays no heed to the focus conditions on the subject constituents. More specifically, "mao2lan2$_{LianSB-RF}$" and "mao2lan2$_{ShiSB-RF}$" resemble each other in duration distribution. The least magnitude of lengthening is the object constituent that locates in the rhematic focus condition with the syntactic structure unmarked. Durational values of these three constituents are: 45.01ms, 45.21ms, and 39.98ms[68].

In Summary from the above analysis, it can be concluded that although there is *syntax*-marked lengthening, the objects that are dwelling in the various focus conditions can perform various durational adjustments. Therefore, durational lengthening on the object constituents further demonstrate that the *nuclear accent* locates on the object position and the *pre-nuclear* one on the subject constituent that are marked by syntactic markers.

---

[68] Results of a One-Way ANOVA demonstrate that there is no significant difference between "mao2lan2$_{LianSB-RF}$" and "mao2lan2$_{ShiSB-RF}$" ($P>0.05$), and that these two elements are different from "liu2min2$_{Un-RF}$" ($P=0.00$ and $P=0.00$).

4.2.3.3   Summary

It has been shown that the intonations resulting from interaction of *syntax*-marked focus and information induced focus are cued by local phonological means. Additionally, the two kinds of focuses can co-existence with each other in one target sentence to perform F_0 rising and durational lengthening simultaneously. The present findings involving the structures 'Lian **Subject**[+LianF] Dou Verb Object Le' and 'Shi **Subject**[+ShiSB] Verb Object De' further support the observations of *nuclear accent* and *pre-nuclear accent* level differences in SC. There are at least three intonation properties that unambiguously place SC within the group of languages that exhibit two levels of accents: (i) SC has focal accent induced by focus marker *lian* or *shi*; (ii) in SC the *syntax*-marked focus and the information induced focus can consist of a string of tonal events that are phonologically distinct pitch accents; specifically, there is a choice from a set of different accents that are associated with *syntax*-marked focus and information induced focus; and (iii) the rightmost accent in the sentence always exhibits the most obvious acoustic manifestations.

4.2.4   Interaction of addition of *syntax*-marked focus and rheme focus with rheme focus

Evidence in part 4.2.2 demonstrates that different kinds of focuses can combine to induce prominence with the consequence of the addition lying in the greater magnitude of pitch range expansion and durational lengthening. The analysis in part 4.2.3 shows that the *syntax*-marked focus and the information induced focus can co-exist with each other in the formation of F_0 prominence and durational lengthening. Additionally, the *wh*-elicited focus can realize the *nuclear accent* and the *syntax*-marked one exhibits *pre-nuclear accent*. Further examination is conducted in this section on the *lian*-structure and *shi*-structure that are put into the context of "rheme focus vs. rheme focus" to investigate the accent patterns conveyed by the rightmost rheme focus and the addition of *syntax*-marked focus and information induced focus. The main concern is with the following aspects: (i) whether the prominence induced by the addition of the *syntax*-marked focus and the rheme focus can co-occur with the following rheme focus; (ii) if the additive focus can compress the rhematic focus on the rightward object position; and (iii) the hierarchical structure of the accent induced by the above mentioned focus conditions. The *asking-answering* pairs employed in this part are:

(i) Lian2 Shei2 Dou1 Ti2 Ba2 Shei2 Le0? (Even who elevated whom?)

 Lian **Liu2 Min2**$^{[+LianF\&+RF]}$ Dou1 Ti2 Ba2 **Mao2 Lan2**$^{[+RF]}$ Le0
  ↓   ↓

 {Rheme focus & *Lian*-marked focus}   {Rheme focus}

(ii) Shi4 Shei2 Ti2 Ba2 Shei2 De0? (It is who that elevated whom?)

 Lian **Liu2 Min2**$^{[+ShiF\&+RF]}$ Ti2 Ba2 **Mao2 Lan2**$^{[+RF]}$ De0
   ↓   ↓

 {Rheme focus & *Shi*-marked focus}   {Rheme focus}

(iii) Lian2 Liu2 Min2 Dou1 Ti2 Ba2 Shei2 Le0? (Even Liumin elevated whom?)

 Lian **Liu2 Min2**$^{[+LianF]}$ Dou1 Ti2 Ba2 **Mao2 Lan2**$^{[+RF]}$ Le0
   ↓   ↓

 {Theme background & *Lian*-marked focus} {Rheme focus}

(iv) *Shi4 Liu2 Min2 Ti2 Ba2 Shei2 De0? (It is Liumin that elevated whom?)

 Shi **Liu2 Min2**$^{[+ShiF]}$ Ti2 Ba2 **Mao2 Lan2**$^{[+RF]}$ De0
   ↓   ↓

 {Theme background & *Shi*-marked focus}   {Rheme focus}

In accordance with the observations of Zubizarreta (1998), which were described in part 4.2.3, the type (i) and type (ii) utterances are grammatically formed a*sking-answering* pairs. The type (iii) and (iv) utterances (designated (i) and (ii) in part 4.2.3) are employed to conduct the informative comparisons by which to explore the underlying causes for the distribution of *nuclear accent*.

4.2.4.1   Overall F_0 patterns

The F_0 contours of the type (i)-(iv) utterances are illustrated in Figure 4.2.4.1.1 with the aim of examining whether *nuclear accent* is restricted by the position of the focus, and, second, whether the *accent* conveyed by the addition of the *syntax*-marked focus and information induced focus can win over the rightward rheme focus in the realization of *nuclear accent*, and eventually in which manner the *nuclear accent* and *pre-nuclear accent* are reflected in the surface form.

In Figure 4.2.3.1.1, the top part describes the content of each syllable in the utterance and the bottom part illustrates the syntactic structures and the focus statuses of the utterances. Specifically, 'LianSB(RF-TB-RF)' denotes the cases in which there are two focuses on the subject constituents (i.e., a *lian*-marked one and information induced one), and also another rheme focus on the object item; 'ShiSB(RF-TB-RF)' denotes the additive focus on the subject constituents (i.e., a *shi*-marked one and information induced one), and another rheme focus locates on the object position. The 'LianSB(TB-TB-RF)' and 'ShiSB(TB-TB-RF)' contours are as previously defined.

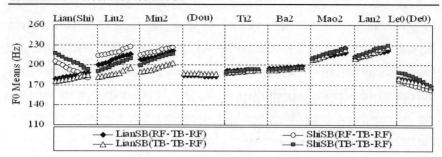

Figure 4.2.4.1.1 Mean F₀ for "Lian(Shi) Liu2 Min2 (Dou) Ti2 Ba2 Mao2 Lan2 Le0(De0)"

In comparison with the 'LianSB(TB-TB-RF)' contour, the 'LianSB(RF-TB-RF)' contour exhibits a similar prominence pattern with the formerly mentioned F_0 pattern in that it contains two prominences in one sentence; i.e., one locates on the *subject* item and the other on the *object* constituent. However, closer examination reveals that the prominence on the subject-item is higher than the one on 'LianSB(TB-TB-RF)', while the prominence exhibited by the object position resembles the prominence contour of 'ShiSB(TB-TB-RF).' As for the specific manner of the phonetic realization of the prominence, there are higher pitch registers on both *subject* and *object* items with each "*H*" and "*L*" tonal feature being raised significantly. Specific minimum and maximum pitch values for each syntactic component in 'LianSB(RF-TB-RF)' are: $liu2min2_{min}$: 200Hz, $ti2ba2_{min}$: 192Hz, and $mao2lan2_{min}$: 210Hz; and, $liu2min2_{max}$: 222Hz, $ti2ba2_{max}$: 198Hz, and $mao2lan2_{max}$: 222Hz. Similar cases on the positions of prominence realization are found in the 'ShiSB(RB-TB-RF)' contour in the subject and object positions. Clearly, the pitch range of the subject constituent under *syntax*-marked focus and rhematic focus is more expanded than the *shi*-marked focus (as illustrated in the 'ShiSB(TB-TB-RF)' contour). This observation is supported by the specific comparisons of the minimum and maximum pitch values of all the syntactic items in the sentence: [$liu2min2_{min}$: 214Hz, $ti2ba2_{min}$: 188Hz, and $mao2lan2_{min}$: 209Hz; and, liu2min2$_{max}$: 227Hz, ti2ba2$_{max}$: 195Hz, and mao2lan2$_{max}$: 225Hz. These results show that the addition of the rhematic focus and the *syntax*-marked focus can exert a more obvious effect on F_0 raising than the solely *lian*-marked or *shi*-marked focus. Moreover, the single rightward rhematic focus cannot be compressed by the addition of the *syntax*-marked focus and the rhematic focus in the proceeding position. Thereafter, no matter what the focus status of the subject position is, the rightmost rheme focus always realizes *nuclear accent*, with the proceeding one realizes a *pre-nuclear accent* in the surface form.

A One-Way ANOVA was conducted on each position of the utterances, the subject, verb, and object positions, with the aim of testing the significance of the differences of each component in a given position. In the subject positions, examination of Figure 4.2.4.1.1 shows that the addition of the *shi*-marked focus and the rhematic focus (rhematic focus on the object) exerts the most obvious effect upon F_0 raising of the subject constituent with all the "*L*" tones and the "*H*" tones being in the highest levels among the four F_0 contours. The pitch contour that is immediately lower than the previous one is the result of the addition of *lian*-marked focus and the rhematic focus induced F_0 pattern with another rhematic focus on the object position. Then, two F_0 contours triggered by the *shi*-marked focus and *lian*-marked focus that also have the rheme focus on the object positions can be observed. Results of the Bonferroni post hoc test show that the lowest point and the highest point of the word 'liu2min2' in the four focus conditions are different from each other. Specifically, 'liu2min2$_{ShiSB(RF-TB-RF)}$' vs. 'liu2min2$_{LianSB(RF-TB-RF)}$' (P_{min}=0.019 and P_{max}=0.028), 'liu2min2$_{ShiSB(RB-TB-RF)}$' vs. 'liu2min2$_{ShiSB(TB-TB-RF)}$' (P_{min}=0.00 and P_{max}=0.00), 'liu2min2$_{ShiSB(RB-TB-RF)}$' vs. 'liu2min2$_{LianSB(TB-TB-RF)}$' (P_{min}=0.00 and P_{max}=0.00), liu2min2$_{LianSB(RF-TB-RF)}$' vs. 'liu2min2$_{ShiSB(TB-TB-RF)}$' (P_{min}=0.019 and P_{max}=0.026), and, liu2min2$_{LianSB(RF-TB-RF)}$' vs. 'liu2min2$_{LianSB(TB-TB-RF)}$' (P_{min}=0.00 and P_{max}=0.00). These results strongly support the evidences observed in the previous part.

Previous discussion has demonstrated that under double-focus conditions (i.e., theme focus vs. rheme focus, double rheme focus, *syntax*-marked focus, and information induced focus) the F_0 of constituents between these two focuses are not compressed. In Figure 4.2.4.1.1, under the verb positions, there are four contours that resemble one another. Results of the Bonferroni post hoc test show that the minimum and maximum values of the words 'ti2ba2 $_{\text{ShiSB(RF-TB-RF)}}$', 'ti2ba2$_{\text{LianSB(RB-TB-RF)}}$', and 'ti2ba2$_{\text{ShiSB(TB-TB-RF)}}$' are not significantly different from each other ($P_{min}>0.05$ and $P_{max}>0.05$ for all). It is thus reasonable to assume that double focus exerts no compressive effect on the constituents between these two focuses.

Under object position, there are also four contours that are induced by the rheme focuses that resemble one another. In the study of the F_0 pattern on the object position in an unmarked structure, no matter what kind of focus is on the subject, the object components always resemble the F_0 contour. In the present part, regardless of the focus status on the subject positions, the object exhibits a similar F_0 pattern under the effect of rheme focus. Results of the Bonferroni post hoc test reveals that the minimum and maximum pitch values of the four words 'mao2lan2' are not different from each other ($P_{min}>0.05$ and $P_{max}>0.05$).

To sum up, the rightward rheme focus can always exhibits similar F_0 prominences regardless of the focus conditions on the subject positions. The non-compression of the prominence on the object position further suggests that the prominence conveyed by the rightward rheme focus is the primary one and the proceeding one occupies secondary status.

4.2.4.2 Duration patterns

Part 4.2.4.1 reports on a systematical examination of the F_0 variations induced by various focus statuses that was conducted. Results demonstrate that the *syntax*-marked focus can form an additive relationship with the information induced focus to induce a more pronounced F_0 raising on the subject positions without any influence on the realization of the prominence on the object position. This fact suggests that there is a level difference between the prominences since the duration data is the secondary cue for the sentential level accent. Therefore, further evidence for a level difference in the accents of SC is examined in this part. In addition to the subject constituents, the durational data of the object components that always observe rheme focus are also adopted as the anchor with the aim of investigating the accent status on the object.

Figure 4.2.4.2.1 depicts the durational distribution of the subjects that are designed to have various focus statuses. The abscissa axis describes the focus statuses exhibited by the subject constituents 'Liu2Min2.' The designation 'LianSB-RF' denotes the condition in which the focus marker *lian* is used to mark the subject that also exhibits rheme focus through the context, 'ShiSB-RF' denotes the *shi*-marked focus on the subject constituent that also contains rheme focus, 'LianSB-TB' and 'ShiSB-RF' have the same meaning as in part 4.2.3.2. Moreover, the ordinate axis illustrates durational distribution in ms.

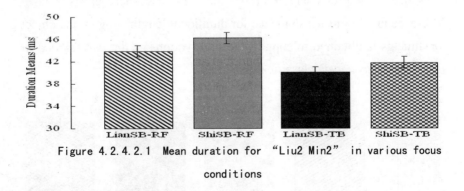

Figure 4.2.4.2.1 Mean duration for "Liu2 Min2" in various focus conditions

Here, we can examine the effect from the addition of *syntax*-marked focus and information induced focus on durational lengthening. Examination of the above figure illustrates that the greatest magnitude of lengthening lies in the effect from the addition of the *shi*-marked focus and the rhematic focus. The secondary position is occupied by the addition of the *lian*-marked focus and the rhematic focus condition. Then comes the duration distribution of the constituent bearing the *shi*-marked focus and *lian*-marked focus. The specific duration values for each item in the graph are: 43.89ms, 46.25ms, 40.01ms, and 41.85ms. A One-Way ANOVA was conducted to test the significance of the differences among each constituent. Results of the Bonferroni post hoc test shows that "liu2min2$_{LianSB-RF}$" significantly differs from other constituents: "liu2min2$_{ShiSB-RF}$" (P=0.012), "liu2min2$_{LianSB-TB}$" (P=0.01), and "liu2min2$_{ShiSB-TB}$" (P=0.023). Moreover, other constituents also differ from each other: "liu2min2$_{ShiSB-RF}$", "liu2min2$_{LianSB-TB}$", and "liu2min2$_{ShiSB-TB}$" (P<0.05). These values further demonstrate that no matter what focus condition locates on the object, the additive effect from *syntax*-marked focus and information induced focus can realize a greater magnitude of lengthening.

Figure 4.2.4.2.2 is the mean duration for the object constituents that have identical rheme focuses with different focus categories on the subject items. Findings with regard to the durational adjustment on the subject items discussed previously reinforce the view that there exists a level difference in SC. Further evidence for durational lengthening on the object constituents is obtained to support the observations of the *nuclear accent* and *pre-nuclear accent* classifications in SC.

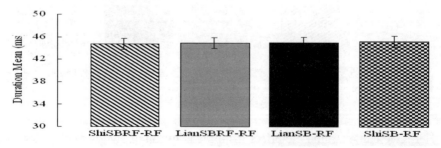

Figure 4.2.4.2.2 Mean duration for "Mao2 Lan2" in various focus conditions

Although the focus status of the subject constituents is designed differently, the manifestation of the effect on durational lengthening of the object remains much the same. Specifically, the four *wh*-elicited rheme focus constituents exhibit no obvious durational differences. Specific values are: 44.72ms, 44.93ms, 45.01ms, and 45.21ms. Results of the Bonferroni post hoc test confirm that the duration of the four constituents are not different from each other (P>0.05). Therefore, the right rheme focus can always realize similar durational lengthening according to the focus status on the object item, which pays no heed to the focus condition on the subject positions.

So far, durational lengthening is consistent with F_0 prominence in that the additive exerts a more obvious effect on durational lengthening, and such an effect does not affect the durational adjustment on the object constituents.

4.2.4.3 Summary

This section has mainly investigated whether the rightward rheme focus can be compressed by a stronger focus status. Results for F_0 pattern and durational distribution of the subject constituents varied by virtue of various focus statuses regardless of the focus status on the object constituents. However, their corresponding object constituents can realize similar F_0 and durational lengthening. The F_0 prominence and duration lengthening data provide further support for the evidence that the *nuclear tone* and *pre-nuclear tone* can co-occur with each other in one sentence. The underlying cause for the appearance can be the *syntax*-marked focus or the rhematic focus. When there is no information induced focus, the *syntax*-marked focus can serve as the major cause for the generation of the *nuclear accent*. When the information induced focus is inserted into the target sentence, the *syntax*-marked focus loses its effect on the generation of the *nuclear accent* and the accent induced focus by the addition of *syntax*-marked focus and information induced focus can be taken as the *pre-nuclear accent*. The essential cause for the location of the *nuclear accent* is also due to the *rightmost position* in SC. This result can be obtained from the non-compression of the accents on the object constituents that is proceeded by the addition of the rheme focus and the *syntax*-marked focus. The phonological domain for the *nuclear tone* and *pre-nuclear tone* is addressed in the following part.

4.2.5 Prosodic phrasing of the '*lian*+S+*dou*+V+O+Le' construction

The above analysis provides phonetic details of focuses in the '*shi*+S+V+O+De' and '*lian*+S+*dou*+V+O+Le' structures. However, whether the *syntax*-marked focus has an effect on prosodic phrasing of the intonation pattern is still unknown. It has been shown in a cross-language study involving Hungarian (Vogel and Ken 1987) that focus determines phrasing at the intonational phrase level. A similar analysis, but at the intermediate phrase[69] level (Cho 1990), has been proposed for Korean. According to Cho, the role played by 'prominence' on phrasing in Korean is manifested by the fact that 'prominent' elements are mapped into the domain of the intermediate phrase boundary. Further, SC presents itself as another language in which *wh*-elicited focus determines *phrasing* at the immediate phrase boundary (see section 3.5). With regard to *syntax*-marked focus, such as the *shi*-marked focus, a study by Jia et al (2009) that systematically investigated the phrasing phenomenon in the sequences '...*de*...*shi*...', '*shi*...+V+*de*+NP', and '*shi*...*de*', demonstrates that the *shi*-marked focus correlates with the intermediate phrase boundary; that is, the intermediate phrase boundary usually locates after the marked focus[70]. Following previous studies, this part assesses the relation between prosodic phrasing and the '*lian*+S+*dou*+V+O+Le' structure. To investigate

---

[69] In their study, they adopt the term 'phonological phrase' that is identical in meaning with the term 'intermediate phrase' used in this research.

[70] Previous discussion on the phrasing effect of the '*shi...de*' construction includes the aspect of '*shi*+subject...+*de*.' This part mainly deals with the relation between *lian*-marked focus and prosodic phrasing.

whether syntactic structure controls the occurrence of phrasing phenomenon in SC, three main types of evidence are considered: (i) durational distribution of pauses, (ii) lengthening, and (iii) prosodic boundary labeling.

4.2.5.1   Durational distribution of pauses

The examination of the pause distribution is conducted from two aspects，firstly, the pause distribution in the pre-boundary position is compared for each target word in a given utterance. Specifically, in the target sentence 'Lian+Subject+Dou+Verb+ Object', the position between 'Lian and subject', 'subject and dou' 'dou and verb', 'verb and object', and 'object and le', is examined. The sentence is guided by the question "Fa1 Sheng1 Le0 Shen2 Me0 Shi4? (What happened?)." Results[71] demonstrate that there are no obvious durational differences among the five positions. Secondly, the duration of the post-focus position marked by *lian* in various information statuses are further examined. Results of the Bonferroni post hoc test show that there is no obvious difference among the four constituents (P>0.05). Thus, we may say that focus statuses variations exert no obvious pause in the '*lian...dou*' construction. Additionally, similar to the information induced focus in the unmarked focus (see section 3.5), the *lian*-marked focus exerts no effect on the pauses. Further evidence for the prosodic phrasing effect are investigated in (ii) and (iii).

4.2.5.2   Lengthening

Previous discussions on the effect of *syntax*-marked focus on lengthening in part 4.2.5.1 establishes that focus can not trigger lengthening in relation to other positions in the '*lian...dou*' structure. This

---

[71] Due to the space limitations, the statistical data is not listed.

part compares the lengthening differences of every syllable in each word in various focus conditions to explore whether the *lian*-marked focus has the property of placing the constituents in other phonological domains.

Figure 4.2.5.2.1 depicts the mean duration for the target words "Liu2Min2." Within the figure, each rectangle illustrates the durational distribution of "Liu2" and "Min2." Also, the specific content of each syllable is described in the bottom part of the X-Coordinate, while the top part of the X-Coordinate expresses the focus status for each word. The Y-Coordinate is measured in milliseconds (ms) and marks the range of the variations in the durational changes in the range of 0-30ms based on the observed range of durational changes.

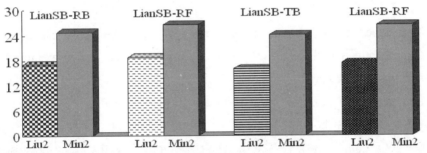

Figure 4.2.5.2.1 Mean duration for "Liu2" and "Min2" in various focus conditions

For each tone2 target word "liu2min2" in the four focus conditions of rheme background, rheme focus, and theme background the second syllable, "min2", exhibits a longer duration than the first syllable, "liu2." Thus, no matter what kind of focus environment the word bears, the second syllable exhibits a longer duration. Specific durational values for each syllable are: liu2: 16.93ms, min2: 24.69ms and liu2: 18.72ms, min2: 26.49ms and liu2: 15.95ms, min2: 24.03ms and liu2: 17.33ms, and min2:26.35ms. A One-Way ANOVA was conducted to compare the durational differences in one word between each syllable. Results demonstrate that under the rhematic background condition "min2" significantly differs from "liu2" (P=0.013). Moverover, under the focus statuses of "rheme focus", "theme background", and "theme focus" the durational differences between "min2" and "liu2" are significant (P<0.05). A additional question concerns the reason why there is a difference between the lengthening results found in the first and the second syllable. Prosodic boundary can be taken as the major cause to explain this phenomenon.

The *non*-symmetric durational lengthening between the two traget syllables in each word, exhibited under various focus statuses, demonstrate that the second syllable serves as the anchor for the greater magnitude of lengthening on the second syllable.

4.2.5.3   Prosodic boundary labeling

This part provides the prosodic boundary labeling results to test the argument that the phrase boundary is in the position before *dou*. For each target sentence, there were 8 speakers, four kinds of focus statuses, and two kinds of tonal combinations. Only the speech data from 4 speakers were selected as samples for prosodic boundary labeling. Further, 4 skilled people were invited to give their subjective judgments on the levels of the prosodic boundary; e.g., prosodic word, intermediate phrase boundary, and intonational phrase boundary. Thus, there are 128 labeling results for each constituent in the sentence. Table 4.2.7.3.1 depicts the results of the prosodic boundary.

Table 4.2.5.3.1   Labeling results of prosodic boundary

Prosodic boundary/Position	Lian	Subject	Dou	Verb	Object
Intonational phrase	0	7	0	3	6
Intermediate phrase	10	119	17	10	9
Prosodic word	118	2	111	115	113

From the above table we can see that the position after '*lian*' received the greatest amount of judgments on the prosodic word boundary, while the position immediately after the subject and before *dou* mainly contains the *intermediate phrase boundary*. Further, after *dou*, the verb constituents and object items mainly exhibit prosodic word boundary. Thus, from the labeling results, it can observe that the intonational phrase boundary is in the position after the subject and before *dou*.

To sum up, the *nuclear tone* and *pre-nuclear tone* are realized in one intonational phrase. The evidence was obtained from: (i) pause evidence (there exists on obvious boundary between the subject and *dou*), (ii) lengthening (the second syllable of the subject constituents exhibits more clearer lengthening), and (iii) prosodic boundary labeling (subjective judgments on the prosodic boundary labeling demonstrate that there is an intonation phrase boundary after the subject constituents).

4.2.5.4   Summary

The intonation-phrasing phenomena described in the '*lian* Subject[+LianS]...*dou*' structure have been shown to bear on important issues of focus. On the one hand, the SC findings of *syntax*-marked focus have contributed to focus phenomenon that is cued by phrasing. On the other hand, SC presents itself as a language in which the focus (*syntax*-marked focus or information induced focus) determines phrasing at the intermediate phrase level.

4.3   Co-existence and conflict of *syntax*-marked focus and *information* induced focus in 'S+*lian*+O+*dou*+V+ le' constructions

Part 4.2 investigates the interaction of the *syntax*-marked subject and different information induced focuses on the subject in the formation of accent patterns exhibited the surface form. The findings suggest that when the *syntax*-marked focus locates in the positions before the information induced focus, the information induced focus can always be realized as the *nuclear accent* in the surface form. Based on this result, it would appear that the *rightward position* plays the determining role in restricting the distribution of the *nuclear accent*. However, one aspect that needs to be further tested to support the above argumentation is the case in which the *syntax*-marked focus distributes after the information induced focus. Therefore, the present part mainly deals with accent placements induced by the interaction of various information categories upon the word order 'Syntactic   component+*Syntax*-marked   focus+...   .'   Based   on   the observation of Fang (1995), Liu and Xu (1998), and Wu (1998), in the '*Subject+Shi*...' structure, the function of *shi* is *copula*, but not focus marker. Since the major aim of this part is to address the relation between *focus* and *accent* with the *syntax*-marked focus locating after the *wh*-elicited focus, the shi-marked structure is excluded.

Thus, 'Subject+*Lian*+Object+*dou* Verb+le' structure, in which the 'Object' receives the *syntax*-marked focus, is adopted. In particular, when the information categories are designed differently, the *lian*-marked focus and the information induced focus in the target sentence form various focus relationships that exert different effects upon the variations of F_0 and duration patterns. The basic syntactic elements in the sentences are **Liu2Min2** for subject, **Ti2Ba2** for verb, and **Mao2Lan2** for object. Previous investigations have shown that tonal combinations contribute differently to the specific realizations of the accent, but exert no influence upon the distribution and levels of accent. Therefore, in this part, the tone2 constituents are selected to reduce the amount of data yet still meet the comparative needs with the constituents in other structures. The relationships of the *lian*-marked focus and the information induced focus are displayed in (i)-(iv):

(i)　　Fa1 Sheng1 Le0 Shen2 Me0 Shi4?(What happened?)

　　　　Liu2 Min2　*Lian*　**Mao2 Lan2**$^{[+LianF]}$　*Dou*　　**Ti2 Ba2**$^{[+RF]}$　Le0

　　　　　　　　　　　　　　↓　　　　　　　　　　　↓

　　　　{*Lian*-marked focus & Rheme background}　　{Rheme focus}

(ii)　　Shei2　Lian2　Mao2 Lan2　Dou1 Ti2 Ba2 Le0? (Who even elevated whom?)

　　　　Liu2 Min2$^{[+RF]}$ *Lian* **Mao2 Lan2**$^{[+LianF]}$　*Dou*　　　Verb　　　Le0

　　　　　↓　　　　　　　↓　　　　　　　　　　　　↓

　　　　{Rheme focus}　{*Lian*-marked focus}　　　{Theme background}

(iii)　　Liu2 Min2　Lian2　Shei2　Dou1　Verb　Le0? (Liumin even elevated whom?)

　　　　Liu2 Min2 *Lian*　**Mao2 Lan2**$^{[+LianF\&+RF]}$　*Dou*　Verb　　Le0

　　　　　↓　　　　　　　↓　　　　　　　　　　　↓

{Theme background} {*Lian*-marked focus&Rheme focus} {Theme background}

(iv)　　Shei2　Lian　Shei2　Dou　Verb　Le0? (Who even elevated whom?)

　　　　Liu2 Min2$^{[+RF]}$　*Lian* **Mao2 Lan2**$^{[+LianF\&+RF]}$ *Dou*　Verb　　Le0

　　　　　↓　　　　　　　↓　　　　　　　　　　　↓

{Rheme focus} {*Lian*-marked focus& Rheme focus} {Theme background}

4.3.1　F_0 contour of rhematic focus constituent after *lian*-marked focus

This sub-section investigates the conflicting relationship of the *lian*-marked verb and the rhematic focus upon F_0 prominence realization. Specifically, the *wh*-operator for the target sentence is "Fa1 Sheng1 Le0 Shen2 Me0 Shi4? (What happened?)", through which the subject constituents are placed into the rhematic background condition and the object items in the rhematic focus environment. Further, as mentioned immediately above, the verb constituents in this part alway serve as the *syntax*-marked focus. Figure 4.3.1.1 depicts the mean F_0 for the target sentence "Liu2 Min2 Shi4 **Mao2 Lan2**[+LianF] Dou1 **Ti2 Ba2**[+RF] Le0 (Liumin even elevated Maolan)." The labels of axises are identical to the F_0 figures in part 4.2.

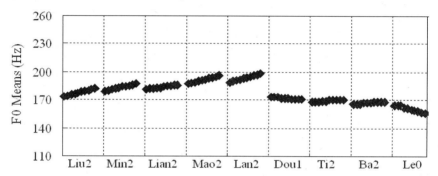

Figure 4.3.1.1   Mean F_0 for "Liu Min2 Lian2 Mao2 Lan2Dou1 Ti2 Ba2 Le0"

Based on the analysis of Fang (1995), the constituent immediately following the marker *lian* is the focus-bearing unit, and can function as subject, adverbial, predicate, etc. Therefore, the focused element in this sentence dwells on the object item "mao2lan2." From the *wh*-question, it is known that the rhematic focus locates on the object item; hence, the *lian*-marked focus is located in the proceeding position of the rhematic focus. It can be seen in Figure 4.3.1.1 that only the *shi*-marked focus position exhibits F_0 prominence of relatively higher pitch registers compared to the other elements in the target sentence. Except for the pitch value of the focus marker *lian* and operator *dou*, the minimum and maximum pitch values of each syntactic item are: liu2min2$_{min}$: 173Hz, mao2lan2$_{min}$: 187Hz, and ti2ba2$_{min}$:168Hz; and, liu2min2$_{max}$: 187Hz, mao2lan2$_{max}$: 198Hz, and ti2ba2$_{max}$: 170Hz. Thus, the lowest point of the word "mao2lan2" is 0.51ST and 0.69ST higher than the subject and the verb items, respectively. With regard to the maximum pitch values, the verb item is 0.43ST and 0.65ST higher than the subject and object items, respectively. Since, as pointed out by Xu (1999), the focused bearing unit exerts a compression effect upon the F_0 of the object and retains the F_0 of the pre-focus position much intact, the differences in the pitch values of the subject and the verb were compared in order to further test for any compression effect upon the verb items. Specifically, the minimum and maximum pitch values of the subject are higher than the verb item. From the pitch value differences for both subject and verb items, it can be determined that the object item is the prominence bearing unit. Hence, the rhematic focus under the present environment is compressed completely.

Therefore, the above analysis establishes that *lian*-marked focus can trigger F_0 prominences with the pitch registers of the whole word being obviously raised and the pitch registers of the following verb item significantly compressed. These results demonstrate that when the subject distributes in the rhematic background condition and the object distributes in the rhematic focus environment, the *lian*-marked focus can compress the rhematic focus.

4.3.2 F$_0$ contour of rhematic focus constituent before *lian*-marked focus

In this part, through the *wh*-operators "Shei2 Shi4 Mao2 Lan2 Dou1 Ti2 Ba2 Le0? (Who even elevated Maolan?)", the rhematic focus locates in the position before the *lian*-marked constituent; therefore, it can be observed whether or not the *lian*-marked focus and the rhematic induced focus can realize prominences simultaneously or only one anchor serves as the prominence bearing unit. Figure 4.3.2.1 illustrates the mean F_0 for the target sentence "**Liu2 Min2**[+RF] Lian2 **Mao2 Lan2**[+LianF] Dou1 Ti2 Ba2

Le0" with the subject items serving as the rhematic bearing unit and the object item as the *lian*-marked focus.

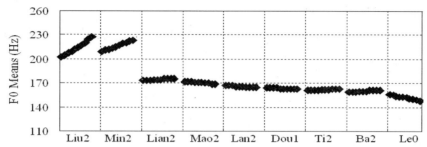

Figure 4.3.2.1   Mean F_0 for "Liu Min2 Lian2 Mao2 Lan2 Dou1 Ti2 Ba2 Le0"

As shown in Figure 4.3.2.1, the sentence contains only one prominence since the subject item "liu2min2" exhibits a much higher pitch register than the other items in the target sentence; moverover, the pitch registers of the constituents following the subject exhibit a compressive effect with all the syllables being compressed with the phenomenon extending to the very end of the target sentence. It is known that in the target sentence, the object item exhibits *lian*-marked focus and it can be ascertained from Figure 4.3.2.1 that there is no prominence on the object item. Further evidences can be obtained from detailed comparisons of the minimum and maximum pitch values of the syntactic items in the sentence: liu2min2$_{min}$: 202Hz, mao2lan2$_{min}$: 165Hz, and ti2ba2$_{min}$: 159Hz; and, liu2min2$_{max}$: 227Hz, mao2lan2$_{max}$: 167Hz, and ti2ba2$_{max}$: 163Hz. Thus, the minimum and maximum pitch values of the word "liu2min2" are much higher than the verb and the object items. Therefore, it can be concluded that the *lian*-marked focus, which is distributing after the subject items, is completely compressed by the proceeding subject item.

In general, when the rhematic focus locates before the *lian*-marked focus and the *lian*-marked focus is placed into the thematic background condition, the *lian*-marked prominence is restricted in that there is absolutely no F_0 raising. The only sentential prominence bearing unit is the rhematic focus induced F_0 raising. This phenomenon constitutes the condition in SC where the focus is not marked by prominence.

4.3.3 F_0 contour of rhematic focus and addition of *lian*-marked focus and rhematic focus in one sentence

As for the syntactic item in the target sentence in this part, the object exhibits two focus-statuses. Specifically, the subject element is designed to have rhematic focus, and the object constituent is both the *lian*-marked focus and the rhematic focus bearing unit. In order to achieve the intended focus environment, the *wh*-operator adopted in this part is "Shei2 Shi4 Shei2 Dou1 Ti2 Ba2 Le? (Who even elevated whom?)." Consequently, the overall conflicts in the realization of the prominences can be investigated. Figure 4.3.3.1 is the mean F_0 for "**Liu Min2**$^{[+RF]}$ Shi4 **Mao2 Lan2**$^{[+RF\&+LianF]}$ Dou1 Ti2 Ba2 Le0", with two rhematic focuses on both the subject and object item and the *lian*-marked focus on the object constituent.

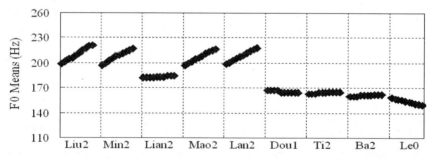

Figure 4.3.3.1   Mean F_0 for "Liu Min2 Lian2 Mao2 Lan2Dou1 Ti2 Ba2 Le0"

Figure 4.3.3.1 shows that there are two prominences in the target sentence, one on the subject item "liu2min2" and one on the object item "mao2lan2." Between these two items, the object constituent and subject constituent exhibit similar pitch registers. In contrast with these two items, the verb item exhibits a relatively lower pitch register. The pitch values of the lowest and highest points of each syntactic element are: liu2min2$_{min}$: 197Hz, mao2lan2$_{min}$:197Hz, and ti2ba2$_{min}$: 163Hz; and, liu2min2$_{max}$: 221Hz, mao2lan2$_{max}$: 218Hz, and ti2ba2$_{max}$: 167Hz. Thus, the minimum pitch values and maximum pitch values for the subject and object constituents show no obvious difference, and the verb constituent is lower than either the object or subject constituents. Hence, it can be concluded from this target sentence that there are two prominences in this sentence: the subject and the object items. This result is mainly due to the effect from the double rheme focus; the *lian*-marked focus exerts no obvious effect.

On the whole, when the syntactic items in the target sentence are put into two focus conditions on object constituents, the rhematic focus and *lian*-marked focus, the additive effect from the object constituent shows no obvious prominence difference with the prominence on the subject constituent.

4.3.4   Mean duration among the words in various focus conditions

Jia et al (2008) proposed that the five-syllable focused constituents exhibit a relatively unified adjustment pattern with the final syllable being lengthened to the greatest magnitude, and with the first syllable occupying the primary position. In this part, the parameter of duration is adopted to investigate the effect induced by *lian*-marked focus and different information focuses upon the constituents in the "Liu2 Min2 Shi4 Mao2 Lan2 Dou1 Ti2 Ba2 Le0" structure. The target sentence gets three information statuses as in parts 4.3.1 and 4.3.3. A One-Way ANOVA was selected as the statistical means.

4.3.4.1   Duration patterns of subject constituents

In this section, durational variations induced by different information categories upon the subject constituents are examined: rheme background, rheme focus, and theme background. It is proposed in the introduction to part 4.3 that the *lian*-marked focus always locates on the verb constituents. Therefore, we can observe the conflicts of the information induced focus and the *lian*-marked focus on the elongation of the duration.

Figure 4.3.4.1 is the duration adjustments of the subject items that are put into various information categories. The X-coordinate describes the status of the information categories; specifically, the left part of each symbol is the description of the position of the *lian*-marked focus and the right part is the information status. For example, "LianOB-RB" denotes the *lian*-marked focus locating at the object item and "RB" denotes the rhematic background condition. The Y-coordinate is the magnitude of durational lengthening measured in milliseconds (ms).

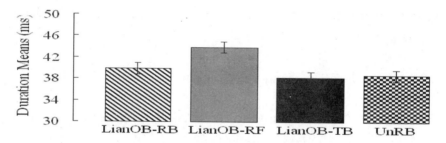

Figure 4.3.4.1 Mean duration for "Liu2 Min2" in various focus conditions

It is known that the target sentence for the tone2 sentence is "liu2min2 Shi4 mao2lan2 dou1 ti2ba2 le0." This indicates that the *lian*-marked focus locates on the object item. Additionally there is no *syntax*-marker before the subject item. Examination of Figure 4.3.4.1 reveals that the greatest magnitude of durational elongation is triggered by the rhematic focus. The secondary position is due to the effect of the rhematic background condition. Further, the thematic background-bearing unit in the *lian*-marked object structure exhibits similar durational adjustment with the unmarked rhematic background bearing unit. Specific duration values of each word are: 39.89ms, 43.85ms, 38.25ms, and 38.7ms[72]. A One-Way ANOVA was conducted to test the observations obtained in Figure 4.3.4.1. Results of the Bonferroni post hoc test establishes that the duration of "liu2min2$_{\text{LianOB-RF}}$" is significantly different from the other constituents in various conditions: "liu2min2$_{\text{LianOB-RB}}$" (P=0.015), "liu2min2$_{\text{LianOB-TB}}$" (P=0.00), and "liu2min2$_{\text{Un-RB}}$" (P=0.001). Additionally, the rhematic background item in the *lian*-marked object structure is significantly different from "liu2min2$_{\text{LianOB-TB}}$" (P=0.0034), however, there is no obvious difference with "liu2min2$_{\text{Un-RB}}$" (P>0.05). Additionally, "liu2min2$_{\text{LianOB-TB}}$" bears no difference with the word "liu2min2$_{\text{Un-RB}}$" (P>0.05). From these results we know that the durational distribution difference lies in the differences of the information categories; specifically, the units exhibit a similar duration elongation when they are put into identical information status regardless of the syntactic structure of the target sentence.

This part mainly discusses the durational adjustment of the subject items in both the *lian*-marked object structure and the unmarked structure. The finding is that although there is *lian*-marked focus on the verb item, the durational differences of the subject constituents are induced by the variations of the information categories.

4.3.4.2   Duration patterns of object constituents

Since the object item is serving as the *lian*-marked focus bearing unit, the present *sub*-section mainly discusses the durational distribution of the object constituents. Figure 4.3.4.2.1 is the durational pattern of the object items "Mao2 Lan2" distributing in *lian*-marked focus position and various information categories. The X-coordinate describes the specific content.

---

[72] Specific duration values are presented from the left most rectangle to the right most rectangle.

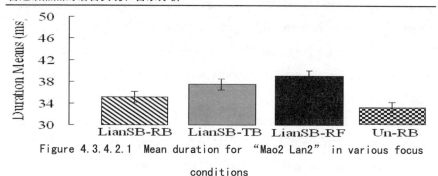

Figure 4.3.4.2.1 Mean duration for "Mao2 Lan2" in various focus conditions

Clearly, Figure 4.3.4.2.1 shows that the overall durational distribution of the word "mao2lan2" which exhibits a shorter duration than the subject constituents. This result is due to the medium position on which the object-items are located. Within these four constituents, the word "mao2lan2$_{LianOB-RF}$" locates in the rhematic focus condition and exhibits the greatest magnitude of lengthening. Additionally, the secondary position is occupied by the word "mao2lan2$_{LianOB-TB}$" due to the spill-over effect from the subject item. Then, "mao2lan2$_{LianOB-RB}$" occupies the ternary position, and "mao2lan2$_{Un-RB}$" shows the least magnitude of lengthening. Specific durational values of each word are: 35.13ms, 37.53 ms, 39.04 ms, and 33.09 ms. Results of the statistical analysis show that "mao2lan2$_{LianOB-RF}$" is different from other constituents: "mao2lan2$_{LianOB-RB}$" (P=0.001), "mao2lan2$_{LianOB-TB}$" (P=0.00), and "mao2lan2$_{Un-RB}$" (P=0.00). Additionally, "mao2lan2$_{LianOB-TB}$" is different from "mao2lan2$_{LianOB-RB}$" (P=0.029) and "mao2lan2$_{Un-RB}$" (P=0.023). Further, "mao2lan2$_{LianOB-RB}$" exhibits a difference with the "mao2lan2$_{Un-RB}$" (P=0.031). This evidence can be accounted for by the investigation of the information statuses of the subject items. With regard to "mao2lan2$_{LianOB-TB}$", its corresponding subject exhibits a rhematic focus that can exert an obvious rightward lengthening (Chen 2006). As for "mao2lan2$_{LianOB-RB}$", its subject item is the rhematic background- bearing unit; therefore, there is an obvious spill-over effect from it. Moreover, the word "mao2lan2$_{LianOB-RB}$" shows a longer duration than "mao2lan2$_{Un-RB}$."

The reason for this phenomenon can be accounted for by the existence of the *lian*-marked focus in the former case.

With regard to the durational distribution of the *lian*-marked focus bearing unit, the durational distributions are affected by the spill-over effect from the subject items and also the focus marking function from the marker *lian*.

4.3.5 Summary

The relation between *lian*-marked focus and information-induced focus, as defined in the previous part and further discussion, was dealt with in the "Subject+*Lian*+Object+*Dou*+Verb+Le" structure. Based on the data examined, the following conclusions were reached: in SC, the *syntax*-marked focus can be taken as the anchor for *nuclear tone* association when there is no information induced focus. Whereas, when there is an insertion of information-induced focus, the *nuclear tone* is always related to the information induced focus and distributes in the rightmost position in the target sentence. What is of more importance in this part is that the focused constituents in part 4.3.2 are not signaled by any kind of accent. It is proposed by Ladd (1996) that English also observes the phenomenon of 'focus-without-accent': cases where focus is signaled by phonetic cues such as duration and vowel quality *without any pitch accent*. This evidence further suggests that there are no bi-directional relations between *focus* and *accent*. The distribution of focus and accent belongs to different aspects, the former one is specified by the context reason and the second one is determined by language specific structural rules.

4.4 Discussion

The relation between *syntax*-marked focus and information-induced focus on the formation of *nuclear* and *pre-nuclear accent* is dealt with in this chapter. Based on the data examined, the following conclusions are reached: (i) in SC, F_0 raising and durational lengthening in the under focus position is the relevant acoustic cues for the *syntax*-marked focus (*lian* or *shi* marked focus); (ii) the *syntax*-marked focus and the information induced focus can form different kinds of relations to induce systematic variations in F_0 and duration pattern; (iii) the phonological means involved in the expression of the focus-related systematic manifestations are *nuclear accent* and *pre-nuclear accent*; (iv) the *nuclear accent* reflects obligatory and unique characteristics in that it can associate with both the *syntax*-marked focus and the information induced focus. The phonetic realization of *nuclear accent* can be varied in the magnitude of its acoustic realization, and its distribution is identified by the obvious F_0 raising and durational lengthening in comparison with other constituents in the same utterance; (v) the *pre-nuclear accent* bears an optional and non-unique nature in that its appearance is highly restricted by the focus status. In SC, only the double focus conditions are reflected by both the *nuclear* and *pre-nuclear accent* distinction. Further, the *pre-nuclear accent* always distributes before the *nuclear accent*. The difference between these two kinds of accents lies in the magnitude of acoustic manifestations; i.e., the former one exhibits secondary performances; and (vi) the *syntax*-marked focus in SC is also assigned a crucial role in determining phonological phrasing at the intermediate phrase level.

It has also been shown that the above focuses in SC exhibit prominence-related effects and crucially effects phrasing at the intermediate phrase level. Specifically, focus is found to be phonologically expressed by means of the phrasal accent pattern; i.e., *nuclear accent* and *pre-nuclear accent*. The two accents are realized in one intonational phrase with only the intermediate phrase boundary locating between these two accents. As noted in the introduction to this research (sections 1.2.3.2 and 1.2.3.3 in particular), the prosodic literature reports on two main types of effects induced by focus: (i) accent effects and (ii) phrasing effects. The former have been reported to play a crucial role in languages such as English, Dutch, and Italian. The latter have been claimed to conspicuously cue focus in languages such as Hungarian, Hausa, and Korean. Furthermore, in these languages, focus seems to determine phrasing in a basic and strict way, and is thus included in the language phrasing algorithms. Clearly, SC behaves like English and Italian with regard to the accent effects, and like Hausa and Korean with regard to the phrasing effects.

Furthermore, the above findings may contribute greatly to the debate on the 'Focus-to-Accent'(FTA) approach in that it provides further evidence in support of the structure-based approach as a result of the observaton that accent distribution is assigned after the specification of the focused items. The accents are also hierarchically structured as in the unmarked structure.

In short, the integrative work of phonological and phonetic analysis on *syntax*-marked focus and information induced focus is shown to offer a coherent account of intonation and prosodic structure in SC.

Chapter Five

Phonological Representation of Accent Patterns in SC

5.1 Introduction

The difficulties in the phonological representation of intonation are that the term means different things to different people. There are multiple sources of variations that characterize intonation phenomena. For example, sex, age, and emotion, not all of which are of a linguistic nature. Therefore, it is not easy to generate the linguistically significant rules or principles governing variations in intonation. Specifically, instrumental work may lead to more or less rigorous findings about the manifestations of physical properties, but may not contribute to an understanding of the linguistic categories (refer to, for example, Sosa 1991 and Ladd 1996, among others).

SC is a typical contour tone language (Yip 2002) in which both tone and intonation rely on pitch to signal tonal contrast and intonation variation. Among modern linguists, Chao (1929) was the first to conduct an investigation of SC intonation and provide a systematic description. He proposes that SC speech melody or pitch movements are comprised of three components: lexical tones, neutral intonation, and modal intonation. Following Chao, Wu (1988; 1996) also contributes greatly to the study of SC tone and intonation. Wu (1988) holds that melodic movement is divided into three levels: citation form, sandhi form, and re-sandhi form that correspond to Chao's distinction among lexical tones, neutral intonation, and modal intonation, respectively. He further takes the tone sandhi patterns (disyllabic, trisyllabic, and quadric-syllabic word combinations) as the basic units to be modified by the effect of intonation. Wu (1996) develops his idea by proposing the 'transposition rule' at the phrase level: the tone sandhi patterns form chunks in connected speech and the requirements of logical and attitudinal prominence can be met through an upper or lower position of their registers as a whole. As for a study of intonation modeling, Shen (1994) proposes an important model of SC intonation concentrating on the modification of the topline and the bottom-line of tonal contours (obtained by connecting the top points and bottom points of the lexical tones, respectively). In general, he holds that in tone languages such as SC, tone and intonation are derived by different means. Specifically, intonation is pitch modification organized by a sequence of tonal pitch ranges, while tones are the contours gliding within the tonal pitch range. Cao (2002; 2004) points out that SC intonation modifies lexical tones mainly in terms of the algebraic sum of pitch register instead of pitch contours.

Specifically, three major factors are involved. The first factor concerns the position of a syllable in a phrase or sentence. The second factor involves stress (or accent) that the lexically specified pitch contour of an accented tone retains with its pitch range being expanded and the specific behavior of its register being closely conditioned by its intrinsic category. The third factor concerns the mood of a sentence, with respect to which Cao proposes that the average pitch level of the sentence uttered with an interrogative intonation is always higher than that of a sentence uttered with a declarative intonation. Lin (2000; 2002) has advocated and pioneered the introduction of the AM (Autosegmental-Metrical) approach to SC intonation studies. Lin (2000; 2002) proposes that the prosodic structure of SC is organized hierarchically into five levels that, in a bottom-up order, are: syllables, prosodic words, minor prosodic phrases, major prosodic phrases, and intonation groups.

Based on an overall survey of some of the most important existing studies concerning SC intonation and prosody mentioned above, as well as a comparative study of the prosodic features of read and spontaneous speeches, Li (2002) proposes the latest version (3.0) of C-ToBI, a prosodic labeling system for Chinese. Xiong (2003) reviewed the pitch features of the ending particle word 'ma0' in 'yes-no' questions. The results show that (a) no matter whether they have the final modality word 'ma0' or not, *'yes-no'* questions have identical types of boundary tones with the pitch being realized in the feature of {*H*} or {Raised}, (b) the position of the focus has no substantial impact on the boundary tone, and (c) the changes of the tones in the sentences also have no fundamental influence on the boundary tone. Therefore, the final boundary tone in SC is an intonation pitch feature that is relatively independent from the focal accents and the tones. Additionally, it has stable pitch representation as well. Li (2005), based on an acoustic analysis of friendly speech and the corresponding neutral speech of an expressive dialogue corpus, proposes that the acoustic patterns of pitch and duration of friendly declarative and interrogative utterances are quite different from those of neutral utterances that are varied in terms of the patterns of sentences stress.

Friendliness of synthesized speech could be achieved via adjusting the perceptually distinctive acoustic parameters. Tonal pitch is the most important cue for better expression of friendliness. Xiong (2006), after investigating three kinds of pitch variations in the running speech of SC, proposes four intonation patterns: (i) the down-step effect on the second *H* tone in a *HLH* tonal sequence motivated by the *L* tone; (ii) the up-step effect on the focal *H* tone and the drop-step effect on the following *H* tone in the same sentence; and (iii) the lift-step effect on the *H* tone when it follows a focal *L* tone in the same sentence. Based on these observations, Xiong further proposes that the pitch values of running speech in SC are determined by two factors: the pitch features of syllabic tones and some kind of modificational effect that raises or lowers the pitch register of the syllabic tone.

Following a widely accepted definition (particularly in the intonation phonology approach), in this research, *intonation* refers to the linguistically significant non-lexical configurations of phonological events. These phonological events are assumed to be formed by a string of categorically distinct entities. The phonetic representation of the abstract string of tonal categories is the fundamental frequency (F_0) contour and duration lengthening. This view of intonation, which is the version followed here, is based on (a) a study of IPO theory by Pierreumbert and colleagues (particularly Pierrehumbert 1980, Beckman and Pierrehumbert 1986, and Pierrehumbert and Beckman 1988), (b) the ToBI transcription system (Silverman et al 1992), (c) the IViE Labeling system (Grabe 2001), (d) the intonation structure of Ladd (1996), and (e) the intonation model of Gussenhoven (2004). These theoretical models clearly imply that there is a phonological level of description in which the structure of tonal patterns is captured. The assumption of such a level has (at least) three important consequences: (a) an intuitively identical contour should be accounted for by the same phonological representation, whereas intuitively different contours should be represented by differences in the structured string of tonal categories; (b) systematic differences of intonational form are a reflection of distinct tonal categories, and systematic differences of intonational meaning should be reflected by a categorical distinction; and (c) if an intonational property is correlated with another linguistic property, this correlation should be expressed in terms of the phonological categories of intonation, and not in terms of variations in physical continua.

Following the path suggested by previous intonational patterns, the major goal of this chapter is to provide the phonological representation of *accent patterns* in SC that should be explicitly defined regardless of the syntactic category of the words and phrases involved or the particular length of an utterance. Further, a consistent correlation between an intonation property and information structure are expressed in terms of the phonological categories of intonation. This means that in case focus (*syntax*-marked focus or information-induced focus) is found to be consistently signaled by specific intonation means in SC, the intonation effects of the focus should be captured in the tonal structure of the language. In contrast, if no such systematic intonation effects associated with the expression of focus are found, the assumption of any tonal means of phonological *focus*-marking would be preempted.

In section 5.2, previous phonological models of intonation structure are provided Within this account, the phonological events involved in each model in the expression of focus are described as accent patterns and phonological units. In section 5.3, the phonological account of accent patterns in SC are observed based on the results of production and perceptual experiments in chapter three, chapter four, and the previous intonation structure. In section 5.4, the underlying causes for the distribution of the accent in the surface form are analyzed by (a version of) the theory of *Prosodic Hierarchy*.

5.2   Phonological structure of intonation

In the literature dealing with the phonological account of intonation, the IPO theory ('t Hart, Collier and Cohen 1990) is, in many ways, the first to make a serious attempt to combine an abstract phonological level of description with a detailed account of the phonetic realization on the phonological elements. However, it was the seminal dissertation 'The Phonetics and Phonology of English Intonation' (Pierrehumbert 1980) that presented a descriptive framework of intonation that separates the phonological representation from its phonetic implementation. Earlier introductions to intonational phonology are Ladd (1996), who coined the term 'Autosegmental-Metrical (AM) Model.' The model is auto-segmental because it has separate tiers for segmentals (vowels and consonants) and tones (H and L). It is metrical because it assumes that the elements in these tiers are contained within the hierarchically organized set of phonological constituents. The theoretical models of a phonological account of intonation in the following research are much along the lines of AM theory; e.g., the ToBI transcription system (Silverman et al. 1992); the IViE Labeling system (Grabe 2001), etc. In this section, the major theoretical models of intonational structure in the previous studies are sketched.

5.2.1   The IPO theory of intonational structure

5.2.1.1   Basic assumptions of IPO

The IPO[73]approach is in many ways the first to make a serious attempt at combining an abstract phonological level of description with a detailed account of the phonetic realization of the phonological elements. It is proposed in this theory that the most essential aspect of pitch variation is due to the difference between a relatively high and a relatively low pitch level. Speech melody is considered to be the continual alternation between relatively high and relatively low pitch levels ('t Hart and Cohen 1990). Pitch events in the IPO model are said to be of two types: (i) 'Prominence-lending': a term adopted to indicate the pitch movements, including both a rise and a fall, occurring relatively early in the stressed syllable; an extremely late rise; and a kind of half-fall. These pitch movements are only taken as phonetic variations; and (ii) 'Non-prominence-lending': a term used to describe the pitch movements, including a rise and a fall, at phrase boundaries; plus a rise and a fall that may span several syllables. These pitch events are phonologically distinctive in the sense that they may turn one contour type into a different one;for example, one of the important functions of a boundary rise is to distinguish a question from a statement.

---

[73] "IPO" is an abbreviation of the Dutch name "Instituut voor Perceptie Onderzoek (Institute for Perception Research) ", which is a perpetual research institute in Eindhoven in the Netherlands.

5.2.1.2　Phonetic realization

The well known phonetic description of pitch movement in the IPO model is the pattern that consists minimally a 'Type 1 Rise' (low to high early in an accented syllable) followed by a 'Type A Fall' (high to low early in an accented syllable). These two movements may occur as part of the same accent in which case it is referred to as a 'pointed hat' or 'flat hat.' The stretches of contour preceding the rise and following the fall, and the transcription in between the two, are idealized as straight line segments annotated as "Ø" (for the upper line) and "0"(for the lower line). Thus, the abstract description of the hat pattern can be expressed as: (0) 1 (Ø) A (0). Within this representation, there is an obligatory "1" and an obligatory "A" with the "Ø" and "0" contours on any non-prominent syllables.

Further, the best-known feature of the IPO approach to phonetic realization is the notion of *declination*. This term was coined by Cohen and 't Hart (1967) to describe the downward trend of F_0. In the IPO model, declination refers specifically to the trend of the top and bottom lines that define the limits of the local pitch movements: the lines annotated "Ø" and "0" in the abstract phonological formulas that represent contours. This indicates that even if nothing happens phonologically in the contour, F_0 continues to go down slightly.

Thus, there are two important properties that make the IPO approach phonological in nature: a linear description and a phonetic identification. With regard to linearity, an IPO description consists of a string of discrete intonation elements. As for phonetic identification, the pitch movements are defined in terms of their phonetic realization. Meaning or function plays no role in the analysis.

5.2.2　Pierrehumbert's model of tonal structure

This part offers an account of Pierrehumbert's model for the description of the intonational structure in English. Her seminal thesis (Pierrehumbert 1980) presents a descriptive framework for intonation that separates a phonological representation from its phonetic implementation. The basic assumption contains three types of pitch events L pitch accents, phrase accents, and boundary tone that are analyzed as consisting of primitive level tones or pitch targets, *High* (*H*) and *Low* (*L*). There are actually two distinct versions of the Pierrehumbert analysis: (i) the original version presented by Pierrehumbert (1980), and (ii) a revised version, intended to supersede the original, developed by Pierrehumbert in collaboration with Mary Beckman (Beckman and Pierrehumbert 1986; Pierrehumbert and Beckman 1988). The discussion in this section presents an account of both versions.

5.2.2.1   The original model

In the original notation, Pierrehumbert represents the contour as a string of pitch accents and edge tones. All pitch accents consist of a single *H* or *L* tone or a combination of these two tones. The central tone of a pitch accent is indicated with an asterisk, either *H** or *L** (hence 'starred tone'). In addition to this central or starred tone, a pitch accent may contain a 'leading' (preceding) or 'trailing ' (following) tone that is written with a following raised hyphen (*H* ‾ or *L* ‾). Boundary tones in the original model are also single tones, either *High* or *Low*, that are associated with the end of an intonation phrase, and are indicated by *H*% or *L*%. The specific phonetic details corresponding to these notations are described in the following part.

5.2.2.2   Pitch accents

Pierrehumbert's original analysis posited seven possible pitch accent types: *H**, *L**, *L*+H*, *L+H**, *H+L**, *H*+L*, and *H*+H*. Specifically, (a) *H**

165

is a local peak aligned with the accented syllable; (b) *L** corresponds to the local valley; (c) *L*+H* is an accent contour that is low for a good portion of the accented syllable and then rises sharply into the following unstressed syllable; (d) *L+H** is similar to *H** with the exception that it rises from a much lower level; (e) *H+L** involves a local drop from a preceding syllable; (f) *H*+L* indicates a high accent that triggers a downstep in the following *H* tone; and (g) *H*+H* indicates that the pitch accent locates on a relatively high pitch and follows the rising of the pitch.

5.2.2.3 Phrase accents

The idea of the phrase tone is borrowed from the 'phrase accent' of Bruce's (1977) analysis of Swedish. Pierrehumbert's (1980) proposal is that in English, the last pitch accent of each phrase is followed by two distinct tonal events. The "*L*" phrase tone can be straightforwardly interpreted as low pitch following the final pitch accent of the phrase. The "*H⁻*" phrase tone represents a high pitch following the last pitch accent.

5.2.2.4 Boundary tones

The "*H%*" boundary tone also indicates a final rise. This is straightforward after the *L* phrase tone, but requires an 'upstep rule' (Pierrehumbert 1980) after an *H* phrase tone. The "*L%*" boundary tone can best be described as indicating the absence of a final rise. After an *L* phrase tone, *L%* indicates a fall to the bottom of the speaking range, but after an *H* phrase tone, it indicates a level sustention of the previous tone.

5.2.2.5 Framework

The basic framework of Pierrehumbert (1980) is considered to be a finite-state grammar that can be used to generate all the legal tunes of English.

Boundary tone   Pitch accents   Phrase accents   Boundary tone

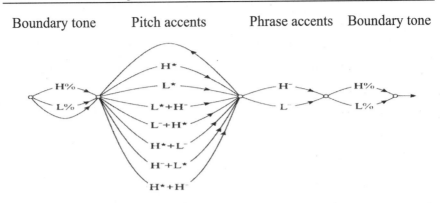

Figure 5. 2. 2. 5. 1   Intonation model of Pierrehumbert (Pierrehumbert 1980: 29)

This grammar states that tunes are made up of one or more pitch accents, followed by an obligatory phrase tone and an obligatory boundary tone. It implies three interrelated theoretical claims about the structure of tunes: (i) the grammar allows all the combinations of pitch accents with phrase and boundary tones; (ii) there is no restrictions on the number of the pitch accents; and (iii) it also implies that there is no primary or secondary distinctions between the pitch accents.

5.2.2.6   Modifications to the original framework

Beckman and Pierrehumbert (1986) propose a revision to the permissible structure of tunes in English. This revision grows out of their work on applying AM theory to Japanese (Pierrehumbert and Beckman 1988). The essence of their proposal is the explicit formulation of a distinction between *intonation phrase* and *intermediate phrase* as levels of prosodic structure in English. Pierrehumbert and Beckman relate this proposal to the issue of separate phrase tones. They suggest that the edge of an intermediate phrase is marked by a phrase tone, while the edge of an intonation phrase is marked by both a phrase tone and a boundary tone, therefore, each type of domain has its own type of edge tone. There is also included some modifications to the types of pitch events; specifically, six pitch accents are described: *H**, *L**, *L*+H*, *L+H**, *H+L**, and *H*+L* with an optional initial boundary "*%H*" preceding the intonation phrase for high initial pitch.

Thus, the notation of Pierrehumbert (1980) bears four characteristics: (i) Linear combination of pitch events: the tonal structure is linear and consists of a string of local events; (ii) Local description for global trends: the overall pitch contour is composed of discrete pitch events; (iii) Pitch events are analyzed in terms of level tones, pitch accents, and phrase accents with boundary tones being described as combinations of the level tones, *High* (*H*) and *Low* (*L*); and (iv) Two levels of prosodic phrases which distinguishes the intermediate from the intonation phrases that are two components in the formulation of the intonation structure.

5.2.3　ToBI labeling system

The ToBI (for Tones and Break Indices) system is a distinct version of the Pierrehumbert analysis. It is a framework for developing community-wide conventions for transcribing the intonation and prosodic structure of spoken utterances in a particular language variety (Silverman et al 1992, Beckman and Ayers 1994, Beckman and Hirscberg 1994). A ToBI framework system for a particular language variety is grounded in careful research on the intonation system and the relationship between intonation and the prosodic structures of a target language (e.g., tonally marked phrases and any smaller prosodic constituents that are distinctively marked by other phonological means).

5.2.3.1　Tiers in ToBI

A complete ToBI transcription contains four tiers. The four tiers are: *Tone Tier*, *Orthographic Tier*, *Break Index Tier*, and *Miscellaneous Tier*.

These four tiers are strings of symbols anchored in time to specific points in the waveform of an utterance that includes the orthographic transcription and a tier reserved for comments on influences and the like. The two most important tiers are those indicating the "Tone Tier" and "Break Index Tier" that label the F_0 contour variations and the strength of a prosodic boundary. Prosodic boundary labeling contains essentially a five-point scale running from '0' to "4." Among these five numbers, "0" denotes a connection of the two words; "1" denotes a prosodic word boundary, "2" denotes a mismatch between the acoutic cues and the perception of the prosodic boundary; "3" denotes an intermediate phrase boundary, and "4" denotes an intonational phrase boundary.

5.2.3.2   Accent inventory in ToBI

The main difference between Pierrehumbert (1980) and Beckman and Pierrehumbert's (1986) analysis is that downstep is explicitly indicated in the transcription in the spirit of Ladd (1983). The following specific changes were made:

(i)   A downsepped *H** is given as *'H**. For instance, {*L+H* L+H* L-L%*} is {*L+H* L+'H* L-L%*} in ToBI.

(ii)   A new pitch accent was introduced to describe a high-level pitch followed by a downstep, *H+'H**. For example, {*H* H+L* L-L%*} is now {*H* H+'H* L-L%*} in ToBI. Since *H+L** was no longer needed to function as *H+'H**, it was deleted from the pitch accents set.

(iii)   Since *H*+L* was in effect a downstep trigger, with realization of *L*, it was removed from the symbol set. For instance, {*H*+L H* L-L%*} is now {*H* 'H* L-L%*} in ToBI.

The pitch event inventory can be further illustrated in the following graph:

Boundary tone   Pitch accents   Phrase accents   Boundary tone

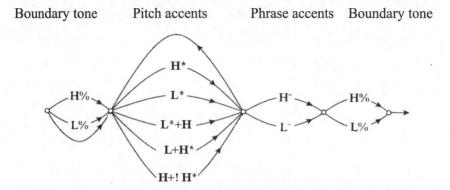

Figure 5.2.3.2.1 ToBI System

Thereafter, the pitch accent inventory in ToBI grammar is: *H**, *L**, *L*+H*, and *H+*$^{|}$*H**. The boundary tones and their phonetic interpretations retained intact. The only change in convention here is that in the final position of an intonation phrase, the phrase accent "*H -* " or "*L -* " is given as part of a complex symbol together with the boundary tone, for instance as "*L-H%*".

5.2.4 IViE labeling system

IViE (Intonational Variation in English) is also a prosodic labeling system that originated from ToBI, but unlike the original ToBI, IViE allows for directly comparable transcriptions of several varieties of English in a single labeling system. Additionally, IViE transcriptions capture rhythmic differences between varieties, and differences in phonetic realization (Grabe and Farrar 2000). In the IViE system, prosody is transcribed on three levels: (a) rhythmic structure, (b) acoustic-phonetic structure, and (c) phonological structure.

5.2.4.1 Tiers in IViE

IViE has five levels of transcription (two orthographic, and three prosodic), described as:

(i)   Orthographic Tier: transcriptions of the words spoken.

(ii)   Prominence Tier: location of prominent syllables (stressed and accented).

(iii)   Target Tier: syllable-based phonetic transcriptions: allow transcribers to draw up a first set of hypotheses about accent alignment.

(iv)   Phonological Tier: formal linguistic representations of speakers' intonational choices.

(v)   Comment Tier: notes on the para-linguistic phenomenon.

5.2.4.2   Accent inventory in IViE

The phonological account of pitch events in IViE is composed step-by-step: (i) identification of accented syllables; (ii) a syllable-based phonetic transcription of the alignment of F_0 patterns surrounding prominent syllables; and (iii) phonological accounts of pitch events based on the phonetic descriptions. Totally, there are seven kinds of pitch accents in the IViE system:

(i)   *H**: High target, common in initial position in so-called flat hats in IPO theory;

(ii)   *L**: Low target;

(iii)   *H*L*: High target on a prominent syllable followed by a low target;

(iv)   *L*H*: Low target on a prominent syllable followed by a high target;

(v)   *H*LH*: internal or final fall-rise for an intonation phrase: high target on a strong syllable;

(vi)   *L*HL*: internal or final rise-fall for an intonation phrase: Low target on a prominent syllable, and high target on the next syllable followed by a low target;

(vii)   *'H*L*: Downstepped high target to a low target;

171

The tonal structure in IViE is illustrated in the following graph:

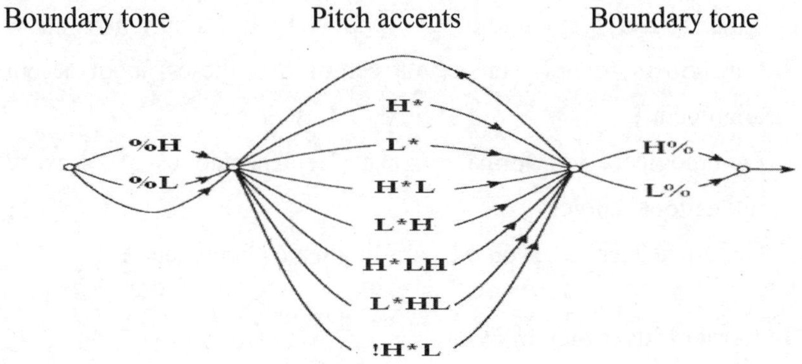

Boundary tone   Pitch accents   Boundary tone

Figure 5.2.4.2.1 IViE System

Although the IViE system includes the differences in the types of pitch accents, it does not include the phrase accents in the overall grammar. The representation of the initial boundary tone also bears slight differences from the original Pierrehumbert model and the ToBI system. Similar implications among these three systems are the legal property of each combination of the pitch event in the grammar.

5.2.5 Ladd's notation of tonal structure

The central idea of Ladd's (1996) tonal structure is that one part of the contour is both obligatory and potentially unique and can be considered as the nucleus while other parts of the contour are taken as optional. This claim has, in one way or another, been a part of theorising about intonation structure at least since the beginning of the British tradition (Crutteden 1992)[74]. According to the founding work in the British school (Palmer 1992), the contour is divided into three parts, called head, nucleus, and tail. Only the nucleus is obligatory, so that on a monosyllabic

---

[74] He extended a discussion of pre-twentieth-century precursors to the nucleus idea.

utterance the contour consists of the nucleus alone. In an utterance with more syllables, the nucleus is normally the last stressed syllable. Pike (1945) draws a distinction between 'primary contour' and 'pre-contour' that almost exactly matches the distinction between nucleus (or nucleus-plus-tail) and head (or prehead-plus-head) of the British school. Pierrehumbert (1980), however, rejects the head/nucleus/tail division and asserts that contours are strings of accents generated by the finite-state grammar. Pierrehumbert does not continue to refer informally to the last accent in the sequence as the 'nuclear' accent. It is worth noting, however, that Pierrehumbert's argument against the nucleus is in effect an argument against the 'head' of the British tradition. It is an argument that follows from her argument against global contour shapes; that is, she denies that the head is an identifiable component of contours primarily because traditional British descriptions of the head are often expressed in terms of global shapes.

5.2.5.1   Types of pitch accents

Within the model, Ladd (1996) distinguishes the nucleus from other accents – and hence recognizes in some way the existence of the head without banning Pierrehumbert's basic assumption that intonation contours are strings of pitch accents or tones. Therefore, the pitch accents are divided into two parts: *nuclear accents* and *pre-nuclear accents*. These two kinds of accents contain identical accent inventory. Specifically: {H^*, L^*, L^*+H, $L+H^*$, H^*+L, and $H+L^*$}. This grammar states that contours consist obligatorily of one accent that corresponds to the nucleus. It states that the nucleus may be preceded by one or more accents, but that any preceding accents must be identical. Thus, this grammar gives us something corresponding to the head in which this kind of pitch event is neither a global shape nor even a obligatory constituent of a contour, but merely a substring of the contour.

5.2.5.2   Post-nuclear accents

Both Grice (1995) and Vella (1995) writing on Palermo Italian and Maltese respectively, show that in sentences where the main focus is early, there may be a secondary accent on a word that occurs after the focused word – a post-nuclear accent. Based on the observations from Grice (1995) and Vella (1995), Ladd (1996) further proposes that similar phenomenon can be observed in the location of post-nuclear L in English falling-rising tunes. Therefore, Ladd postulates a special category of pitch accents (Hp or Lp) referred to as 'boundary accent' or 'phrase accent.' This term refers to pitch phenomena at the ends of phrases that are definitely accentual, but are also clearly distinct from the accentual phenomena in the main body of the phrase. Specifically, they behave like pitch accents when there is an acceptable word available, but like boundary tones when there is not. The 'phrase accents' are associated with a lexically stressed syllable; there is no distinction between these accents and pitch accents in the phonetic realization of the pitch. Furthermore, Ladd did not treat the post-nuclear accents as the optional accents following the obligatory *nuclear accent* that would be analogous to the way the *pre-nuclear accents* are generated. This is because, unlike *pre-nuclear accents*, the post-nuclear tones are in some sense obligatory: they are always present in the contour in one form or another. What is optional and rule-governed is whether they surface as accents or boundary tones. The overall grammar of the Ladd model is illustrated in the following figure:

Boundary Tone Pre-nuclear Accents   Nuclear Accent Phrase Accents Boundary Tone

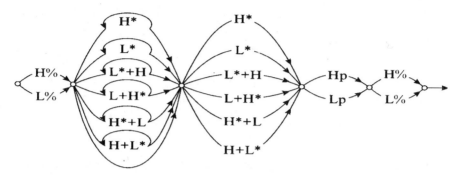

Figure 5. 2. 5. 2. 1   Intonation model of Ladd (1996: 217)

The intonational grammar of Ladd (1996) distinguishes former tune structure from two aspects: (i) the distinction between the obligatory and optional accents, and (ii) the implications of the phrase accents that bear both the underlying and surface meaning.

5.2.6   Gussenhoven's representation of tonal structure

Based on the phonological account of middle-class southern British English[75] and the intonational studies of phonologists (Palmer 1922, Pike 1945,Crystal 1969, Liberman 1975, Pierrehumbert 1980, Ladd 1996 and Gruttenden 1997), Gussenhoven (2004) proposes a model for the phonological structure of English tunes. The grammar mainly contains four kinds of pitch events: nuclear contours, pre-nuclear pitch accents, onsets, and boundary tones.

---

[75] Its intonational grammar is very similar to that of Standard Dutch, American English, and North German.

5.2.6.1 Nuclear contours and boundary tones

There are four kinds of nucler tones: $\{H^*, L^*, L^*H$ and $H^*L\}$, and three kinds of boundary tones: $\{H_l^{76}, L_l$ and $\emptyset\}$, in the inventory of the Gussenhoven (2004) model. Through the combinations of the unclear tones and the boundary tones, the grammar can describe the following ten kinds of pitch movements: (a) $H^*\ L\ L_l$: fall; (b) $H^*\ L\ H_l$: fall-rise; (c) $H^*\ H$ $_l$: high rise; (d) $L^*\ H\ H\ _l$: low rise; (e) $H^*\ \emptyset$: high level; (f) $L^*\ H$ $\emptyset$: half-completed rise; (g) $H^*\ L\ \emptyset$: half-completed fall; (h) $L^*\ H_l$: low low rise; (i) $L^*\ L_l$: scathing intonation; and (j) $L^*\ L_l$: low level.

It is known that through exhaustive combinations of the nuclear tones {H*, L*, L*H and H*L} and the boundary tones {H$_l$, L$_l$ and $\emptyset$}, it should be possible to produce twelve neutral tones; however, the above analysis only contains ten types of combinations. The two missing combinations are $L^*H\ L_l$ and $H^*\ L_l$, both of which describe a fall on the $_l$-final syllable, the counterpart of the final rise; while the accented syllable is low and followed by a rise (L^*H), or has a rise early in the accented syllable (H^*). Gussenhoven proposes that the standard BrE does not contain these two kinds of pitch movements; therefore, the combinations of the nuclear contours and the boundary tones can be illustrated as:

$$\begin{Bmatrix} H^*(L) \\ L^*(H) \end{Bmatrix} \begin{Bmatrix} H_l \\ L_l \\ \phi \end{Bmatrix}$$

$$\text{NoS}_{\text{LUMP}}{}^{77}$$

Figure 5.2.6.1.1　Combinations of nuclear tones and boundary tones

(Gussenhoven 2004)

5.2.6.2 Pre-nuclear pitch accents

Although there are just four nuclear pitch accents, the pre-nuclear

---

[76] The symbol "$_l$" denotes the boundary of the intonation phrase.

[77] NoS$_{\text{LUMP}}$ indicates that the combinations contain no "L*H L$_l$ and H* L$_l$" pitch events.

paradigm consists of five pitch accents. Specifically: pre-nuclear fall (*H** *L*), pre-nuclear rise (*L* H*), pre-nuclear high level (*H**), pre-nuclear low level (*L**), and pre-nuclear fall-rise (*H* L H$_l$*). The corresponding phonetic realization of these pre-nuclear tones are:

(i)   pre-nuclear H* L: it is like the nuclear fall, except that it usually tends to slope down more gradually, and take up the space between it and the next tone;

(ii)   pre-nuclear L* H: it is like the nuclear pitch accent, except that the rise may take up the space available before the next accent;

(iii) pre-nuclear H*: if it occurs before H* H$_l$, the second H* may be a little higher than the first; if it appears before L* H, there is some slumping down in the syllables before the L*;

(iv)   pre-nuclear L*: describes a low level pre-nuclear stretch;

(v)   pre-nuclear H* L H: it may appear as a rise-plus-steep fall on a pre-nuclear accented syllable followed by a gradual rise.

5.2.6.3   Onsets

The unaccented syllables in the intonation boundary preceding the first accent, known as the 'prehead' (O' Connor and Arnold 1973) or 'onset' as "H$_i$ and L $_i$" (Gussenhoven 1983), have so far exhibited a low or mid pitch. This neutral pronunciation is generally considered to be the result of the absence of a boundary tone (Liberman 1975, Pierrehumbert 1980, Beckman and Pierrehumbert 1986) that could be seen to explain the fact that the pitch tends to be mid, but might be low without changing the identity of the contour. The "L $_i$" onset contrasts with "H$_i$", where the " L $_i$" onset is several syllables long, in that it typically falls somewhat from mid, while a longer "H $_i$" onset may fall slightly from high pitch. The frequency of the high onset may be biased towards occurrences before L*, except in the case of the low scathing contour, L* L$_l$. Thus, the standard mini-grammar of the Gussenhoven model can be illustrated as:

$$\left\{ \begin{matrix} H_l \\ L_l \end{matrix} \right\} \left\{ \begin{matrix} H^*(L) \\ L^*(H) \end{matrix} \right\}_0^n \left\{ \begin{matrix} H^*(L) \\ L^*(H) \end{matrix} \right\} \left\{ \begin{matrix} H_l \\ L_l \\ \phi \end{matrix} \right\}$$

NOSLUMP

Figure 5.2.6.3.1　Standard model of tonal structure of Gussenhoven

(Gussenhoven 2004)

5.2.6.4　Expanding the tonal grammar

5.2.6.4.1　Delay

The results of an experiment by Pierrehumbert and Steele (1989) suggests that the 'scooped' contours of Vanderslice and Ladefoged (1972) and Ladd (1980) are discretely different from the 'unscooped' $H^*L\ L_l$ and H^*LH_l. In the scooped version, low pitch appears in the accented syllable, while the peak is shifted towards the right. Rise-fall(-rise) nuclear tones have in fact generally been recognized as distinct categories from the fall(-rise) tones (Crystal 1969, Halliday 1970, O' Connor and Arnold 1973, and Pierrehumbert 1980). Gussenhoven (1983) proposes a morpheme [D$_{ELAY}$] or L-prefixation with the meaning 'significant' that could apply to $H^*L(H)$ and L^*H, causing the stared tone to be realized late.

5.2.6.4.2　Downstep and Leading H

The downstep phenomenon had been described earlier (e.g., O' Connor and Arnold's 1973 'terraced contour'). Pierrehumbert (1980) was the first to incorporate downstept, which up to then had been applied to lexical tone, in the analysis of an intonation-only language. In Beckman and Pierrehumbert (1986), downstep applies to H^* and their phrase accent "H - ", when occurring after a bi-tonal pitch accent. Gussenhoven (2004) further proposes that H^*, whether or not delayed, can undergo downstep and the H feature on its left can come from different sources. This feature is described as [DOWNSTEP] in the tonal structure.

Gussenhoven (2004) also points out that the leading H (+H) is a feature of English intonation, and is possible adjacent to the nuclear pitch accents. The phonetic realization of "+H" exhibits differently with !$H*$, therefore it is taken as an independent feature in Gussenhoven's model.

If the downstept, L-prefixation, and leading-H are added to the standard mini-grammar of Figure 5.2.6.3.1, the extended grammar can be illustrated as:

$$([\text{DOWNSTEP}]) \begin{Bmatrix} H_l \\ L_l \end{Bmatrix} (L) \begin{Bmatrix} H^*(L(H)) \\ L^*(H) \end{Bmatrix}_0^n (H+)(L) \begin{Bmatrix} H^*(L) \\ L^*(H) \end{Bmatrix} \begin{Bmatrix} H_l \\ L_l \\ \phi \end{Bmatrix}$$

NOSLUMP

Figure 5.2.6.4.2.1 Gussenhoven's extended model of tonal structure

(Gussenhoven 2004)

On the whole, compared with the previous theoretical model, the characteristics of Gussenhoven's model can be described as: (i) it contains obligatory and optional distinctions between the pitch accents; i.e., the nuclear and *pre-nuclear accents*; (ii) the L-prefixation and Leading H feature are the newly proposed features in Gussenhoven's model, thus it provides a more detailed description of the connecting or transcription feature.

5.3   Intonation structure of SC

This part concentrates on the phonological representation of the tonal structure of SC based on the phonetic evidences observed in Chapter Three and Chapter Four. It is known that in all languages, vowel height and consonant place of articulation are central to conveying the meaning of a word, and there are some languages, classified as 'tone languages', that employ tone for this purpose. SC is a kind of tonal language that uses variations in tone to convey different meanings. Phonological representation of the tonal structure of SC needs to take tonal types into consideration. The earliest distinction within the group of tone languages was between those that just have *level tones*, which require the syllable to reach a certain pitch height, and those that also have *contour tones*, which require the syllable to be said with a pitch movement. Pike (1948) termed these 'register tone languages' and 'contour tone languages', respectively. Additionally, tone contrasts have a paradigmatic dimension: the number of tonal contrasts possible on a given syllable; as well as a systematic dimension: the number of positions in a word where these contrasts are used. As for the first dimension, many tone languages have only a binary level contrast that is represented by the symbols *H* (*High*) and *L*(*Low*); thus, the notations for the two values of a binary feature such as [±Hightone] often suffice to describe them. The number of level tone contrasts may, with increasing rarity, reach three, four, or five (Maddieson 1978).

5.3.1 Autosegmetal representation of tone

SC belongs to the group of contour tone languages. Chao (1930) proposes a five-scale tone system to present the tonal movement of SC: (i) ma^{55} : *H* 'mother' (tone1); (ii) ma^{35}: *LH* 'hemp'(tone 2); (iii) ma$^{21(4)}$: *L(H)* 'horse'(tone3); and (iv) ma^{51}: *HL* 'scold'(tone4). Autosegmetal phonology represents tones on a separate tier from the rest of the representation: the tones are autonomous segments, or autosegments. Basically, there are three kinds of representations that have different implications (Gussenhoven 2004):

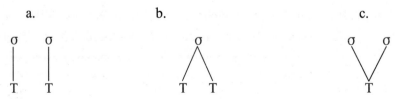

If the representation of "a" were needed, tone would form an integral part of the syllable, or the vowel in it: they would share each other's fate in deletions and insertions. In allowing "b" and "c", the theory predicts that a tone can disappear while the vowel it occurred on remains, or vice versa. Presentation of "b" is that of a contour tone, which frequently arises at the edges of words or phrases, while the continuation of a tone's pitch value on an adjacent Tone Bearing Unit (TBU)[78] can be presented as in "c" , a multiple association of a tone.

It is proposed by Duanmu (2000) and Yip (2002) that one heavy syllable in SC can have two moras. SC belongs to the group of languages that can have mora and syllable as the tonal bearing units. The tonal features of SC can be presented as in (i)-(iv) (Wang 2002):

(i)   tone1   (ii)   tone2   (iii)   tone3   (iv)   tone4

As described in chapter three and chapter four, when dealing with F_0 prominence, the research renders each of the syllables into its original tonal target to observe the specific effect induced by different information statuses. The instrumental research has shown that focused constituents (theme focus, rheme focus, and *syntax*-marked focus) present the same kind of correlates: a consistent F_0 prominence and durational lengthening under the scope of focus. Specifically, within the tone1 target sentence, the two tonal targets "*HH*" are raised by the information focus and this effect can be reflected on both syllables of the words. When information status remains identical, the elongation and the prominence location of the sentence with various tonal combinations exhibit a consistent pattern; i.e., durational lengthening and prominence under focus scope with the only difference due to the specific manner of tonal realization. The target of the tone2 and tone4 constituents, '*LH*' and '*HL*' are also raised as a whole

---

[78] The 'Tone Bearing Unit' , or TBU, is the element in the segmental structure to which tone associates. Duanmu (2000) proposes that SC can be taken as a syllable or mora bearing unit language.

entity with the 'H' tone as the major anchor. Based on a study of the five-syllable focused constituents in SC, Jia et al (2008) propose that the focus can trigger an effect on all the five syllables under focus. The major effect manifests on the '*H*' tone of the syllable. Although the present study adopts no *L* tone-target syllable, the study of Jia et al (2006; 2008) demonstrates that focus exerts no obvious effect on the '*L*' tone. All these results demonstrate that SC as a tonal language has some form of intonation structure, and the structure is configured above the lexical level. The evidence presented in the following paragraph accounts for the phonological structure of intonation in SC.

5.3.2　Phonological pattern of intonation structure in SC

It is assumed in chapter three and chapter four that the accent pattern in SC can be classified into two types: *nuclear accent* and *pre-nuclear accent*. *Nuclear accent* is always related to the rightmost focused constituent, and its appearance is necessary with variations on specific phonetic realizations in different contexts. However, the appearance of *pre-nuclear accent* is optional and can only locate in the position preceding the *nuclear accent*. Therefore, the central goal of theories of the intonation structure of SC is to be able to provide an explicit phonetic characterization of all the phonological events regardless of how phonetic realization varies with to each other. In particular, it should be able to make explicit predictions of how a given tune is realized when it is applied to different texts.

5.3.2.1　Types of phonological events

5.3.2.1.1　Nuclear tone

The idea that one part of a contour is both obligatory and potentially unique can readily be related to the idea of the nucleus, which in one form or another has been a part of theorizing about intonation structure at least since the beginning of the British tradition (see Cruttenden 1992 for an interesting discussion of pre-twentieth-century precursors to the nucleus idea). According to the founding work in the British school, Palmer (1922) points out that the contour is divided into three parts, called head, nucleus, and tail. Only the nucleus is obligatory and associated with the most prominent syllable that is normally also the last stressed syllable. The tail is the stretch of contour following the nuclear syllable, and is largely or entirely dictated by the choice of nuclear tone. The head is the stretch of contour preceding the nuclear syllable, and is an independent choice. Although Crystal (1969) and Halliday (1967) provide penetrating theoretical criticisms of many of the assumptions of the British tradition, they retained the idea of the distinction between the nucleus ('tonic' in Halliday's terminology) and other parts of a contour.

Similar ideas are found outside the British tradition as well. For example, Pike (1945) draws a distinction between 'primary contour' and 'precontour' that almost exactly matches the distinction between nucleus and head. The IPO tradition, though it originally had no such distinction, incorporates a three-way distinction between prefix, root, and suffix that is comparable in many respects (through not identically) to the British distinction between head, nucleus, and tail ('t Hart, Collier, and Cohen 1990). Ladd (1996) also mentions that it is entirely possible to distinguish the *nucleus* from other accents, and hence recognizes in some way the existence of the head. Ladd further defined the pitch event associate with the head as a *pre-nuclear accent*.

SC also exhibits the phonological entity *nuclear accent* based on the observations from the previous chapter as described in the following aspects: (i) there always exists an accent associated with the single focus status; i.e. rheme focus, *lian*-marked focus, or *shi*-marked focus, and the accent has a corresponding relationship with the focus. However, the only difference among the three kinds of focuses is due to the magnitude of the

F_0 prominence and durational lengthening that belongs to the variation in the phonetic aspect, (ii) under a dual focus condition, the rightmost accent exhibits the primary acoustic performance; specifically, theme focus vs. rheme focus, *lian*-marked focus vs. rheme focus, the addition of *lian*-marked focus to rheme focus vs. rheme focus, rheme focus vs. addition of *lian*-marked focus and rheme focus, and (iii) under multiple rheme focuses, only the rightmost focus can realize accent in the surface form. Therefore, because the primary accent in SC exhibits the characteristics of obligatoriness and uniqueness, it is defined as a *nuclear accent* following the British tradition.

As for the inventory of the nuclear tone in SC, tonal contrast is presented in the first step. It is mentioned in chapter one that the prominence realization of the focused constituent has the property of intonation at the post-lexicon level, i.e., the syntactic component under the scope of the focus (theme focus, rheme focus, or *syntax*-marked focus) exhibit F_0 prominence or durational lengthening. The realization of F_0 prominence is above the level of lexical tone, and the tone is the determining factor for the local F_0 contour of the syllable. Also, information induced focus extensively modulates the global shape of the F_0 contour that in turn affects the height and even the shape of the local contour. Thereafter, the basic account of the nuclear tone should be generated from tonal combinations: {HH(tone1), LH(tone2), LL(tone3), and HL(tone4)}. As described in the original model of Pierrehumbert (1980), the central tone of an accent is indicated with an asterisk, as either '*H**' or '*L**' (thereinafter 'starred tone'). The present study and the study from Jia (2006; 2008) point out that the central tone for accent realization is the tonal target '*H*', thus, the accent bearing unit of tone1 is represented as '*H**' to meet the economy need for phonological representation. For the tone2 and tone4 items, the representation is '*LH**' and '*H*L*'. With regard to the tone3 constituent, although it has '*L L*' tonal targets and bears no obvious F_0 prominence, the constituent exhibits obvious lengthening under focus; therefore, the designation 'L*' denotes the focused item of the tone3 item. It is proposed by Jia Yuan et al (2008) that the F_0 and duration of the five-syllable constituent under the scope of the focus can be modulated by the focus, and the modification can be reflected in each of the syllables under the focus. Thus, the phonological representation of the nuclear tone should align with the syllable in SC.

5.3.2.1.2   Pre-nuclear tone

Ladd (1996) states that nuclear tone may be preceded by one or more accents, but that any preceding accents must be identical. This entity is referred to as 'pre-nuclear tone' by Ladd. This grammar shows that, corresponding to the head, the 'pre-nuclear tone' is neither a global shape nor even a constituent in any strict sense—it is merely a substring of the contour. The British tradition's terminology is thus substantially redefined in accordance with AM assumptions, but the basic descriptive insight (as we have just seen, forms part of most traditions) is retained. Note that this definition also defuses Pierrehumbert's arguments against assigning special status to the nucleus. She attaches considerable importance to the fact that there appears to be no phonetic difference between nuclear and pre-nuclear accents in English. The largest study of this question is by Silverman and Pierrehumbert (1990) who show that a number of phonetic condition factors in the alignment of 'H' accent peaks affect nuclear tone and pre-nuclear tone in identical ways. This means that the nuclear tone is not in any way phonetically distinct from pre-nuclear accents.

As for the phonetic realization of pre-nuclear tone in SC, important pieces of evidence in that direction are: (i) pre-nuclear tone is not phonetically distinct from nuclear tone; Specifically, two rheme focuses can induce similar F_0 performances; and (ii) pre-nuclear tone exhibits a different phonetic realization with nuclear tone: under the condition of theme focus vs. rheme focus and *syntax*-marked focus vs. rheme focus, the pre-nuclear tone shows a small magnitude of phonetic variations (F_0 prominence and duration lengthening) than nuclear tone. Therefore, the pre-nuclear tone is not always distinct from nuclear tone in the phonetic realization of the phonetic aspect in SC. We follow Ladd (1996) and argue that the pre-nuclear tone has an identical tonal inventory as the nuclear tone: {*H**; *L**; *LH** and *H*L*}.

5.3.2.1.3   Onsets

The unaccented syllables in the proceeding positions of the first accent, are known as the 'prehead' (O'Connor and Arnold 1973) or 'onset'(Gussenhoven 1983). Similar pitch events exist in SC. This phenomena has been shown in chapter three and chapter four as described here: (i) the pitch movement of the constituent in the position proceeding the focus (rheme focus or *syntax*-marked focus) remains largely intact and exhibits a contour similar to its original tone, and (ii) the pitch contour between the two focues remains largely the same as their original tone (no lowering or raising); i.e., two rheme focus, theme focus vs. rheme focus, and *syntax*-marked focus vs. rheme focus. Therefore, the study proposes that SC observes the phonological entity as 'onset' and the specific phonetic realization resembles its original tonal target. Thus, the symbol 'T' is adopted to represent it. The inventory is presented based on the tonal types in SC: {*H*; *L*; *LH* and *HL*}. The location of the *onset* is in two positions: between the pre-nuclear and nuclear tone and proceeding the pre-nuclear tone.

5.3.2.1.4   Boundary tone

All the intonational models in the above part contain the phonological event of boundary tone (refer to Pierrehumbert (1980), Ladd (1966), and Gussenhoven (2004), to list just a few). The '*H%*' boundary tone always indicates a final rise and the '*L*%' boundary tone can best be described as indicating the absence of final rise. In SC, Lin (2006) proposes that the '*H*%' boundary tone be adopted to mark the distinction between the declarative and interrogative mood. We also adopt the 'H%' and 'L%' boundary tones in this study to mark the initial and final variations of the pitch in the intonation structure of SC.

5.3.2.2   Phonological pattern of accents

Based on the observations, the intonation structure of SC can be presented as follows:

$$\left\{ \begin{array}{c} H\% \\ L\% \end{array} \right\} (T) + \left\{ \begin{array}{c} H^* \\ L^* \\ LH^* \\ H^*L \end{array} \right\} + (T) \left\{ \begin{array}{c} H^* \\ L^* \\ LH^* \\ H^*L \end{array} \right\} \left\{ \begin{array}{c} H\% \\ L\% \end{array} \right\}$$

Figure 5.3.2.2.1   Tonal structure of SC

This grammar states that the contours of {*H**; *L**; *LH** and *H**L} locate at the right position is the nuclear tone that is the obligatory phonological event in SC. The accent with an identical inventory as the nuclear tone is the pre-nuclear tone that bears optional and secondary characteristics. The symbol 'T' is the onset that is adopted to mark the transitional unaccented constituents. The features are determined by its tonal combination, and its appearance is also optional. The '*H*%' or '*L*%' denote the boundary tones to indicate the relative '*H*' or '*L*' pitch of the initial or boundary tones.

5.3.3   Hierarchical structure of accents

The observations in the previous section show that the essence of the nuclear tone is not its serial position in the tonal structure but the fact that it is the most important accent from the point of view of focus. As for the hierarchical structure of accents, Ladd (1996) proposes the general structure for intonation through updating the proposals in terms of the X-bar theory of constituent structure (Kornai and Pullum 1990):

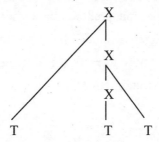

Figure 5.3.3.1 Hierarchical structure of tunes (Ladd 1996)

Such a structure has the following four implications: (i) a tune has one element, the nucleus, that is in some sense its central or most prominent point; (ii) a tune has a constituent structure in which the most major break is that between the nucleus and all that precedes, and the distinctive post-nuclear tone elements of a tune are more closely bound to the nucleus than are the prenuclear elements; (iii) post-nuclear elements in at least some languages may surface either as accents or as edge tones depending on the metrical structure of the segmental materials to which they are associated; and (iv) the pre-nuclear element in a tune is a single linguistic choice. The occurrence of multiple *pre-nuclear accents* depends on the metrical structure of the segmental material to which the tune is associated.

It is worth noting that the principle proposed by Ladd (1996) indicates that the intonation structure bears the property of a phrase. The elements of tunes are abstract tones, and they are not intrinsically either accent tones or boundary tones. Rather, they are intrinsically nuclear, pre-nuclear, or post-nuclear. A pre-nuclear tone can surface as one or more accents or may be deleted/truncated. The post-nuclear tones often surface as accents or boundary tone, and form a group with the nuclear tone.

This structure can be taken to account for the hierarchical levels of accents in SC: (i) the essential part of the intonation structure is a nuclear tone, (ii) post-nuclear tone can only surface as a boundary tone in SC, (iii) the pre-nuclear tone can only surface as one accent in a given intonational phrase, and (vi) the major break in the phrase exists at the nuclear tone and all the constituents after it.

5.3.4   Underlying causes for restricting the distribution of accents

Obviously, the hierarchical structure demonstrated in the above section does not actually describes in detail how prenuclear and nuclear elements are associated with segmental strings of different metrical structure, and what is the underlying causes for the realization of the accents in the surface form. This assumption has important implications for the relation between *focus* and *accent* that is mentioned in Chapter Three. According to 'Focus-to-Accent (FTA)' theory (Gussenhoven 1983), focus is signaled by pitch accents that are assigned directly to focused words or constituents. The argument of FTA theory implies that focus can determine the appearance of accent. Different from the FTA view, Selkirk (1984)'s account of the focus-accent relation is what she calls an 'accent-first' account. According to Selkirk, focus can be identified by the appearance of pitch accent. In her model, a metrical grid representing various features of the utterance's rhythm and stress pattern is constructed for each utterance. Independently, pitch accents are assigned to individual words. The assignment of pitch accents is purely based on the syntactic-semantic constituent in accordance with the 'Focus-to-Accent' theory. The following parts are two kinds of cases that ought to be fatal counterexamples for Gussenhoven's and Selkirk's argument; namely, focus that is not signaled by accent ('focus without accent'), and accents that do not signal focus ('accent without focus'). Both cases of which occur in SC. Hereinafter, the presentation relates both *focus and accent to prosodic structure*. Specifically, evidence is presented showing that it is the *relative metrical strength* in the prosodic structure that serves as the underlying causes for determining the accent distribution in the surface form in SC.

5.3.4.1   Focus without accents

In the preceding chapter (section 4.3.2), the study alluded to the fact that the *syntax*-marked focus (*lian*-marked focus) is compressed by the rheme focus. Under that given context the target sentence '**Liu Min**[+RF] *Lian* **Mao Lan**[+LianF] *Dou* Ti Ba Le (Liumin even elevated Maolan)' , exhibits rheme focus and *lian*-marked focus on the subject and object positions, respectively. As for the accent realization in the target sentence, the rheme focus wins the conflicts with the *lian*-marked focus in the formation of the sentential accents. Therefore, the *lian*-marked focus is not signaled by accents in this case. The phenomenon of 'focus without accent' has also been shown by Ladd (1996) who proposes that many such cases in English involve prepositional phrases with pronoun or adverb objects, such as *for him* and *in there*. He pointed out that these two words can of course occur with pitch accent on either word, but exactly the same focus distinctions can be made when the entire phrase is completely de-accented. Under this case, focus is not signalled by accent, but by other phonetic cues such as duration and vowel quality. From this evidence, accents do not always respond directly to focus.

5.3.4.2   Accents without focus

Although the present experiment has not provided any evidence of 'accent without focus', in the study of accent distribution in the *shi*-construction of SC, Jia et al (2009) propose that accent is not always determined by focus. This phenomenon is exemplified through the accent distribution on the word 'Beijing' in the target sentence 'Jiao4 Ta1 Qü4 Bei3 Jing1 De0 Shi4 Wo3 (It is me that asked him to go to Beijing).' The study argues that the focus in the utterance is symbolized by the marker *shi,* and that the accent on the word is induced by other causes. Selkirk (1984) has provided evidence for 'accent without focus' in English. She mentions that single word utterances such as *California* can constitute the focus in a single-word utterance, and therefore, it should have a pitch accent. Unfortunately, it frequently has two pitch accents, one on the primary stressed syllable *-for-* and one on the secondary stressed syllable *Cal-*. Selkirk admitts that she had no explanation for the 'additional' accent.

5.3.4.3   A metrical account of accent distribution

Evidence of 'focus without accent' and 'accent without focus' in SC demonstrate that sentence-level prominence is not a primarily matter of where accent is located, but involves a specification of a relatively 'strong or weak' relation in the prosodic structure that determines the distribution of the accent in the surface form.

The search for the theory of a '*w-s*' relation in the metrical structure is the work within what has come to be known as metrical phonology. Metrical phonology begins with Liberman's (1977) notation that linguistic prominence crucially involves a *relation* between nodes in a binary-branching tree. According to Liberman and Prince (1977), in any such relation one node is strong and the other weak: permit (verb) '*w-s*'and permit (noun) '*s-w.*'

It is important to emphasize that absolute degree of prominence is not implied by the labels 'strong' and 'weak.' There is no direct phonetic interpretation whatsoever of either label, but only of the entire structure. What the notation means is that one node is structurally stronger than the other; this relative strength may be manifested phonetically in a great variety of ways. Liberman and Prince (1975) further proposed the Designated Terminal Element (DTE for short) to analyze the accent realization in the surface form. Within this theory, the pitch accent in

English is determined in both citation and sentence-level by 'DTE.'

Ladd (1996) adopts the 'DTE' to distinguish between the accent realization of *broad focus* and *narrow focus*[79] conditions. He takes the phrase 'Five France' as an example, and pointed out that the broad focus condition is '*w-s*' with the word 'France' as the accent bearing unit. As for the narrow focus condition, the relation is '*s-w*' and the accent locates on the word 'five.'

The present study also adopts the DTE to analyze accent realization in the surface form in SC. Evidence in chapter three and chapter four strongly indicate that the DTE in a given unit serves as the anchor for primary accent realization in the surface form. The observations are: (i) the single focus (rheme focus or *syntax*-marked focus) pattern in SC can be generated as 's-w,' since the focused constituent bears the *nuclear accent* and the pitch registers of the following items are compressed; (ii) under a double focus condition (theme focus vs. rheme focus and *syntax*-marked focus vs. rheme focus), the primary accent is always related with the DTE focused item; and (iii) in a multiple focus environment, although there are more than two constituents serving as the rheme focus, the only accent is due to the DTE.

All of the above observations suggest that the metrical structure of SC is presented as '*w-s*' that is, the rightmost position is the metrically strongest position. Xu (2004) proposes that, compared with the focus in European languages that have a systematic manifestation in pitch accents, Chinese is a language in which there is a reverse relationship between syntactic positioning and phonological prominence of focus. It is the sentence-final position, and usually the most deeply embedded position on the recursive side of branching, where dwells the informational focus as default in Chinese. As for the phonetic realization of the five-syllable constituents of SC, Jia et al (2008) argue that the final syllable of a constituent exhibits the greatest magnitude of F_0 prominence and

---

[79] The deifinition of broad and narrow focus is in chapter one.

durational lengthening. Thus, the rightmost position is considered to be the metrically strongest position in SC, and is the underlying cause for determining the magnitude of phonetic realization.

5.4 Discussion

The phonological representation of accent patterns and underlying causes for restricting the accent distribution are mainly dealt with in this Chapter. The intonation phenomena discussed here are shown to bear on important issues of intonation structure. On the one hand, the accent patterns of SC have contributed to two long-standing debates: the classifications of the nuclear tone and prenuclear tone, and the hierarchical structures of accents. On the other hand, they have strengthened the views of the non-bidirectional relation between *focus* and *accent* in languages. Based on these observations the phonological description of accent realization in SC can be expressed as: (i) single focus condition: [Focus]→[Nuclear accent]; (ii) dual focus condition: [Focus]→[Nuclear accent] /_ [DET]; [Focus]→[Prenuclear accent]/_ [Non-DET]; (iii) multiple focus condition: [Focus]→[Nuclear accent] / _ [DET].

Chapter Six

OT Analysis of Tonal Structure

6.1 Introduction

Optimality Theory (OT) is a grammatical model that aims to explain the relation between the underlying forms and the surface representation (Prince and Smolensky 1993, McCarthy and Prince 1993, McCarthy and Prince 1995, Kager 1999, McCarthy 2002). Previous studies using OT in an analysis of SC mainly concentrate on the word level, in particular, the analysis of tone sandhi in various dialects of SC. For example, Wang (2002) proposes that the classical generative phonology cannot provide a satisfactory explanation of the tone sandhi disyllabic sequences in the Tianjin dialect and analyzes the phenomenon through a series of ranked constraints. Also within the framework of OT, Ma (2005) investigated the direction of tone sandhi of tri-syllabic constituents in the Tianjin dialect and provides a satisfactory solution to this paradox. As for the OT analysis of other dialects, Ma et al (2009) examines the tone sandhi of the disyllabic words in the Nanjing dialect. Ma argues that tone sandhi plays a key role in tonal shape, and tone sandhi in tonal register explains the differences between the old and new Nanjing dialects.

In the prsent section, it deals with the post-lexical phenomenon in SC under the model of OT. Specifically, this goal is approached through three steps: (i) the analysis of accent pattern generation; i.e. H^*, L^*, LH^* or H^*L, (ii) the association of the accent, and (iii) the location of the prosodic boundary. All the constraints adopted to explain accent related issues come from the study of Gussenhoven (2004).

194

6.2   Grammatical model of OT

The central idea of OT is that surface forms of a language reflect resolutions of conflicts between competing demands or *constraints*. A surface form is 'optimal' in the sense that it incurs the least serious violations of a set of violable constraints ranked in a *language-specific* hierarchy. Constraints are universal, and directly encode markedness statements and principles enforcing the preservation of contrasts. Languages differ in the ranking of constraints, giving priorities to some constraints over others. Such rankings are based on 'strict' domination: if one constraint outranks another, the higher-ranked constraints have priority, regardless of violations of the lower-ranked constraint. However, such a violation must be minimal. This condition predicts the *economy* property of grammatical processes.

OT is a development of Generative Grammar, a theory that deals with formal description and a quest for universal principles, on the basis of empirical research of linguistic typology and first language acquisition. However, OT differs radically from earlier generative models in various ways. To accommodate cross-linguistic variation within a theory of Universal Grammar, OT assumes that universal constraints are violable, while earlier models assumed 'parametric' variation of inviolate principles. Moreover, OT is surface-based in the sense that well-formedness constraints evaluate surface forms only, no structural conditions are placed on lexical forms. Earlier models have assumed Morpheme Structure Constraints, resulting in the duplication of static and dynamic rules in phonotactics. In contrast, OT entirely abandons the notion of a rewrite rule, dissociating 'triggers' and 'repairs.' This serves to explain conspiracies: multiple processes triggered by a single output-oriented goal. Finally, OT also eliminates derivations, replacing these with parallelism: all constraints pertaining to some type of structure are evaluated within a single hierarchy. OT is not a theory of representations, but a theory of interactions of grammatical principles. More accurately, the issue of representations exhibits similarities to that of constraint interaction. Therefore, the divergence from earlier generative models is less clear-cut in this respect.

OT comprises a component G_{val} that freely generates a large set of candidate output forms by improvising on the input form. The set of possible output forms generated by G_{EN} is vetted by the constraints in a process known as [E_{Val}]. The set of universal constraints, referred to as $C_{ONSTRAINS}$, is ranked for the language in question, and it is this ranking that constitutes the language's grammar. E_{VAL} involves taking the total group of competing output forms produced by G_{EN} to the highest constraint, allowing it to remove forms from the set, and taking the remainder to the next highest, and so on. Any form that violates it more where one or more other forms violate it less, is discarded from the set of competing candidates. Whenever more than one forms violates the same constraint in equal measure, these all proceed to the next constraint, for as long as is needed for a single, winning candidate to emerge.

6.3   Constraints in the analysis

6.3.1   Markedness constraints

Two classes of markedness constraints are OCP and NoC_{ONTOUR}. The Obligatory Contour Principle (OCP) (Goldsmith 1976, with reference to Leben 1973) militates against the occurrence of adjacent like tones. The strictest interpretation occurs in Bengali that disallows any *L...L* or *H...H* regardless of far apart their targets are. The OCP is functionally explained by the lack of contrast presented by sequences of similar signals. That is, the hearer is best served by acoustic differences, and thus repeating phonological elements is not in the hearer's interest (Flemming

1995, Boersma 1998). Articulatory motivations are behind the class of markedness constraints generally referred to as NoC$_{ONTOUR}$ that ban complexity in tonal representations. Again, there are more or less lenient enforcements with *LHL* being more marked than *HL*. NoC$_{ONTOUR}$ bans associations of more than one tone with the same TBU. Some languages with moraic associations curb tonal complexity within the syllable even though no tone is multiply associated. There are also two markedness constraints, NoR$_{ISE}$ and NoF$_{ALL}$, that forbid *LH* and *HL* contours within the syllable.

6.3.2   Faithfulness constraints

There are three faithfulness constraint 'families' that formulas with variables:

(i)   MAX-IO(Element[80]): 'Maximality': Every element in the input has a correspondent in the output that disallows deletion.

(ii)   IDENT(Element): stipulates that any element in the output should be a faithful reproduction of the corresponding element in the input.

(iii)   DEP(Element): forbids insertion: every element in the output has a corresponding element in the input.

6.3.3   Association constraints

Anttila and Bodomo (2000) create associations with the help of a constraint family requiring TBUs to be associated with a tone, TBU←T and another requiring tones to be associated with TBUs, T→TBU. These constraints have the combined effect that exactly *one* tone is associated with a TBU and exactly *one* TBU is associated with a tone, respectively.

---

[80] By 'element', Gussenhoven (2004) refers to any phonological substance, such as a feature, a segment, a tone, an accent, a constituent such as an intermediate phrase or intonation phrase, but not a relation such as association or an alignment.

Further, Gussenhoven (2000) also proposed separate constraints banning and spreading contouring: NoSPREAD and NoCROWD, respectively. These five constraints are described as:

(i)   TBU←T: TBUs are associated with T[81];

(ii)   T→TBU: Tones are associated with TBU;

(iii)   NoS$_{PREAD}$: A tone is associated with only one TBU;

(iv)   NoC$_{ROWD}$: A TBU is associated with only one tone;

(v)   NoA$_{SSOC}$: TBUs are not associated with tone.

6.3.4   Alignment constraints

The alignment of the tonal feature associates with some constituents also be analyzed the interaction of constraints. Selkirk (2000) captures the feature in English based on the following constraints:

(i)   WRAPXP[82]: requires that be contained in a single major phrase;

(ii)   ALIGNXP: requires that the boundary aligns with the right boundary of the prosodic domain;

(iii)   ALIGNFOC: requires that the boundary right aligns with the focused constituent.

6.4   OT analysis of accent patterns

The phonological representation of accent patterns of SC as generated in section 5.3.2.2, is dealt with in the framework of OT. Based on the inventory of the types of accents, the accent features are analyzed according to the tonal combinations of the focused constituents: H^*, L^*, LH^* and H^*L. The central tone is assigned to the H target in the sequence 'LH^*' and 'H^*L' due to the phonetic realizations of the focused items that are mainly manifested on the H feature in SC.

---

[81] 'T' is the abbreviation for tone.

[82] 'XP' denotes any syntactic component.

The constraints adopted in this section are: (i) OCP, (ii) NoC$_{\text{ONTOUR}}$, (iii) IDENT(Element), (iv) TBU←T, (v) T→TBU, and (v) ALIGNXP. When the order is arranged differently, it can generate different types of accents. For an analysis of accent patterns, the underlying form of each target syllable is assumed to be '*LH*'.

6.4.1   Generation of H* tone

Table 6.4.1.1 provides the process of the generation of the accent pattern of H*. The top part of the table displays the ranked constraints and the left part, which is separated by the two solid lines, is the candidates. The symbol "*" in the table indicates the validation of the constraints. When a candidate violates a higher ranked constraint and is eliminates by the constraint, it is marked by the symbol "!". As for the optimal candidate, it is expressed by the sign "☞".

In the above table, the ranking of the constraints are: OCP >> NoF$_{\text{ALL}}$ >> No$_{\text{RISE}}$ >> ALIGN(*, Rt) >> ALIGN(*, Left) >> H*→TBU >> L*→TBU >> MAX-IO(LH). According to these constraints, the accent patterns '*HH**', '*H*H*', "*LL**" and '*L*L*' violate the OCP that requires that identical tonal feature can not connect with each other. Thus, these four accents are deleted by the constraints. The two falling tones, *H*L* and *HL**, the two rising tones, *LH** and *L*H* violate the constraints 'NoF$_{\text{ALL}}$' and 'No$_{\text{RISE}}$', therefore, they are eliminated in the competitions. Compared with the *L** and *H** tones, the former one violates H*→TBU, L*→TBU, and MAX-IO(LH), and the latter only violates the last two constraints; thereafter, the *H** wins over the competition and serve as the optimal candidate with least violation of the constraints.

Tableau 6.4.1.1 H* tone generation

(LH, σ)	OCP	NoFALL	NoRISE	ALIGN(*,Rt)	ALIGN(*,Left)	H*→TBU	L*→TBU	MAX-IO(LH)
σ | ☞ H*							*	*
σ | L*						*!	*	*
σ /\ H H*	*!				*		*	*
σ /\ H* H	*!			*			*	*
σ /\ L L*	*!				*	*		*
σ /\ L* L	*!				*	*		*
σ /\ L H*			*!		*			
σ /\ L* H			*!	*		*	*	
σ /\ H L*		*!			*	*		
σ /\ H* L		*!			*		*	

6.4.2 Generation of L* tone

The following table demonstrates the process of the generation of the L* accent in SC. The constraints are identical with the previous part, only the ranking is varied. The symbols in the table bear the same implications as the previous one.

Tableau 6.4.2.1 L* tone generation

(LH, σ)	OCP	NoF$_{ALL}$	NoR$_{ISE}$	ALIGN (*,Rt)	ALIGN (*,Left)	L*→TBU	H*→TBU	MAX-IO (LH)
σ | H*						*!		*
σ | ☞ L*							*	*
σ ∧ H H*	*!				*	*		*
σ ∧ H* H	*!			*		*		*
σ ∧ L L*	*!				*		*	*
σ ∧ L* L	*!			*				*
σ ∧ L H*			*!		*	*		
σ ∧ L* H			*!	*			*	
σ ∧ H L*		*!			*		*	
σ ∧ H* L		*!			*	*		

The generation of the L* tone shows only a slender difference with the process of *H** tone generation. The bi-tonal constituents, *HH*, H*H, LL*, L*L, LH*, L*H, H*L,* and *HL*, are eliminated from the ranked constraints: 'OCP >> NoF$_{ALL}$ >> No$_{RISE}$ >> ALIGN(*, Rt) >> ALIGN(*, Left)'. The deletion of the *H** tone is due to the violation of the higher constraint 'L*→TBU' compared with the *L** tone, therefore, the L* tone is the optimal candidate.

6.4.3　Generation of LH* tone

Crucially, in the discussion of the accent pattern of the contour tones, the level tones are deleted in the first step. Then, the contour tone with the feature of '*HL*' is ruled out. When the rising tone is left for further competition, the constraints of 'ALIGN(*, Rt)' and 'ALIGN(*, Left)' are adopted to eliminate the incorrect association of the central tone.

Examination of table 6.4.3.1 shows that the bi-tonal targets of level tones such as *HH**, *H**H, *LL** and *L**L are excluded due to violation of OCP. The single tonal features *H** and *L** are deleted by the 'MAX-IO(LH) constraint,' since the *H** and *L** reduces the feature of *L* and *H*, respectively. Further, the falling tone of '*H**L' and '*HL**' violate the 'NoF$_{ALL}$' constraint of 'NoF$_{ALL}$', which that outranks the 'No$_{RISE}$' constraint, thus they are ruled out. Then, the location of the central tone that associates with the *H* or *L* tone on the *LH* sequence is determined. Due to the higher ranking of the 'ALIGN(*, Rt)' constraint over the 'ALIGN(*, Left)' constraint, '*L**H' is deleted and '*LH**' is left as the optimal candidate.

Table 6.4.3.1 LH* tone generation

(LH, σ)	OCP	MAX-IO (LH)	NoF_ALL	NoRI SE	ALIGN (*, Rt)	ALIGN (*,Left)	H*→TBU	L*→TBU
σ │ H*		*!						*
σ │ L*		*!					*	*
σ ∧ H H*	*!	*				*		*
σ ∧ H* H	*!	*			*			*
σ ∧ L L*	*!	*				*	*	
σ ∧ L* L	*!	*			*		*	
☞ σ ∧ L H*				*		*		*
σ ∧ L* H				*	*!		*	
σ ∧ H L*			*!			*	*	
σ ∧ H* L			*!			*		*

6.4.4   Generation of H*L tone

In the generation of 'H*L', the important steps to approach the goal are to rule out the tonal sequences of 'H', 'L', 'HH', 'LL' and 'LH'.

Tableau 6.4.4.1　H*L tone generation

(LH, σ)	OCP	MAX-IO(LH)	No_RISE	NoF_ALL	ALIGN (*,Left)	ALIGN (*, Rt)	H*→TBU	L*→TBU
σ | H*		*!						*
σ | L*		*!					*	*
σ /\ H H*	*!				*			*
σ /\ H* H	*!					*		*
σ /\ L L*	*!				*		*	
σ /\ L* L	*!					*	*	
σ /\ L H*			*!		*			*
σ /\ L* H			*!			*	*	
σ /\ H L*				*!	*		*	
σ /\ ☞H* L				*				*

Based on the above argument, when the constraints are rank as: OCP >> MAX-IO(LH) >> No_RISE >> NoF_ALL, the tonal sequences of '*H*', '*L*', '*HH*', '*LL*' and '*LH*' can be ruled out. Then, the ranking 'ALIGN(*, Left)' >> 'ALIGN(*, Rt)' is emloyed to determine the association of the central tone that is located on the *H* tone in the *HL* sequence.

6.5   OT analysis of accent distributions

This section is concerned with the search of the rankings in the OT framework for the analysis of the accent distribution in SC. As mentioned in chapter three and chapter four, *nuclear accent* corresponds with single-focus condition (rheme focus, *lian*-marked focus, and *shi*-marked focus) with the accent distributing on the positions of subject, verb, object, or subject and object.

The constraints used to analyze the accent distribution phenomenon are: (i) NOASSOC, (ii) ALIGNXP, and (iii) T→TBU. The constraints are ranked differently to analyze the different location of the accents, since the accent pattern is determined by tonal combinations of the constituents. The distribution of accent shows no corresponding relation with the accent pattern; therefore, we adopt '*LH**' as an anchor to investigate the distribution of the accents.

6.5.1   Accent on subject position

Acoustic evidence of rheme focus, *lian*-marked focus, and *shi*-marked focus has shown that focus status on the subject can trigger *nuclear accent* with the whole register being obviously raised. In this *sub*-section, the accent distribution is mainly discussed under the model of OT. The basic word order of the target sentence, the underlying form of the accent distribution, is designed to associate with all the three syntactic components. Specifically, subject, verb, and object are each set to have the accent pattern *LH**. The top part of the table displays the ranked constraints and the left most column provides all the possible candidates in the surface form. The symbol '☞' indicates the optimal candidate.

Table 6.5.1.1 Accent on subject position

(LH*+LH*+LH*, σσσ)	ALIGN (LH*,Left)	NOASSOC	LH*→TBU	ALIGN (LH*,Mi)	ALIGN (LH*,Rt)
(S) (V) (O) σ σ σ, ☞L H*		*	**	*	*
(S) (V) (O) σ σ σ, L H*	*!		**		*
(S) (V) (O) σ σ σ, L H*	*!	*	**	*	
(S) (V) (O) σ σ σ, L H*L H*		**!	*		*
(S) (V) (O) σ σ σ, L H* L H*		**!	*	*	
(S) (V) (O) σ σ, L H*L H*	*!	**	*		

In table 6.5.1.1, A_{LIGN}(LH*, Left) is ranked in the highest position to rule out the incorrect distribution of the accent on the verb and constituents. This constraint can also exclude the association of the accents on the verb and object positions. Apart from the A_{LIGN}(LH*, Left) constraint, the constraint that locates immediately following the previous constraint is NOASSOC, which requires no association of the on the tonal bearing unit. Therefore, the *LH** locating on the subject position violates this constraint once, and the *LH** feature distributes in subject and verb, also subject and object violates the constraint twice. Also, the candidates of the distribution on the subject win over the competitions. In this research, although no evidences on the distribution of the accent on verb element is provided, the verb can be taken as the accent bearing anchor in SC. This results can be analyzed from the ranking of 'ALIGN(LH*,Mi)>> NOASSOC>> LH*→TBU>> ALIGN(LH*,Left) >> ALIGN(LH*,Rt)'.

6.5.2   Accent on object position

Within both unmarked structure and *lian*-marked structure in previous chapters, the object items have the *nuclear accents* due to the effect from the rheme focus. This sub-part is applied to investigate the accent distribution on the object constituent. Table 6.5.2.1 displays the constraints and the results.

The constraints for the generation of the accent on the object constituent exhibit a similar nature with the accent on the subject constituent. The only difference lies in the constraint 'A$_{LIGN(LH*, Rt)}$' that requires the accent to associate with the right most constituent. When this constraint ranks in the highest position, the candidates with the accent on the subject, verb, and both the subject and verb positions are excluded in the competition. The association of the accents on the subject and object positions, and the verb and the object positions are also ruled out for twice violating the constraint NOASSOC.

Table 6.5.2.1 Accent on object position

(LH*+LH*+LH*, σσσ)	ALIGN(LH*, Right)	NOASSOC	LH*→TBU	ALIGN (LH*, Left)	ALIGN (LH*,Mi)
(S) (V) (O) σ σ σ L H* (under V)	*!	*	**		*
(S) (V) (O) σ σ σ L H* (under O-side)	*!	*	**	*	
☞ (S) (V) (O) σ σ σ L H* (under O)		*	**	*	*
(S) (V) (O) σ σ σ L H* L H*	*!	**	*		
(S) (V) (O) σ σ σ L H* L H*		**!			*
(S) (V) (O) σ σ L H*L H*		**!	*	*	

6.5.3 Accents on subject and object positions

Under double focus condition; i.e., theme focus vs. rheme focus, *lian*-marked focus vs. rheme focus, addition of *lian*-marked focus vs. rheme focus, rheme focus vs. addition of *lian*-marked focus, and rheme focus locating on the subject and object constituents, there are two accents on the surface form. The *nuclear accent* is always lead by the rightmost focus with the proceeding one serving as the *pre-nuclear accent.*

Table 6.5.3.1   Accents on subject and object positions

(LH*+LH*+LH*, σσσ)	ALIGN (LH*,Left)	ALIGN (LH*,Rt)	NOASSOC	LH*→TBU	ALIGN (LH*,Mi)
(S) (V) (O) σ σ σ L H*		*!	*	**	*
(S) (V) (O) σ σ σ L H*	*!	*	*		
(S) (V) (O) σ σ σ L H*	*!		*	**	*
(S) (V) (O) σ σ σ L H* L H*		*!	**	*	
☞ (S) (V) (O) σ σ σ L H* L H*			**	*	*
(S) (V) (O) σ σ L H* L H*	*!		**	*	

In Table 6.5.3.1, the single accent patterns; i.e., on subject, verb, and object positions are ruled out by the higher level of constraints ALIGN(LH*,Left) >> ALIGN(LH*,Rt). The distribution of the dual accents on the subject and verb constituents, and verb and objects are also eliminated by the constraints ALIGN(LH*,Left) >> ALIGN(LH*,Rt). The optimal candidate is the accent pattern with the *nuclear accent* on the object and *pre-nuclear accent* on the subject.

6.6　OT analysis of prosodic phrasing

The results of the acoustic experiments have shown that the right edge of the focus, roughly the theme focus, rheme focus, or *syntax*-marked focus tend to coincide with some prosodic constituents. Specifically, there is an intermediate phrase-boundary after the focused constituents that is mainly trigger by the lengthening of the final syllable of the focused words. Since the intermediate phrase boundary also associates with the focused constituent, the target sentence 'Lian2 Liu2 Min2 Dou1 Ti2　Ba2 Mao2 Lan2 Le0 (Even Liumin elevated Maolan)' , is taken as an example for prosodic phrasing analysis. The top part of Table 6.6.1 depicts the constraints for the analysis of the prosodic phrasing phenomenon. The left column displays the target sentence with all the possible phrasing locations in the sentence. The symbol 'I' denotes the intermediate phrase boundary.

The ranking of the constraints for prosodic phrasing: ALIGNFoc >> ALIGN(Word) >> WRAPXP. The phrasings located on the positions of the non-post-focus are eliminated by the constraint of ALIGNFoc. The phrasing that distributes within the focus scopc, and not the boundary of the prosodic word, is deleted by the constraint 'ALIGN(Word).' Thus, the candidate with the prosodic boundary distributing after the focus and coinciding with prosodic word boundary is the optimal option with the violation of the lowest rank of constraint.

Tableau 6.6.1 Prosodic phrasing

(Lian2Liu2Min2Dou1Ti2 Ba2Mao2Lan2Le0)	ALIGNFoc	ALIGN(Word)	WRAPXP
(Lian2) Liu2Min2Dou1Ti2Ba2Mao2Lan2Le0)	*!		*
(Lian2Liu2) Min2Dou1T2 Ba2Mao2Lan2Le0)		*!	*
(Lian2Liu2Min2Dou1) T2 Ba2Mao2Lan2Le0)	*!		*
☞(Lian2Liu2Min2) Dou1Ti2Ba2Mao2Lan2Le0)			*
(Lian2Liu2Min2Dou1Ti2) Ba2Mao2Lan2Le0)	*!		*
(Lian2Liu2Min2Dou1Ti2Ba2) Mao2Lan2Le0)	*!		*
(Lian2Liu2Min2Dou1Ti2Ba2Mao2) Lan2Le0)	*!		*
(Lian2Liu2Min2Dou1Ti2Ba2Mao2Lan2) Le0)	*!		*

6.7   Discussion

This chapter mainly deals with the accent pattern, accent distribution, and prosodic phrasing effect of focus in SC under the framework of OT. This research goal is approached through three steps: (i) different accent patterns are generated by the same constraints with various rankings; specifically,

a.   **H***: OCP>>NoFALL>>NoRISE>>ALIGN(*,Rt)>>ALIGN(*,Left)
      >>$H^* \rightarrow$TBU>>$L^* \rightarrow$TBU>>MAX-IO(LH),

b. **L***: OCP>>NoFALL>>NoRISE>>ALIGN(*,Rt)>>ALIGN(*,Left)>>
→TBU>>*H**→TBU>>MAX-IO(*LH*),

c. **LH***: OCP>>MAX-IO(*LH*)>>NoFALL>> NoRISE>>ALIGN(*,
Rt) >>ALIGN(*,Left) >>*H**→TBU>>*L**→TBU,

d. **H*L**: OCP>>MAX-IO(*LH*) >>NoRISE>> NoFALL ALIGN(*,Left)
>>ALIGN(*, Rt) >>*H**→TBU>>*L**→TBU,

(ii) identical constraints are also adopted to analyze the accent
association:

a. **Subject**: ALIGN(*LH**,Left) >>NOASSOC >>*LH** → TBU
>>ALIGN(*LH**,Mi)>> ALIGN(*LH**,Rt),

b. **Object**: LIGN(*LH**,Left)>>NOASSOC>>*LH**TBU>>ALIGN(*LH**,Left)
>>ALIGN(*LH**,Mi),

c. **Subject and object:** ALIGN(*LH**,Left) >>ALIGN(*LH**,Rt)
>>NOASSOC>>*LH**→TBU >>ALIGN(*LH**,Mi)

(iii) prosodic phrasing locating after the focus is generated from the
following constraints: ALIGNFoc>>ALIGN(Word) >>WRAPXP.

Chapter Seven

Concluding Remarks

The present chapter will summarize the main findings of the research and will discusse, from a cross-linguistic perspective, some of their implications for the understanding of prosodic effects of the focus and intonation structure of SC. It will also give some of the suggestions and ideas of what need to be done in the future research.

7.1　Major findings

The major goal of this research to address the relation between the intonation structure, prosodic structure, and focus in SC. It is mainly concerned with the following aspects: (i) the examination of the acoustic manifestations of different kinds and numbers of focuses in SC, (ii) the phonological description and analysis of accent patterns conveyed by the focus under discussion, (iii) the hierarchical structures of accents with the relation between *focus distribution* and *accent distribution* being accessed within the framework of Prosodic Hierarchy Theory, the Autosegmetal-metrical Theory of Intonational Phonology, and Optimality Theory. The chosen approach was both theoretical and empirically based, along the lines of laboratory phonology research.

In chapter two, the methodology adopted in this research is described. Both the acoustic and perceptual experiments have been explored in this research with the aim of exploring the accent patterns induced by different kinds (*syntax*-marked focus or information induced focus) and numbers (single, double, or multiple) of focuses in SC. It describes in detail the experimental procedures: the selection of the experimental materials (including the selection of the syntactic structure and the composing elements), the implementation of the intended focus conditions, the recording procedure, and the measures of the "wav" files.

In chapter three and four various types of evidence were considered in the investigation of the accent patterns of SC. In chapter three, the acoustic effects of one or more focuses upon F_0 and durational patterns in unmarked structures are examined. The conclusions are: (i) single rheme focus realizes with F_0 raising and durational lengthening *under-focus* position and F_0 compression of the *post-focus* constituents. Tonal combinations only contribute to the specific manner of the prominence that exerts no influence on the distribution of the prominence; (ii) double focus can trigger F_0 raising and durational lengthening simultaneously; i.e., theme focus vs. rheme focus, and double rheme focus. However, different focus levels (TF vs. RF[1]) can lead to different magnitudes of acoustic manifestations with the primary focus being marked by the greatest magnitude of acoustic performances. On the other hand, dual rheme focus can induce similar acoustic realizations in the under-focus positions.

As for the constituents between the two focuses, they show no lowering; (iii) multiple rheme focuses can not lead to multiple prominences, with the rightmost focus serving as the only anchor to realize prominence in the surface form; (iv) the phonological explanation to analyze the surface the acoustic performances are *nuclear accents* and *pre-nuclear accents*. The *nuclear accent* is the obligatory part of the intonation contour and its distribution is usually determined by the rightmost focus. The *pre-nuclear accent* is the substrings of the contour that can resemble contours with the *nuclear accent*, but its appearance is optional and in the position proceeding the *nuclear accent*; (v) the focus also shows phrasing effect on the intonation that reconstructs the intonation into two intermediate phrases.

---

[1] As is mentioned in chapter one, the primary focus is rheme focus, and theme focus occupies the secondary focus position.

In chapter four, the acoustic cues for symbolizing the *syntax*-marked focus in SC were the main concern. The intonation patterning was established based on the following findings: a) regardless of the kinds of focus marker (*shi* or *lian*), the constituents marked by *lian* or *shi* exhibit similar acoustic effect with the *wh*-question elicited focus; therefore, under a single focus condition, the *syntax*-marked focus can trigger *nuclear accent* at the phrasal level; b) the *syntax*-marked focus can co-exist with the *wh*-elicited focus on the same syntactic component to induce a greater magnitude of F_0 raising and durational lengthening for the *nuclear accent*; c) *syntax*-marked focus can distribute in the position proceeding the *wh*-elicited focus to realize *pre-nuclear accent* and *nuclear accent* in the surface form; d) when the *syntax*-marked focus locates after the *wh*-elicited focus, the accent is compressed completely with other phonetic cues to mark the existence of the *syntax*-marked focus; e) the *syntax*-marked focus also reorganizes the intonation structure into the intermediate phrases.

In chapter five, the intonation structures of SC were established based on the following phonetic facts: (i) the consistent presence of focus-related F_0 raising and durational lengthening; (ii) the distinction between *nuclear accent* and *pre-nuclear accent*; (iii) the selection of a special accent to express focus, whether the focus is early or late; (iv) the consistent phrasing effects from different kinds of focuses. The intonation pattern of SC is constructed in the linear sequence by the categorical distinctive phonological events: *nuclear tone, pre-nuclear tone, onset* and *boundary tone*. The essential property of the nuclear tone and boundary tone are the obligatoriness and uniqueness in the contour, while the pre-nuclear tone and onset are of the nature of optional. This suggests that the relation between the nuclear tone and the pre-nuclear tone is essentially a matter of the relation between the primary accent and secondary accent. As to the underlying causes for restricting the distribution of the *nuclear accent* and *pre-nuclear accent* in the surface form, it is determined by the metrical structure of SC that tends to be 'strong-weak' under a single focus condition and *'weak-strong'* under dual focus conditions. Thereafter, the metrically stronger position needs to realize the nuclear accent at the phrasal level.

In chapter six, the theoretical model of Optimality Theory is adopted to analyze the generation of accent patterns in SC. A series of ranked constraints are adopted to analyze the types of accents, and the association of the accent and the phrasing distribution. With regard to accent pattern generation, the following constraints are adopted: OCP; NoFALL; NoRISE; ALIGN(*, Rt); ALIGN(*, Left); $H^* \rightarrow$ TBU; $L^* \rightarrow$ TBU;MAX-IO(*LH*). When these constraints rank differently, various types of accent patterns can be generated; i.e., H^*, L^*, LH^* and H^*L. As for the association of the accents, the constraints are: ALIGN(*LH**, Left); NOASSOC; $LH^* \rightarrow$ TBU; ALIGN(*LH**, Mi); ALIGN(*LH**, Rt). To analyze the phrasing phenomena, the constraints are: ALIGNFoc; ALIGN(Word); WRAPXP.

7.2   The cross-linguistic perspective

The prosodic reflexes of focus in SC were shown to be prominence-related effects, and crucially, not phrasing effects. Specifically, focus is found to be phonologically expressed by means of the phrasal accent pattern and the selection of a particular accent type, while the prosodic phrasing is at the intermediate phrase level.

As noted in the introduction to this research (section 1.2.3.3 in particular), there are two reports on two main types of effects induced by focus in prosodic literature: (i) accent effects and (ii) phrasing effects. The former have been reported to play a crucial role in languages such as English and Italian. The latter have been claimed to conspicuously cue focus in languages such as Hausa and Korean. Furthermore, in these languages focus seems to determine phrasing in a basic and strict way, and is thus included in the language phrasing algorithms. In contrast, a focus effect on phrasing in languages of the English or Italian type seems to be best expressed by reconstructing conditions that affect, and therefore presuppose, 'default' phrasing. Clearly, SC is taken to instantiate a clear case of the type of language that behaves like Hausa with regard to accent effects, and like Korean with regard to phrasing effects.

The phonological properties noted above can be taken as language universals concerning the way in which intonation features are organized. As (Type I) shows: on the one hand, English and Italian are all 'intonation' languages (in the sense that they have post-lexical pitch accents associated with stressed positions); on the other hand, (Type II) languages such as Hausa and Korean, have both lexical tone and intonation properties. The two types of languages are described as follows:

(i)   **Type I**: English: Pitch accents,

(2 levels of) boundary tones

Italian: Pitch accents,

(2 levels of) boundary tones

Type II: Hausa: Lexical tones and intonational properties

Korean: No stress accent, (post-lexical) intonation

properties and boundary tones

(Sources: Beckman and Pierrehumbert 1986, Grice 1995, Inkelas and Leben 1973, Jun 1996).

These two types of languages are generally distinguished; specifically, in Type I, irrespective of the various approaches to focus phenomena; the phonological means of focus is always present. There is no clear and visible focus morphology and syntax, and the phonological means suffice to mark a constituent as focused. In Type II, this place is taken by specific focus-related syntax and/or morphology. Notably, in those types of languages, phonological phenomena are reported to be insufficient to render a constituent focused. Putting these two pieces together, there seems to be a correlation between the kind of prosodic reflexes of focus found in a language and its focus related morpho-syntax. Phrasing effects crucially cue focus in languages, such as Hausa and Korean, that are known to realize focus in a particular syntactic position in sentence structure (and that in some cases may also use morphological focus markers). These cases are described in studies on the morphological marker and structural focus position of Hausa (Zec and Inkelas 1990, Kiss 1995).

SC presents itself as a Type II language. Evidence in both Chapter Three and Chapter Four have shown that the post-lexical intonation features (*nuclear accent* and *pre-nuclear accent*) and syntactic approach (focus marker *shi* and *lian*) are taken to mark focus in SC. Xu (2004) also claims that informational focus is always grammatically realized in natural languages, but in different ways across languages. Compared with the focus in European languages, that have a systematic manifestation in pitch accents, SC is a language in which there is a reverse relationship between syntactic positioning and phonological prominence of focus. It is the sentence-final position, and usually the most deeply embedded position on the recursive side of branching, where the informational focus resides as default in SC. Phonological realization is a compensatory device where the expression intended to be focused cannot occur in the default position due to some structural limitation. All of these observations suggest, in one way or another, SC is characterized by the intonation properties of languages like Hausa and Korean.

7.3　Suggestions for future research

In the two previous sections, significant major areas of research that should inform future work on the syntax-phonology interface on SC have been suggested. Namely, the extent of interlanguage variation concerning the syntax-phonology mapping conditions (illustrated by the *end-based* and the *relation-based* proposals, and the debates about the role played by branchingness as mentioned in section 1.2.2), and the study of the prosody of focus in SC from the point of view of the syntax-phonology mapping (that is, taking into consideration the presence/absence of focus-related morpho-syntactic properties).

Another important area for future work concerns the issues of intonation structure. The status of the *pre-nuclear accent* of the SC declarative tune needs clarification, and a specific intonation study addressing this issue is called for. Further work on the perception of intonation differences is also required, especially with regard to tonal alignment distinctions and the role they play in the expression of focus. An obvious approach would be to systematically vary this specific aspect of the contour by means of resynthesis of modified natural speech. Also, particularly interesting would be an investigation of whether the difference of *pre-nuclear accent* and onset in the early position of utterances in SC is in fact perceived by speakers regardless of the size of the contour excursion found in the F_0 contour.

Finally,the integration of work on prosodic phrasing with work on the phonology and phonetics of intonation has shown that the various types of phenomena observed reflect the same phrosodic structure (either the intermediate phrase or the intonational phrase levels of phrasing). This finding assigns to the prosodic hierarchy a pivotal phrase in phonological structure. However, the database needs to be enlarged with the observation of the prosodic properties of diverse sentential types before a conclusion can be drawn on the general adequacy of this view. Such improvements in the converge of the SC database is certainly a direction to pursue in future research that should also include an examination of eventual prosodic and/or intonational dialectal differences.

Bibliography

Anttila, Arto & Bodomo, Adams. 2000. Tonal polarity in Dagaare. In Carstens and Parkinsons(Eds.) *Trends in African Linguistics* 4: *Advances in African linguistics* 119-134.

Beckman, Mary & Pierrehumbert, Janet. 1986. Intonational Structure in Japanese and English. *Phonology Yearbook* 3: 255-310.

Beckman, Mary & Ayers M. Ayers. 1994. Guidelines for ToBI labelling, vers 2.0. Ms. and accompanying speech materials, Ohio State University.

Beckman, Mary & Hirschberg Julia. 1994. The ToBI annotation conventions. Ms. and accompanying speech materials, Ohio State University.

Boersma. P. 1998. *Functional Phonology: Formalizing the Interactions between Articulatory and Perceptual Drives*. The Hague: Holland Academic Graphics.

Bolinger, Dwight. 1972. Accent is predictable (if you're a mind-reader). *Language* 48: 633-644.

Bolinger, Dwight. 1972. *Intonation and Its Uses*. Stanford, California: Stanford University Press.

Bolingcr, Dwight. 1989. *Intonation and Its Uses: Melody in Grammar and Discourse*，Stanford, California: Stanford University Press.

Botinis, Antonis & Robert Bannert. 1997. Tonal perception of focus in Greek and Swedish. *Intonation: Theory, Models and Applications － Proceedings of an ESCA Workshop*, 47-50. Athens: ESCA/University of Athens.

Bruce, Gösta. 1977. *Swedish Word Accents in Sentence Perspective*. Lund: Gleerup.

Cai, Weitian (蔡维天). 2004. Tan zhi yu lian de xingshi yuyi(On the formal semantics of *zhi* or *lian*). *Chinese Language* 2: 99-111.

Cambier-Langeveld, Tina. 1999. A cross-linguistic study of accentual lengthening: Dutch vs. English. *Journal of Phonetics* 27: 255-280.

Cao, Jianfen (曹剑芬). 2002. Hanyu shengdiao yu yudiaode guanxi (The relationship between tone and intonation in Mandarin Chinese). *Chinese Language* 3: 195-202.

Cao, Jianfen (曹剑芬). 2004. Jiyu yufa xinxide hanyu Yunlü jiegou yuce (Prediction of prosodic organization based on grammatical information). *Journal of Chinese Information Processing* 3: 41-46.

Chao, Yuanren (赵元任). 1929. Beiping yudiao de yanjiu (Study of Beijing intonation). In *Chao, Yuanren yuyanxue lunwenji* (Collection of Chao, Yuanren's linguistic papers) 2002. Beijing: The Commercial Press.

Chao, Yuanren (赵元任). 1930. A system of tone letters. *Le Maître Phonétique* 45: 24-27.

Chao, Yuanren (赵元任). 1968. *A Grammar of Spoken Chinese*. Berkerley and Los Angeles: University of California Press.

Chen, Hu (陈虎). 2006. *English and Chinese Intonational Phonology: A Contrastive Study*. Henan: Henan University Press.

Chen, Matthew (陈渊泉). 1990. What must phonology know about syntax? In Sharon Inkelas and Draga Zec (eds.) *The phonology-syntax connection*, 19-46. Chicago: University of Chicargo Press.

Chen, Yiya (陈轶亚). 2003. *The Phonetics and Phonology of Corrective Focus in Standard Chinese*. PhD dissertation, State University of New York at Stony Brook, Stony Brook.

Chen, Yiya (陈轶亚). 2006. Durational adjustment under corrective focus in Standard Chinese. *Journal of Phonetics*, 34, 176-201.

Chen, Yiya (陈轶亚) & Bettina Braun. 2006. Prosodic realization of information structure categories in Standard Chinese. Speech Prosody. Dresden. Germany.

Cho, Young-mee Y. 1990. Syntax and phrasing in Korean. *The Phonology-syntax connection*, 47-62. Chicago: University of Chichago Press.

Chomsky, Noam. 1971. Deep structure, surface structure, and semantic interpretation. *Semantics —a Interdisciplinary Reader in Philosophy, Linguistics and Psychology*, 183-216. Cambridge: Cambridge University Press.

Condoravdi, Cleo. 1990. Sandi rules of Greek and prosodic theory. *The phonology-syntax connection*, 63-84. Chicargo: University of Chicargo Press.

Chu, Chauncey (屈承熹). 1998. *A Discourse Grammar of Mandarin Chinese*. New York: Peter Lang Publishing.

Cohen, Antonie & 't Hart, Johan. 1967. On the anatomy of intonation.

Lingua 19: 177-192.

Condoravdi, Cleo. 1990. Sandhi Rules of Greek and Prosodic Theory. *The phonology-syntax connection*, 63-84. Chicago: Cambridge University Press.

Cooper, William E, Eady Stephen J, & Mueller, Pamela R. 1985. *Journal of the Acoustical Society of America* 77: 2142-2156.

Cruttenden, Alen. 1992. The origins of nucleus. *Journal of the International Phonetic Association* 20: 1-9.

Crystal, David. 1969. *Prosodic Systems and Intonation in English.* Cambridge: Cambridge University Press.

Crystal, David. 1997. *A Dictionary of Linguistics and Phonetics.* Oxford: Blackwell Publishers.

Culicover, Peter W & Michael Rochemont. 1983. Stress and Focus in English. *Language* 59: 123-165.

Dik, Simon C. 1981. *Functional Grammar.* Dordrecht: Foris Publications.

Dresher, B. Elan. 1994. The prosodic basis of the Tiberian Hebrew system of accents. *Language* 70: 1-52.

Duanmu, San. 2000. *The Phonology of Standard Chinese.* New York: Oxford University Press.

Eady, Stephen & Cooper, William. 1986. Speech intonation and focus location in matched statements and questions. *Journal of the Acoustical Society of America* 80: 402-415.

Eady, Stephen & Cooper William, Klouda Gayle, Mueller Pamela & Lotts Dan. 1986. Acoustical charactcristics of sentential focus: narrow vs. broad and single vs. dual focus environments. *Language and Speech* 29: 233-251.

Eefting, W. 1991. The effect of "information value" and "accentuation" on the duration of Dutch words, syllables, and segments. *Journal of the Acoustical Society of America* 89: 412-424.

Fang, Mei (方梅). 1995. Hanyu duibi jiaodian de jufa biaoxian shouduan (The syntactic approach to mark contrastive focus in SC). *Chinese Language* 4: 279-288.

Faber, David. 1987. The accentuation of intransitive sentences in English. *Journal of Linguistics* 23: 341-358.

Féry, Caroline. 1992. Focus, Topic and Intonation in German. *Arbeitspapieredes Sonderforschungsbereichs* 340. Bericht Nr. 20.

Féry, Caroline. 1993. *German Intonational Patterns.* Tübingen: Niemeyer.

Firbas, Jan. 1964. On defining the theme in functional sentence analysis.

Tracaux Linguistiques de Prague 1: 267-280.

Firbas, Jan. 1966. Non-thematic subjects in contemporary English. *Tracaux Linguistiques de Prague* 2: 229-236.

Flemming, Edward. 1995. *Auditory Representations in Phonology*. PhD dissertation. Stanford University Press.

Frota, Sónia. 1993. On the prosody of focus in European Portuguese. *Proceedings of the Workshop on Phonology*, 45-66. Lisboa: APL.

Goldsmith, J. 1976. *Autosegmental Phonology*. PhD Dissertation. Massachusetts Institute of Technology.

Grabe, Esther, Post, Brechtje, Nolan, Francis & Farrar, Kimberley. 2000. Pitch accent realization in four varieties of British English. *Journal of Phonetics* 28: 161-185.

Gribe, Esther. 2001. The IViE labelling guide. Version 3. <http://www. phon. ox. ac. uk/esther/ivyweb/guide.html>.

Grice, Martine. 1995. *The Intonation of Interrogation in Palermo Italian: Implications for Intonation Theory*. Tübingen: Niemeyer.

Gussenhoven, Carlos. 1983. Focus, mode and nucleus. *Journal of Linguistics* 19: 377-417.

Gussenhoven, Carlos. 1984. *On the Grammar and Semantics of Sentence Accents*. Dordrecht. Foris.

Gussenhoven, Carlos. 1994. Focus and Sentence Accents in English. Focus and Natural Language Processing. *Working Papers of the Institute for Logic and Linguistics*. Heidelberg, 83-92.

Gussenhoven, Carlos. 2004. *The Phonology of Tone and Intonation*. Cambridge: Cambridge University Press.

Halliday, Michael. 1967. Notes on transitivity and theme in English. *Journal of Linguistics*, 3: 199-244.

Halliday, Michael. 1970. Language structure and language function. *New horizons in linguistics*, 140-165. Harmondsworth: Penguin.

Hayes, Bruce. 1989. The prosodic hierarchy in meter. In Paul Kiparsky and G. Youmans (eds.) Phonetics and Phonology. *Rhythm and Meter*, 201-260. New York: Academic Press.

Hayes Bruce & Aditi Lahiri. 1991. Bengali Intonational Phonology. *Natural Language and Linguistic Theory* 9: 47-96.

Hayes, Bruce and Aditi Lahiri. 1991. Bengali Intonational Phonology. *Natural Language and Lingusitic Theory* 9: 47-96.

Hirvonen, P. 1970. *Finish and English Communicative Intonation*. Publication of the Department of Phonetics, 8. University of Turku.

Ho, Yong. 1993. *Aspects of Discourse Structure in Mandarin Chinese*. Lewiston/Queenston/Lampeter: Mellen University Press.

Huang, Cheng-Teh. James (黄正德). 1982. *Logical Relation in Chinese and the Theory of Grammar*, Massachusetts Institute of Technology Doctoral dissertation, Cambridge.

Hu Jianhua (胡建华). Fouding jiaodian yu xiayu (Negation,focus and scope). *Chinese Language* 2: 99-112.

Inkelas Sharon and Draga Zec. 1995. Syntax-phonology Interface. In John Goldsmith (ed.) *The Handbook of Phonological Theory*, 535-549. Cambridge, Massachusetts: Blackwell.

Itô, Junko & Mester, Armin. 1992. *Weak Layering and Word Binarity*. Univesity of California, Santa Cruz.

Jackendoff, Ray. 1972. *Semantics Interpretation in Generative Grammar*. Cambridge, Massachusetts: Massachusetts Institute of Technology Press.

Jaeggli, O. 1982. *Topics in Romance syntax*. Dordrecht: Foris.

Jia Yuan (贾媛), Xiong Ziyu (熊子瑜) & Li, Aijun (李爱军) 2006. Phonetic and phonological analysis of focal accents of disyllabic words in Standard Chinese. *The 5th International Symposium on Chinese Spoken Language Processing*. Singapore: Springer Press.

Jia Yuan (贾媛), Ma, Qiuwu (马秋武) & Li, Aijun (李爱军). 2007. Putonghua wuzizu jiaodian chengfen shichang fenbu moshi yanjiu (The durational patterns of five-syllable focused constituents in Standard Chinese). *Technical Acoustics* 4: 252-256.

Jia Yuan (贾媛), Xiong, Ziyu (熊子瑜), Li, Aijun (李爱军) 2008. Putonghua jiaodian zhongyin dui yuju yingao de zuoyong (The effect of focal accents upon sentential pitch in Standard Chinese). *Journal of Chinese Phonetics* 1: 118-124. Beijing: The Commercial Press.

Jia Yuan (贾媛), Li, Aijun (李爱军) & Chen, Yiya (陈轶亚). 2008. Putonghua wuzizu jiaodian chengfen yingao he shichang moshi yanjiu (Pitch and duration Patterns of five-syllable consituents in Standard Chinese). *Applied Linguistics* 4: 53-61.

Jia Yuan (贾媛), Li, Aijun (李爱军), Ma, Qiuwu (马秋武) & Xiong, Ziyu (熊子瑜). 2009. Juyou jiaodian biaoji zuoyong de "shi" zi ju zhongyin fenbu yanjiu (Accents distribution in the *focus*-marking Shi construction). *Journal of Chinese Information Processing* 3 : 103-109.

Jun, Sun-Ah. 1996. *The Phonetics and Phonology of Korean Prosody: Intonational Phonology and Prosodic Structure*. New York: Garland Publishing.

Kager Rene. 1999. *Optimality Theory*. Cambridge: Cambridge University Press.

Kanerva, Jonni M. 1990. Focusing on phonological phrases inChichewa. *The Phonology-syntax Connection*, 145-161. Chicargo: University of Chicargo Press.

Kingdon, Roger. 1958. *The Groundwork of English Intonation*. London: Longman.

King, Patricia H. 1995. *Configuring Topic and Focus in Russian*. Stanford: Center For The Study of Language and Information Publications.

Kiss, Katalin. 1996. The focus operator and information focus. *Working Papers in the Theory of Grammar*, Vol. 3, N2, Budapest.

Kornai, Andras & Geoffrey K. Pullum. 1990. The X-bar Theory of phrase structure. *Language* 66: 24-50.

Ladd. D. Robert. 1980. *The Structure of Intonational Meaning: Evidence from English*. Bloomington, Indiana: Indiana University Press.

Ladd. D Robert. 1983. Phonological features of intonation peaks. *Language* 59: 721-759.

Ladd. D Robert. 1983. Even, focus, and normal stress. *Journal of Semantics* 2: 157-170.

Ladd. D. Robert. 1990. Intonation: emotion vs. grammar. *Language* 66: 806-816.

Ladd. D. Robert. 1992. *Compand Prosodic Domains*. University of Edinburgh.

Ladd, D. Robert. 1996. *Intonational Phonology*. Cambridge: Cambridge University Press.

LaPolla, Randy J. 1995. Pragmatic relations and word order in Chinese. In *Word Order in Discourse*, Downing, Pamela A. and Michael Noonan (eds.), 297-332.

Leben, William. 1973. *Suprasegmental Phonology*. PhD dissertation, Massachusetts Institute of Technology.

Lehiste, Ilse. 1970. *Suprasegmentals*. Cambridge, Massachusetts: Massachusetts Institute of Technology.

Leusen, Noor van & L. Kálmán. 1993. *The interpretation of free focus*. University of Amsterdam.

Li, Aijun (李爱军). 2002. Chinese prosody and prosodic labeling of spontaneous speech. *Speech Prosody*. France.

Li, Aijun (李爱军). 2005. Youhao yuyinde shengxue fenxi (Acoustic analysis on friendly speech). *Chinese Language* 5: 418-431.

Li, Charles. N. 1975. *Word order and Word Order Change*. Austin and London: University of Texas Press.

Li, Charles. N & Thompson Sandy. 1979. An explanation of word order change from SVO to SOV. *Foundations of Language* 12: 201-214 .

Li, Charles. N & Thompson Sandy. 1981. *Mandarin Chinese: A Functional Reference Grammar*. Berkeley and Los Angeles: University of California Press.

Liberman, Mark. 1975. *The Intonation System of English*. PhD dissertation, Massachusetts Institute of Technology.

Liberman, Mark & Prince, Alan. 1977. On stress and linguistic rhythm. *Linguistics* 8: 249-336.

Lin, Maocan (林茂灿). 2000. Putonghua yujuzhong jianduan he yuju yunlv duanyu (Breaks and prosodic phrases in the utterances of Standard Chinese). *Dangdai yuyanxue* 4: 210-217.

Lin, Maocan (林茂灿). 2002. Putonghua yujude yunlvjiegou he jipin (F_0) gaodixian goujian (Prosodic structure and lines of F_0 top and bottom of utterances in Chinese). *Dangdai yuyanxue* 4: 254-265.

Lin, Maocan (林茂灿). 2006. Yiwen he chenshu yuqi yu bianjiediao (Interrogative and declarative mood and boudary tone). *Chinese Language* 4: 364-376.

Liu, Danqing & Xu Liejiong (刘丹青、徐烈炯). 1998. Jiaodian yu beijing huati ji hanyu 'lian' ziju (Focus and background, topic and lian-sentence in Chinese). *Chinese Language* 4: 243-252.

Liu, Danqing (刘丹青). 2004. Identical topics: a more characteristics property of topic prominent languages. *Journal of Chinese Linguistics*: 1-32.

Liu, Danqing (刘丹青). 2004. *Yuxu Leixingxue yu Jieci Lilun* (Toplology of Word Order and Preposition Theory). Beijing: The Commercial Press.

Liu, Tanzhou (刘探宙). 2008. Duochong qiangshi jiaodian gongxian jushi (Constructions containing mutiple strong foci in Chinese). *Chinese Language* 3: 952-962.

Lü, Bisong (吕必松). 1983. Guanyu "shi…de" jiegou de jige wenti (Some problems concerning the *"shi…de"*) construction. *Shijie Hanyu*

Jiaoxu 2: 47-63.

Maddieson, Ian. 1978. Universals of tone. in Greenberg, Joseph H. (ed.) *Universals of human language* 2: 337-465. Stanford: Stanford University Press.

Ma, Qiuwu (马秋武). 2005. Tianjinhua liandu biandiao zhimi (An OT solution to the paradox of Tianjin Tone sandhi). *Chinese Language* 6: 561-568.

Ma, Qiuwu (马秋武). 2009. Nanjign fangyan liangzizu liandu biandiao de youxuanlun fenxi(An OT solution to bisyllabic tone sandhi in Nanjign dialect). *Yuyan Yanjiu* 1: 27-32.

Ma, Qiuwu (马秋武), Jia Yuan (贾媛). 2009. Yudiao Yinxixue Zonglan (Overview of Intonational Phonology). *Nankai Linguistics* 1: (to be published).

Mathesius, Vilem. 1929. Functional linguistics. In *Praguiana: Some basic and less well-known aspects of the Prague Linguistics Circle*, ed. Josef Vachek, 121-142. Amsterdam: Johan Benjamins (1983).

McCarthy J. John. 2002. *A Thematic Guide to Optimality Theory.* Cambridge: Cambridge University Press.

McCarthy J. John & Prince, Alan. 1993. Generalized alignment. In G. Booij and J. v. Marle (eds.) *Yearbook of Morphology* 79-153. Dordrecht: Kluwer.

McCarthy J. John & Prince, Alan. 1995. Faithfulness and reduplicative identity. In J.N. Beckman. L.W. Dickey and S. Urbanczyk (eds.) *Papers in Optimality Theory*, 249-384. University of Massachusetts.

Nespor, Marina & Irene, Vogel. 1986. *Prosodic Phonology.* Dordrecht: Foris.

Nespor, Marina & Irene, Vogel. 1989. On the cleshes and lapeses. *Phonology* 6: 69-116.

Nooteboom, Sieb and J. Kruyt. 1987. Accents, focus distribution, and perceived distribution of given and new information: An experiment. *Journal of the Acoustical Society of America* 74: 1512-1524.

O' Connor, J. D. & Arnold, Gordon Frederick. 1973. *Intonation of colloquial English*(2nd edn). London: Longman.

O' Shaughnessy, Douglas. 1979. Linguistic features in fundamental frequency patterns. *Journal of Phonetics* 7: 119-145.

O' Shaughnessy, Douglas & Jona Allen. 1983. Linguistic modality effects on fundamental frequency in speech. *Journal of the Acoustic Society of America* 74: 1155-1171.

Palmer, Harold. 1922. *English Intonation, with Systematic Exercises*. Cambridge: Heffer.

Peperkamp, Sharon. 1997. *Prosodic Words*. PhD dissertation of Lillehammer University College. The Hague: Holland Academic Graphics.

Pierrehumbert, Janet. 1979. The perception of fundamental frequency declination. *Journal of the Acoustical Society of America* 66: 363-369.

Pierrehumbert, Janet. 1980. *The phonology and phonetics of English intonation*. PhD dissertation, Massachusetts Institute of Technology.

Pierrehumbert, Janet & Beckman, Mary. 1988. *Japanese Tone Structure*. Cambridge, Massachusetts: Massachusetts Institute of Technology Press.

Pierrehumbert, Janet & S.A. Steele. 1989. Categories of tonal alignment in English. *Phonetica* 46: 181-196.

Pike, Kenneth L. 1945. *The Intonation of American English*. Ann Arbor: University of Michigan Press.

Prieto Pilar, Jan van Santen and Julia Hirschberg. 1995. Tonal alignment patterns in Spanish. *Journal of Phonetics* 23: 429-451.

Prince, Allen & Smolensky, Paul 1993. *Optimality Theory: Constraint Interaction in Generative Grammar*. Rutgers University Center for Cognitive Science Technical Report 2.

Purcell. E.T. 1976. Pitch peak location and the perception of Serbo-Croatian word tone. *Journal of Phonetics* 4: 265-270.

Rice, Keren D. 1987. On defining the intonational phrase: evidence from Slave. *Phonology Yearbook* 4: 37-59.

Rochemont, Michael & Peter, Culicover. 1990. *English Focus Constructions and the Theory of Grammar*. Cambridge: Cambridge University Press.

Ross, Claudia. 1983. On the function of Mandarin DE. *Journal of Chinese Linguistics* 11. 2: 214-246.

Schmerling, Susane. 1976. *Aspects of English Sentence Stress*. Austin: University of Texas Press.

Selkirk, Elisabeth. 1984. *Phonology and Syntax: the Relation between Sound and Structure*. Cambridge: Cambridge University Press.

Selkirk, Elisabeth. 1986. On the derived domains in sentence phonology. *Phonology Yearbook* 3: 371-405.

Selkirk, Elisabeth. 1995. Sentence prosody: intonation, stress, and phrasing. *The Handbook of Phonological Theory*, 550-569. Cambridge, Massachusetts: Blackwell.

Selkirk, Elisabeth. 1995. The prosodic structure of function words. *Optimality Theory*. University of Massachusetts Occasional Papers 18: 439-469. Amherst : GLSA.

Selkirk, Elisabeth & Tong, Shen. 1990. Prosodic domains in Shanghai Chinese. *The Phonology-syntax connection*, 313-337. Chicago: University of Chicago Press.

Selkirk, Elisabeth. 2000. The interaction of constraints on prosodic phrasing. See Horne 2000: 231-261.

Shen Jiong. (沈 炯) 1994. Hanyu Yudiao Gouzao he Yudiao Leixing(Construction and type of Chinese Intonation), *Dialect* 4.

Shi, Dingxu (石定栩). 2003. Lilun Yufa yu Hanyu Jiaoxue－cong "shi" de Jufa Gongneng Tanqi (Theoretical grammar and Chinese language teaching－concerning it from the function of the "shi" construction). *Chinese Teaching in the World* 2: 5-12.

Silverman. K. E., Beckman, J. Pitrelli, M. Ostendorf. C. Wightman. P. Prica, Pierrehumbert, Janet and J. Hirschberg. 1992. ToBI: a standard for labeling English Prosody. *Proceedings of the 2nd International Conference on the Processing of Spoken Language*: 867-870.

Silverman. K. E & Pierrehumbert, Janet. 1990. The timing of pre-nuclear high accents in English. See Kingston and Beckman 139-151.

Silverstein, Ro. 1976. A Strategy for Utterance Production in Hausa. *Studies in African Linguistics Los Angeles* 7: 233-241.

Song, Yuzhu (宋玉柱). 1981. Guanyu shijian zhuci "de" he "laizhe" (On tense markers "de" and "laizhe"). *Chinese Language* 4: 271-276.

Sosa, Juan M. 1991. *Fonética u Fonologia de la entonación del Español Hispanoamericano*. PhD dissertation, University of Massachusetts, Amherst.

Steedman, Mark. 2000. Information structure and the the syntax-phonology interface. *Linguistic Inquiry* 31: 649-689.

Szabolcsi, Anna. 1981. The semantics of topic-focus articulation. *Formal Methods in the Study of Language*, 513-540. Amsterdam: Mathematische Centrum.

Tai, James H-Y (戴浩一). 1973. Chinese as a SOV language. *Papers from the Ninth Regional Meeting of the Chicago Linguistic Society*.

659-671.

't Hart, Johan T, Collier Rene & Cohen Antonie. 1990. *A Perceptual Study of Intonation: An Experimental-Phonetic Approach to Speech Melody*. Cambridge: Cambridge University Press.

Tsao, Fengfu (曹逢甫). 1990. *Clause and Sentence Structure in Chinese: A Functional Perspective*. Taipei: Student Book Coorporation.

Thorsen, Nina. 1975. Lexical stress, emphasis for contrast, and sentence intonation in Advanced   Standard Copenhagen Danish. *Proceedings of the IXth International Congress of Phonetic Sciences. Volum II The Relation between Sentence Prosody and Word Prosody*, 417-423.

Toledo, Guillermo. 1989. Señales Prosodicas del Foco. *Revista Argentina de Lingüistica* 5(1-2): 205-230.

Vanderslice, Ralph & Ladefoged, Peter. 1972. Binary suprasegmental features and transforational word accentuation rules. *Language* 48: 819- 838.

Vaissère, Janqueline. 1971. *Contribution á la synthèse par regles du francais*. PhD dissertation, Université des Langues et Lettres de Grenoble.

Venditti, Jennifer J, Jun, Sun-Ah & Beckman, Mary. 1996. *Prosodic cues to syntactic and other linguistic structures in Japanese, Korean and English. Singnal to syntax: bootstrapping from speech to grammar in early acquisition*, 287-311. Hillsdald: Lawrence Earlbaum.

Vella, Alexandra. 1995. *Prosodic Structure and Intonation in Maltese: influence on Maltese English*. PhD dissertation, Edinburgh University.

Vogel, Irene & István, Kenesei. 1987. The interface between phonology and other components of grammar: the case of Hungarian. *Phonology Yearbook* 4: 243-263.

Vogel, Irene & István, Kenesei. 1987. Syntax and senmantics in phonology. *The Phonology-syntax connection*, 339-363. Chicago: University of Chicago Press.

Vogel Irene, Bunnell Timothy & Hoskins Steven. 1995. The phonology and phonetics of the rhythm rule. *Papers in Laboratory Phonology IV*, 111-127. Cambridge: Chicago University Press.

Wang, Jialing (王嘉龄). 2002. Youxuanlun he tianjinhua de liandu biandiao ji qingsheng (On tone sandhi and neutral tone in the Tianjin dialect within the framework of Optimality Theory). *Chinese Language* 4: 363-372.

Welmers, William E. 1973. *African Language Structures*. Berkeley, Los Angeles. University of California Press.

Wells, William E. 1986. An Experimental Approach to the Interpretation of Focus in Spoken English. *Intonation in Discourse*, 53-75. London: Croom Helm.

Winkler, Suanne. 1997. *Focus and Secondary Predication*. Berlin: Mouton.

Wu, Guo. 1998. *Information Structure in Chinese*. Beijing: Peking University Press.

Wu, Zongji (吴宗济). 1988. Hanyu putonghua yudiao de jiben diaoxing (The basic patterns of Standard Chinese intonation). *Wang Li xiansheng jinian lunwenji* (Festschrift for Wang Li). Beijing: The Commercial Press.

Wu, Zongji (吴宗济). 1996. A new method of intonation analysis for Standard Chinese. *Report of Phonetic Research*.

Xu, Jie (徐杰). 2001. *Pubian Yufa Yuanze yu Hanyu Yufa Xianxiang* (Grammatical principles and grammatical phenomena). Beijing: Beijing University Press.

Xu, Liejiong (徐烈炯). 2004. Jiaodian de Yuyin biaoxian (Phonetic realization of focus). In *Jiaodian de jiegou he yiyi yanjiu* (Study of focus structure and meaning), 277-299. Beijing. Foreign Language Teaching and Research Press.

Xu, Liejiong (徐烈炯). 2004. Manifestation of informational focus. *Lingua* 114: 277-299.

Xu, Yi (许毅). 1999. Effects of tone and focus on the formation and alignment of F_0 contours. *Journal of Phonetics*, 27, 55-105.

Xiong, Ziyu (熊子瑜). 2003. Yunlü danyuan bianjie tezheng de shengxue yuyinxue yanjiu (An Acoustic study of the boundary features of prosodic units). *Applied Linguistics* 2: 117-121.

Xiong, Ziyu (熊子瑜). 2006. Pitch Variations in the Running Speech of Standard Chinese. TAL 2006, LA ROCHELLE (France).

Xiong, Zhongru (熊仲儒). 2005. Fouding jiaodian jiqi jufa yunhan (Negative focus and its syntactic implications). *Chinese Language* 4: 300-307.

Xiong, Zhongru (熊仲儒). 2007. "*Shi...de*" de goujian fenxi (On the construction of "shi...de"). *Chinese Language* 4: 321-330.

Yip, Moira. 1980. *The Tonal phonology of Chinese*. PhD dissertation.

Massachusetts Instituent of Technology.

Yip, Moira. 2002. *Tone*. Cambridge: Cambridge University Press.

Yuan, Yulin (袁毓林). 2003. Cong Jiaodian Lilun kan Juwei 'de' de jufa yuyi gongneng (The syntactic and semantic function of utterance final 'de' from the theory of focus). *Chinese Language* 1: 3-16.

Yuan, Yulin (袁毓林). 2006. Shixi "lian" ziju de xinxi jiegou tedian (On the information structure of "lian" structure). *Linguistic Sciences* 2: 14-28.

Zec, Draga & Sharon, Inkelas. 1990. Prosodically constrained syntax. *The Phonology-syntax connection*, 365-378.

Zhang, Bojiang (张伯江) & Fang Mei (方梅). 1996. *Hanyu Gongneng Yufa Yanjiu* (Studies in Chinese Functional Analysis). Nanchang: Jiangxi Eduation Press.

Zhao, Shuhua (赵淑华). 1979. Guanyu "*shi...de*" ju (On "*shi...de*" construction). *Language Teaching and Linguistic Studies* 1: 57-66.

Zhu, Dexi (朱德熙). De zi jiegou he panduanju (The *de* construction and sentences expressing judgment). *Chinese Language* 1: 23-27; 2: 105-109.

Zubizarrreta, Maria Luisa. 1998. *Prosody, Focus, and Word Order*. Cambridge: Massachusetts Institute of Technology Press.

Appendix   Sample Sentences

(I) **Target sentences:**

(i) **Unmarked short sentences:**

    a. Wu1 Yin1 Wei1 Bi1 Wen1 Yin1 Le0.
       wu yin   intimidate wen yin   le
       (Wuyin intimated Wenyin).

    b. Liu Min2 Ti2 Ba2 Mao2 Lan2 Le0.
       liu min   elevate   mao lan   le
       (Liumin elevated Maolan).

    c. Mai4 Li4 Nüe4 Dai4 Lu4 Na4 Le0.
       mai   li4   maltreat   lu   na   le
       (Maili maltreated Luna).

(ii) **Unmarked long sentence:**

    a. Wu1 Yin1 Jin1 Tian1 Wei1 Bi1 Wen1 Yin1 Le0.
       wu yin   today   intimidate   wen yin   le
       (Wuyin intimidated Wenyin today).

    b. Liu Min2 Ling2 Chen2 Ti2 Ba2 Mao2 Lan2 Le0.
       liu min   early morning elevate   mao lan   le
       (Liumin elevated Maolan on the early morning).

    c. Mai4 Li4 Ban4 Ye4 Nüe4 Dai4 Lu4 Na4 Le0.
       mai li4   midnight   maltreat   lu   na   le
       (Maili maltreated Luna at midnight).

(iii) ***lian* marked subject:**

    a. *Lian2* Liu2 Min2 *Dou1* Ti2 Ba2 Mao2 Lan2 Le0.
       even   liu   min   all   elevate   mao lan   le
       (Even Liumin elevated Maolan).

    b. *Lian2* Mai4 Li4 *Dou1* Nüe Dai4 Lu4 Na4 Le0.
       even   mai4 li   all   maltreat   lu   na   le
       (Even Maili maltreated Luna).

(iv) ***lian* marked object:**

    a. Liu2 Min2 *Lian2* Mao2 Lan2 *Dou1* Ti2 Ba2 Le0.
       liu   min   even   mao lan   all   elevate   le
       (Liumin even elevated Maolan).

    b. Mai4 Li4 *Lian2* Lu4 Na4 *Dou1* Nüe Dai4 Le0.
       mai   li   lian   lu   na   all   maltreat   le
       (Maili even maltreated Luna).

(v) *shi* **marked subject:**

    a.   *Shi4* Liu2 Min2 Ti2 Ba2 Mao2 Lan2 *De0.*
        is   liu   min   elevate   mao lan   de
        (It is Liumin that elevated Maolan).

    b.   *Shi4* Mai4 Li4 Nüe4 Dai4 Lu4 Na4 *De0.*
        is   mai4 li4   maltreat   lu   na   de
        (It is Maili that maltreated Luna).

(II)   **Focus conditions of the target sentences:**

(i)   **Theme focus and rheme focus in unmarked short sentences:**

Tone1 sentence:

    a.   Fa1 Sheng1 Le0 Shen2 Me0 Shi4?
        happen   le   what
        (What happen?)
        Wu1   Yin1   Wei1   Bi1   Wen1 Yin1   Le0.

            Rheme background   Rheme focus

    b.   Shei2 Wei1 Bi1 Wen1 Yin1 Le0?
        who   intimdate   wen   yin le
        (Who intimidated Wenyin?)
        Wu1   Yin1   Wei1   Bi1   Wen1 Yin1   Le0.

            Rheme focus   Theme background

    a.   Wu1   Yin1   Wei1   Bi1   Shei2   Le0?
        wu   yin   intimdate   whom   le
        (Wuyin intimdated whom?)
        Wu1   Yin1   Wei1   Bi1   Wen1 Yin1 Le0

            Theme background   Rheme focus

    b.   Wu1 Yin1 Wei1 Bi1 Shei2 Le0? Shei2 Wei1 Bi1 Shei2 Le0?
        wu yin   intimate who   le   who   intimate whom le
        (Wuyin intimidated whom? Who intimidated whom?)
        Wu1   Yin1   Wei1   Bi1   Wen1 Yin1 Le0

    Theme focus   Theme background   Rheme focus

Tone2 sentence:

    a.   Fa1 Sheng1 Le0 Shen2 Me0 Shi4?
        happen   le   what
        (What happen?)

Liu2 Min2   Ti2 Ba2   Mao2 Lan2 Le0.

⎵ Rheme background ⎵ ⎵ Rheme focus ⎵

b.   Shei2   Ti2 Ba2   Mao2 Lan2 Le0?
     who   elevate   mao lan le
     (Who elevated Maolan?)

Liu2 Min2   Ti2 Ba2   Mao2 Lan2 Le0.

⎵ Rheme focus ⎵ ⎵ Theme background ⎵

c.   Liu2 Min2 Ti2 Ba2   Shei2 Le0?
     liu min elevate whom le
     (Liumin elevated whom?)

Liu2 Min2   Ti2 Ba2   Mao2 Lan2 Le0.

⎵ Theme background ⎵ ⎵ Rheme focus ⎵

d.   Liu2 Min2 Ti2 Ba2 Shei2 Le0? Shei2 Ti2 Ba2 Shei2 Le0?
     liu min   elevate who le   who elevate   whom le
     (Wuyin intimidated whom? Who intimidated whom?)

Liu2 Min2   Ti2   Ba2   Mao2 Lan2 Le0.

⎵ Theme focus ⎵ ⎵ Theme background ⎵ ⎵ Rheme focus ⎵

Tone4 sentence:

a.   Fa1 Sheng1 Le0 Shen2 Me0 Shi4?
     happen   le   what
     (What happen?)

Mai4 Li4   Nüe4 Dai4   Lu4 Na4   Le0.

⎵ Rheme background ⎵ ⎵ Rheme focus ⎵

b.   Shei2   Nüe4 Dai4   Lu4 Na4 Le0?
     who   maltreat   lu   na le
     (Who maltreated Luna?)

Mai4 Li4   Nüe4 Dai4   Lu4 Na4   Le0.

⎵ Rheme focus ⎵ ⎵ Theme background ⎵

c.   Mai4 Li4   Nüe4 Dai4   Shei2   Le0?
     mai li   maltreat   whom le
     (Maili maltreated whom?)

235

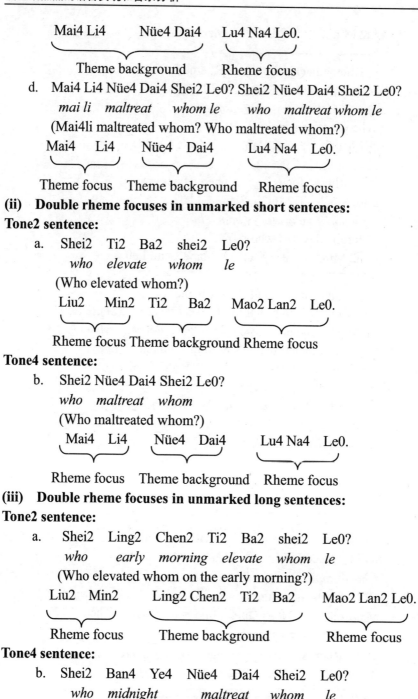

Mai4 Li4　　Nüe4 Dai4　Lu4 Na4 Le0.

Theme background　　Rheme focus

d.　Mai4 Li4 Nüe4 Dai4 Shei2 Le0? Shei2 Nüe4 Dai4 Shei2 Le0?

mai li　maltreat　whom le　who　maltreat whom le

(Mai4li maltreated whom? Who maltreated whom?)

Mai4　Li4　　Nüe4　Dai4　　Lu4 Na4　Le0.

Theme focus　Theme background　Rheme focus

(ii)　Double rheme focuses in unmarked short sentences:

Tone2 sentence:

a.　Shei2　Ti2　Ba2　shei2　Le0?

who　elevate　whom　le

(Who elevated whom?)

Liu2　Min2　Ti2　Ba2　Mao2 Lan2　Le0.

Rheme focus Theme background Rheme focus

Tone4 sentence:

b.　Shei2 Nüe4 Dai4 Shei2 Le0?

who　maltreat　whom

(Who maltreated whom?)

Mai4　Li4　　Nüe4　Dai4　　Lu4 Na4　Le0.

Rheme focus　　Theme background　Rheme focus

(iii)　Double rheme focuses in unmarked long sentences:

Tone2 sentence:

a.　Shei2　Ling2　Chen2　Ti2　Ba2　shei2　Le0?

who　early　morning　elevate　whom　le

(Who elevated whom on the early morning?)

Liu2　Min2　　Ling2 Chen2　Ti2　Ba2　　Mao2 Lan2 Le0.

Rheme focus　　Theme background　　Rheme focus

Tone4 sentence:

b.　Shei2　Ban4　Ye4　Nüe4　Dai4　Shei2　Le0?

who　midnight　maltreat　whom　le

(Who maltreated whom at midnight?)

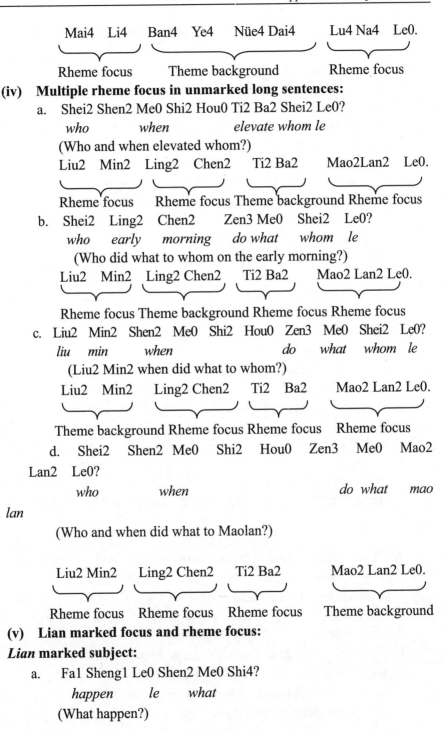

Mai4 Li4   Ban4 Ye4   Nüe4 Dai4   Lu4 Na4   Le0.

Rheme focus   Theme background   Rheme focus

(iv) **Multiple rheme focus in unmarked long sentences:**

   a. Shei2 Shen2 Me0 Shi2 Hou0 Ti2 Ba2 Shei2 Le0?

     who   *when*   *elevate whom le*

     (Who and when elevated whom?)

     Liu2 Min2   Ling2 Chen2   Ti2 Ba2   Mao2Lan2 Le0.

     Rheme focus   Rheme focus Theme background Rheme focus

   b. Shei2 Ling2 Chen2   Zen3 Me0 Shei2 Le0?

     who   *early*   *morning*   *do what* *whom* *le*

     (Who did what to whom on the early morning?)

     Liu2   Min2   Ling2 Chen2   Ti2 Ba2   Mao2 Lan2 Le0.

     Rheme focus Theme background Rheme focus Rheme focus

   c. Liu2 Min2 Shen2 Me0 Shi2 Hou0 Zen3 Me0 Shei2 Le0?

     liu   *min*   *when*   *do*   *what*   *whom* *le*

     (Liu2 Min2 when did what to whom?)

     Liu2   Min2   Ling2 Chen2   Ti2   Ba2   Mao2 Lan2 Le0.

     Theme background Rheme focus Rheme focus   Rheme focus

   d. Shei2   Shen2 Me0   Shi2 Hou0 Zen3 Me0   Mao2

Lan2   Le0?

     who   *when*   *do what*   *mao*

lan

     (Who and when did what to Maolan?)

     Liu2 Min2   Ling2 Chen2   Ti2 Ba2   Mao2 Lan2 Le0.

     Rheme focus   Rheme focus   Rheme focus   Theme background

(v) **Lian marked focus and rheme focus:**

***Lian* marked subject:**

   a. Fa1 Sheng1 Le0 Shen2 Me0 Shi4?

     happen   *le*   *what*

     (What happen?)

Lian2 **Liu2 Min2** *Dou1* Ti2 Ba2　Mao2 Lan2　Le0.

⎵⎵⎵⎵⎵_Lian_-marked focus　　　　　Rheme focus

b.　Lian2　Shei2　Dou1 Ti2 Ba2 Mao2 Lan2 Le0?
even　who　all　elevate　mao　lan　le
(Even who elevated Maolan?)
Lian2 **Liu2 Min2** *Dou1* Ti2 Ba2　　Mao2 Lan2 Le0.

⎵⎵⎵⎵⎵_Lian_-marked focus & Rheme focus

c.　Lian2　Liu2　Min2　Dou1　Ti2　Ba2　Shei2　Le0?
even　liu　min　all　elevate　whom　le
(Even Liumin elevated whom?)
Lian2 **Liu2 Min2** *Dou1* Ti2 Ba2　　Mao2 Lan2　Le0.

⎵⎵⎵⎵⎵_Lian_-marked focus　　　　　Rheme focus

d.　Lian2　Shei2　Dou1　Ti2　Ba2　Shei2　Le0?
even　who　all　elevate　whom　le
(Even who elevated whom?)
Lian2 **Liu2 Min2** *Dou1* Ti2 Ba2　　Mao2 Lan2　Le0.

⎵⎵⎵⎵⎵_Lian_-marked focus Rheme focus　　Rheme focus

Lian marked Object:
　c.　Fa1 Sheng1 Le0 Shen2 Me0 Shi4?
　　　happen　le　what
　　　(What happen?)
　　　Liu2 Min2　　*Lian2* **Mao2 Lan2** *Dou1* Ti2 Ba2　　Le0.

⎵⎵⎵⎵⎵_Lian_-marked focus　　Rheme focus

　b.　Liu2　Min2　Lian2　Shei2　Dou1　Ti2　Ba2　Le0?
　　　liu　min　even　who　all　elevate　le
　　　(Liumin even elevated whom?)
　　　Liu2 Min2　　*Lian2* **Mao2 Lan2** *Dou1* Ti2 Ba2　　Le0.

⎵⎵⎵⎵⎵_Lian_-marked focus & Rheme focus

　c.　Shei2　Lian2　Shei2　Dou1　Ti2　Ba2　Le0?
　　　who　even　whom　all　elevate　le
　　　(Who even elevated whom?)

Liu2 Min2   *Lian2* **Mao2 Lan2**   *Dou1*   Ti2 Ba2   Le0.

Lian-marked focus   Rheme focus

(v) *Shi*-marked focus and rheme focus:

a.   Fa1 Sheng1 Le0 Shen2 Me0 Shi4?
     happen   le   what
     (What happen?)
     Shi4 **Liu2   Min2**   Ti2 Ba2   Mao2 Lan2 De0.

           Shi-marked focus   Rheme focus

b.   Shi4   Shei2   Ti2 Ba2 Mao2 Lan2 De0?
     is   who   elevate   mao   lan   de
     (It is who elevated Maolan?)
     Shi4   **Liu2   Min2**   Ti2 Ba2   Mao2 Lan2   De0.

     Shi marked focus & Rheme focus

c.   *Shi4   Liu2   Min2   Ti2   Ba2   Shei2   De0?
     even   liu   min   elevate   whom   de
     (It is Liumin elevated whom?)
     Shi4   **Liu2   Min2**   Ti2 Ba2   Mao2 Lan2 De0.

           Shi-marked focus   Rheme focus

d.   Shi4   Shei2   Ti2   Ba2   whom   De0?
     even   who   elevate   whom   de
     (It is who elevated whom?)
     Shi4   **Liu2 Min2**   Ti2 Ba2   Mao2 Lan2   De0.

     Shi-marked focus Rheme focus   Rheme focus

后　记

2005 年 2 月，在我的导师马秋武教授的推荐下，我参加了林茂灿先生举办的语音学讲习班，当时我还在南开大学念硕士 2 年级，对于语音学的认识完全处于懵懂状态。语音室的李爱军、熊子瑜和胡方老师的系列讲座，引发了我对语音学研究的强烈兴趣。我的主要研究方向为音系学，在语音室先辈以及导师的鼓励下，便选择了语音学和音系学相结合的研究思路，此后我来到语音室做交流学生，直到后来工作，始终坚持着接口研究的思路。普通话的焦点问题是语言学各个研究领域都感兴趣的话题，无论从焦点的定义还是研究的方法，不同的领域差异大相径庭。但从理论研究和应用角度，都需要对这一问题进行深化和探索。

普通话焦点的语音特征和音系分析，是我硕士期间就开始的研究课题，后来，在博士论文的研究过程中，又将这一问题进行了扩展。本书的研究内容，主要是在博士论文的基础上修改和提炼而成的。书中通过语音学和音系学结合的研究方法，考察了普通话语调结构、韵律结构以及焦点的关系。通过研究普通话不同类别和不同数量焦点的语音表现以及交互作用的韵律特征，揭示普通话重音的层级性差异和不对应性特征，并采用音系学理论（语调音系学和优选论），对普通话的重音类型进行表征，并对普通话焦点和重音的关系以及制约重音分布的底层原因等问题进行系统阐述和解释。书中所采用的语料均为设计的普通话语料，在后续研究中需要扩展到自然语流，以及不同的方言焦点的研究中。在考察自然话语和方言焦点的韵律特征基础上，归纳和总结焦点和重音的对应关系，以验证和完善现在的理论模型。此外，对于重音音系类型的研究，可以进一步扩展到认知层面，考察不同类型的重音的 ERP 加工差异。

经历了漫长的写作和修改过程，这本书终于要出版了，这不只是我个人的努力和付出，也凝聚了很多老师的心血。我首先要感谢的是我的导师马秋武教授，马老师是我攻读硕士和博士的导师，是我学术道路的引路人。在治学的过程中，马老师时常教导我们，一定要一步一个脚印，要勤奋与严谨并重。他对于学术的执着和追求深深地影响着我。在我的论文写作期间，马老师给予了精心的指导，直到今天马老师所说的"细处见功夫"，一直是我在文章写作时遵守的准则。

感谢语音研究室的学术前辈和同仁的帮助和支持，在每次学术讨论中，吴宗济先生、林茂灿先生和曹剑芬先生对语音学的认识和看法，给了我观点和研究方向上的启示。感谢李爱军研究员在本书出版过程中的所有帮助，从出版基金的申请到出版社的选取，都得到了李老师无私的帮助。李老师是我的良师益友，在学术上，她总是能给我指明正确的研究方向，并默默地支持我。在工作和生活中，她给予我最大程度的支持和关心。她面带笑容的鼓励，让我信心倍增，心中颇感温暖。我还要感谢熊子瑜副研究员和胡方副研究员，面对我的琐碎问题，他们总是给予我帮助，同一办公室的讨论总是那么及时和有效。除此之外，感谢语音室陈肖霞老师、华武老师、殷治纲博士、方强博士和高军博士，在日常生活中的帮助与关怀。语音室是和谐与温暖的大家庭，能够在这个集体中工作，我感受到幸福和快乐。成功的团队没有失败者，正是因为集体的力量，我才可以有勇气去面对工作中的各种困难，享受快乐科研的过程。

此外，我要感谢台湾中研院的郑秋豫研究员，在每次国际会议上对我的研究所提的意见和建议。感谢荷兰莱顿大学的陈轶亚博士，我在荷兰学习期间，与陈轶亚老师每周的讨论总给我最大的启发。感谢我的师姐山东农业大学翟红华教授、师兄福建师范大学闫小斌副教授和南开大学冉启斌副教授，在我攻读博士和工作期间给予的无私帮助。

最后，感谢我的家人对于我工作的支持，我长久以来的忙碌总是忽视他们的感受，谢谢他们的理解和支持。离开奋斗与坚持的土壤，天赋的种子便寻不到春华秋实的前程。倘若希望在金色的秋天收获果实，那么在寒意侵人的早春，就该卷起裤腿，去不懈地拓荒、播种、耕耘，直到收获的那一天。借着此书出版之际，我也勉励自己，在日后的研究工作中，日日行，不怕千万里；常常做，不怕千万事。

贾媛

2012 年 8 月 5 日